Three Mothers, Three Daughters

CULTURAL STUDIES

A series of books edited by Samir Dayal

Crisis of the European Subject
Julia Kristeva

Three Mothers, Three Daughters
Michael Gorkin and Rafiqa Othman

Sunlight and Shadow:
The Jewish Experience of Islam
Lucien Gubbay

Three Mothers,
Three Daughters

Palestinian Women's Stories

Michael Gorkin

Rafiqa Othman

OTHER

Other Press

New York

10 9 8 7 6 5 4 3 2

Library of Congress Cataloging-in-Publication Data

Gorkin, Michael.
    Three mothers, three daughters : Palestinian women's stories /
Michael Gorkin, Rafiqa Othman.
      p. cm.
Originally published: Berkeley : University of California Press, c1996.
Includes bibliographical references and index.
ISBN 1–892746–45–X (SC)
    1. Women, Palestinian Arab—West Bank—Social conditions.
2. Women, Palestinian Arab—West Bank—Interviews. 3. Jewish-Arab relations. 4. Women, Palestinian Arab—West Bank—Attitudes.
I. Othman, Rafiqa, 1959– II. Title.

HQ1728.5 .G67 2000
305.48'892'74056953—dc21

                         00–027880

For my daughters,
Maya and Talya

❧

Michael Gorkin

For my parents,
Qasem and Fatma

❧

Rafiqu Othman

CONTENTS

Map of Israel
ix

Acknowledgments
xi

Preface by Michael Gorkin
xiii

Introduction
I

UMM MAHMUD AND MARIANNE
(East Jerusalem)
13

UMM ABDULLAH AND SAMIRA
(Camp Aida)
83

UMM KHALED AND LEILA
(Village of Abu Ghosh)
157

Epilogue by Rafiqa Othman
221

Chronology
229

Glossary
233

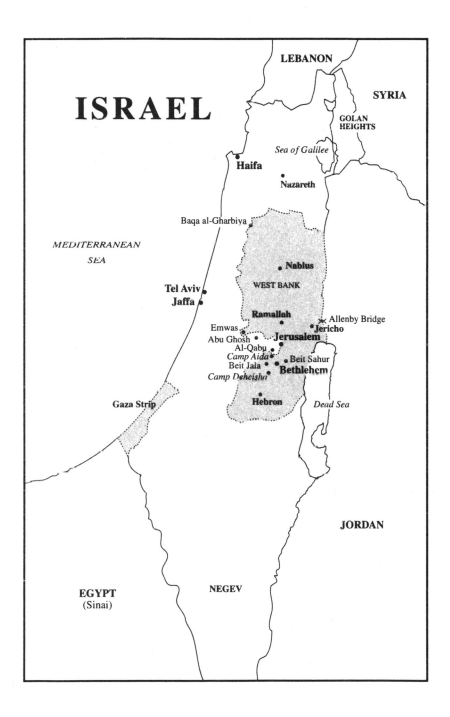

ACKNOWLEDGMENTS

We are, above all, deeply grateful to the six women who agreed to tell us their stories. We are unable to cite their names publicly—in keeping with our promise to them—but we hope that we have made clear to them privately how much we value their courage and candor. We are also thankful to Mufida Abd al-Rahman and Leila Atshan, who first helped us make contact with some of the six women and offered us encouragement and practical suggestions throughout our work with the women.

To Sufyan Kamal, Dafna Ladin-Gorkin, Nuzha Othman, Rifqa Othman, Saliba Sarsar, Avraham and Daniella Stern, and Amnon Toledano we express our appreciation for their helpful comments on the manuscript at various stages along the way. And to the staff at the University of California Press—Suzanne Samuel, Nola Burger, and Edith Gladstone—we wish to express our appreciation for their professional expertise in turning the manuscript into a book; and a special thanks to Lynne Withey, who was behind the project from its inception to its completion.

Finally, we want to state here what we have indicated elsewhere in the book, namely, that our working together on this project would have been inconceivable without the support of our families. Their belief in the value of our collaboration has sustained us throughout the work.

PREFACE

I met Rafiqa Othman in the spring of 1989, shortly after I had begun doing fieldwork for my book on a Palestinian family, *Days of Honey, Days of Onion* (1991). The Arabic language teacher who had been giving me private lessons suddenly left the Jerusalem area, and I was in urgent need of a tutor. A mutual friend suggested Rafiqa. She was then, and still is, a special education teacher—not a language instructor. Our friend suggested that Rafiqa could teach me to speak Arabic well enough, and besides, as one who lives in an Arab village in Israel, she could help me understand some of what I was experiencing in the field. On the latter point, our friend turned out to be absolutely correct. On the matter of my proficiency in Arabic, he was less correct; and to this day Rafiqa and I continue a joking argument as to whether the mediocre results in this area were due more to the teacher or the student.

In any case, such was the beginning of an unusual friendship, of which this book is an outgrowth. I say "unusual" because, as anyone who is familiar with Israel/Palestine sadly knows, friendship between a Jew and an Arab is still rather uncommon, especially if the two happen to be a man and a woman. That Rafiqa and I have been able to continue our friendship and work together in these circumstances is a tribute, above all, to the openmindedness of both our families—to whom we are extremely grateful. It is also a promising sign, perhaps, that despite occasional raised eyebrows we have not been impeded in our fieldwork among Palestinians, though I am inclined to think that part of our success in avoiding unpleasantness came from the shock value of our being the first pair of its kind to show up in this village or that.

The actual decision to do fieldwork together was slow in coming. For a year and a half our contact was limited to the lessons in Arabic. Dutifully, Rafiqa would show up twice a week at the apartment in Jerusalem where my family lives and we would converse, or attempt to do so, in Arabic. More often, we would lapse into speaking Hebrew—in which we are both fluent—so as to discuss more thoroughly my field experiences with the Palestinian family. These discussions proved invaluable in my understanding the family. Moreover, it soon became clear that in Rafiqa I had found, by chance, an insightful interpreter of her own society. I had also found a friend. For Rafiqa (and this I only vaguely sensed at the time) the experience of analyzing Palestinian culture with an outsider was something new and fascinating. She had encountered the anthropology "bug," if I may call it that, and had grown eager to try her own hand at these things.

For my part, this "bug" had long since entered my system, with the result that my work as a sedentary practicing clinical psychologist was no longer the same. I had cut back drastically on the number of clinical hours I was working and found myself drawn to anthropological literature, especially ethnographic studies of Middle Eastern peoples. This peregrination into the realm of anthropology is not one that I regret. I would like to think—in fact, I am sure—that it has added to my clinical understanding, if not to the size of my clinical practice. I hope too that a clinical background has contributed to my ethnographic work, though by now I have read a sufficient number of studies by trained anthropologists to know that the latter are as suspicious of poachers in their domain as are my own psychoanalytically oriented colleagues of anyone who would dare do psychotherapy without psychoanalytic training. Be that as it may, it is hard for me to imagine at this point giving up either activity.

I think it was part of my effort to blend clinical psychology and anthropology, as well as the wish to continue work with Rafiqa, that led to the next project: a study of traditional psychotherapeutic healers in the Palestinian community. My interest in this area had been piqued while I did fieldwork on the Palestinian family. The matriarch of the family had a deep belief in the healing powers of *sheikhs*,* and she herself was a minor practitioner of these arcane arts. I was never able to discuss any of this at length with her because her husband—my main informant—openly scorned this "nonsense," as he called it; and it did not seem worth jeopardizing my relationship with him to pursue this material with his wife. But I did discuss it with Rafiqa. As it happened, her father's mother was also a believer in *sheikhs*, and she had grown up hearing of the dangers of "the evil eye" and "black magic," as well as the magic cures wrought by healers. Not a believer herself, Rafiqa nonetheless was as curious about this material as I was. Thus, after a period of swapping stories and ideas, and reading the relevant literature, we decided to attempt our first project together.

To do fieldwork together in the Palestinian community, to be *seen* together, was a step that potentially exposed Rafiqa to considerable criticism. But she was determined to take it. As a respectful daughter, she felt obliged to inform her parents. Up to that point, Rafiqa was well acquainted with my family, but I still had not met hers. Her parents, with whom she lives, were not even aware of our contacts. At length, a meeting was arranged—a festive lunch at Rafiqa's house, with all her family meeting mine. The lunch was followed by a visit to the family's fields (I can still see my daughter romping through the almond groves with Rafiqa's niece, somehow communicating without a common lan-

---

* The term *sheikh* (fem., *sheikha*) is colloquial Arabic for "traditional healer." *Sheikh* is also a term applied to Muslim religious officials and to teachers, typically of religious subjects.

guage), and then a tour of her village. Not a word was said that day about Rafiqa's and my work together, though later Rafiqa was given to understand that her plans had the parental blessing.

For about a year, we went around Israel and the West Bank leisurely gathering material from male and female healers. Perhaps not surprisingly, a number of healers assumed that we were a couple in search of treatment, and they immediately began working on us—by offering horoscope readings. However, when we truthfully, if humorlessly, apprised them of our real intentions, they were quite cooperative with us. Our success here was due almost entirely to Rafiqa. Although never before having attempted fieldwork per se, she had an immediate and natural way of winning confidence ("I always know if I can trust someone by the gleam in the eyes," one wary *sheikha* said, avoiding my eyes and looking straight at Rafiqa. "And the gleam in *yours* is a good one!"). The data we gathered in these interviews were far more than we needed for a professional paper. At one point, we thought of writing a book on one of the female healers—the wary *sheikha,* to be specific. But we settled for a professional paper, which turned out to be the first journal article to appear in Israel written by a Jewish man and an Arab woman ("Traditional Psychotherapeutic Healing and Healers in the Palestinian Community," *Israel Journal of Psychiatry* 31 [1994]: 221–31).

By this time Rafiqa and I were a team, and we were determined to attempt a larger project. Actually, it was while working on the healers that we alighted on that larger project: a book on Palestinian women. Each of us had a private reason for wanting to tackle this subject. Mine dated back to the book on the Palestinian family, and the frustrations I had experienced, as a man, attempting to interview the women in the family. I knew I had not adequately portrayed the lives of women (and I mentioned the problem in the afterword of the book's 1993 paperback edition). I also knew that the only way I had any chance of writing about women was to work with a female coauthor. In Rafiqa, I had found my coauthor. For Rafiqa's part, the wish to write about Palestinian women was, understandably, far more personal. She will talk about this in the book's epilogue; she feels that her story, and the stories of so many other Palestinian women, have not been adequately told. This book, she felt, is a way of telling some of these stories.

And so we set out to find some Palestinian women, mothers and daughters, who would tell us their stories . . . I would have preferred to end the preface with this sentence, or some other felicitous phrase. But frankly, to do so would leave out a significant, though upsetting, development that took place as we did this book. In retrospect, it was one that I probably should have anticipated, yet when it happened I was taken by surprise.

The reader will gather, I imagine, that up until this book Rafiqa's and my friendship was idyllic, without quarrel. The book changed that. No sooner had we begun our planning than we had our first disagreement. Simply stated, the disagreement was over the inclusion of a particular couple, mother and daughter, with whom we had become acquainted while writing about the healers. I felt they would be excellent subjects for the present book. Rafiqa felt they would not: their family was "too problematic," and therefore they were not representative. She was adamant— a trait I had never before seen in her. With much reluctance, I went along with her.

Other differences soon followed, over some substantive issues to be covered in the book. For instance, I wanted to pursue sexual topics far more than did Rafiqa. She, as an "insider," felt that going into some of this material would be trespassing on the women's privacy and dignity; and I, as an "outsider," believed that this material was essential to any book on women. There were other substantive disagreements too. Yet our most serious disagreement did not involve who or what to include in this book, but rather another, seemingly extraneous, issue: namely, the pace at which we would do the interviewing. In brief, I wanted to go fast, and Rafiqa wanted to go slow. It had taken us months to find appropriate subjects, and once we found them I wanted to be sure we got the material we needed, especially when one woman seemed to lose interest in talking with us. Rafiqa, who in any case had other professional commitments that were weighing on her, advised that we back off some and go about the interviewing at a relaxed pace as we had with the *sheikh*s. The disagreement, muted at first, eventually escalated into a high-decibel quarrel. At that point my wife, also a psychologist (but with a feminine viewpoint), told me that I was losing perspective, and she suggested that I look into my contribution to the fracas.

Which I did. And what became clear to me—or clearer, I should say—is that I was attempting to impose my views on Rafiqa, without much willingness to compromise. I was doing so, I had to admit, because deep down part of me felt it was my prerogative to do so—my prerogative because I was older, more experienced, and yes, because I was a Western male. These issues had not come up before between us, I realized, because up until the book Rafiqa had uncomplainingly played a secondary, even submissive, role. Now, with her personality fully engaged in this project, she sought to assert herself. Indeed, it became obvious that in our own way, Rafiqa and I were painfully playing out a struggle that is at the heart of the stories of the women in this book. Intriguing as all this was to me, it was also a shameful moment of truth. For a while, I considered jettisoning the project altogether in light of this awareness. But, as is apparent, I did not take that path. Instead I sought to work through these problems as best I could with Rafiqa in the course of the book.

I am relieved that our friendship has survived this experience and emerged from it with a few saving blemishes. And the crisis, perhaps inevitable, may have contributed to the book itself. For sure, it brought home to me, as nothing else could, some of the struggles that our subjects discuss in this book. In any event, it is with a clearer understanding, and a somewhat clearer conscience, that I now feel I can say,

And so we set out to find some Palestinian women, mothers and daughters, who will tell us their stories . . .

—*Michael Gorkin*
October 1995

Introduction

Samir Dayal

Three Mothers, Three Daughters offers a glimpse into everyday Palestinian
life under Israeli occupation, as the Palestinians see it. It is the product
of the collaboration between a Muslim woman, Rafiqa Othman, who lives
in an Arab village, and a Jewish male clinical psychologist, Michael
Gorkin. This interdisciplinary collaboration itself is of some interest in
the field of cultural anthropology, but it also has human interest. A
friendship between a Jewish man and an Arab woman is unusual enough,
as the authors themselves remark, but their working together as an interviewing team for this book embodies the hope for a shared future for
the Israelis and the Palestinians, the hope that the two cultural groups
will find it possible to work and live together.

This hope, which informs every page of the book, would surely have
been enough to warrant the book's republication in the new Cultural
Studies series (it was originally published by the University of California Press in 1996). But one could give other reasons. Traditional Muslim rules governing women's participation in public life being what they
are, "insider" accounts of women's daily lives are rare. Yet this book
does not stoke the prurient or Orientalist curiosity that has driven many
outsiders since the Enlightenment. Rather, the personal accounts of the
six women that form the core of the book have a universal appeal. They

show, in their unpretentious and modest way, how much Israeli and Palestinian families actually share, vividly recreating the web of small events and intimate family connections that make up the lives of these Palestinians. But they are also shot through with a sense, simultaneously, of the historic significance and the transitional quality of everyday Palestinian reality.

THE POLITICS OF THE EVERYDAY

We often hear in Cultural Studies about "everyday life." However, it is often precisely the daily experience of ordinary people that is suffocated under the theoretical point or polemic at issue in some expatiation on "the meaning" of the quotidian. We hear, for instance, about "resistance" to institutions or to power in the everyday act of insurgent behavior from subaltern groups. We hear about the agonistic process of negotiations between the Israelis and Palestinians. We hear about the problem of the status of Palestinian citizenship. The attempt in most studies that deal with the issues of Palestinian life and politics today (with the exception of Edward Said and a few other writers of his caliber) is often to present a theoretical framework and illustrate it by a few ethnographic or cultural examples. That is all well and good. But few accounts successfully marry the theoretical or academic discourse with the more unruly and frequently messy testimony of personal life, along with its frustrations and even its inconsequentialities.

From this book, however, we learn something about the significant ordinary things that give experience its materiality and immediacy: dress, food, professional and domestic work done by younger and older women. We are given not only the inert cliché (often presented in Cultural Studies circles as a first principle in cross-cultural understandings of gender politics) about sex segregation in Muslim societies, but an intimate, lived perspective on the actual range of social interactions between and among girls and women as contrasted with the barriers to social interaction between the sexes. Moreover, we learn about this sanctioned sexual segregation from the perspective of the girls and women themselves, in first person narrative. We learn about the intimate joys of their home life even in hard times and about the hardship of being separated from their homes before they are destroyed or taken by the occupying forces.

The interviews give us a window onto many threshold events in the women's lives: their education (when they are afforded formal education), key events in their childhoods, their entry into the adult world through marriage, motherhood, sometimes even their martyrdom, as well as the traditions and ideologies associated with these events. The attention to the grain of daily life bespeaks the authors' appreciation that cultural politics begins in the local and may end in the local, rather than being referenced to the global.

But this is not to say that the interviews are not contextualized within a wider frame. On almost every page the interviewees are acutely aware of how the seemingly intractable deadlock in peace negotiations between the Israelis and the Palestinians transforms the mundane reality of individuals and their families. In the family of Umm Abdullah and in that of Umm Khaled, for instance, the impact of the occupation is truly harsh. These two women must endure the loss of what is dearest to them: home, children, and way of life. However, their politicization is not expressed in ready-made ideological language but emerges from quotidian hardship. For here political engagement is a matter of necessity, a matter of agency and history.

ISLAM AND WESTERN MODERNITY

Given the bad press Islam as a world-historical force has received in the West since the 1980 Iranian Islamic revolution, and more recently in response to the activities of Osama bin Laden (the leader of a militant faction advocating fundamentalist Islamist views), this book usefully presents a truer, more human face to Islam. It reminds students of culture that even those who side with the fundamentalists sincerely and fervently believe that they and Islam are in no sense hostile to women's rights, and that they are not opposed in an undiscriminating way to Western modernity or "progress" and change. It has become increasingly important to resist the lazy equation of Islam with blind and sometimes violent fundamentalism, to be wary of the circulation of unflattering images of the veil, of "bearded mullahs with kalashnikovs," of anti-Western terrorism, and of the oppression of women under shariah law (Haddad and Esposito, p. x).

The authors are sensitive to the need to balance the claims of Western modernity on the one side and Islam on the other, leaving aside for the moment other cultures' claims. This sensitivity is thrown into relief if we contrast Gorkin and Othman's approach with that of someone such as Mervat Hatem. Writing about women in Egypt, Hatem (1998) writes, "Islamists are unequivocal in declaring the importance of science, reason, professional education, and technology in the building of the new society. . . . Islamist, oppositional discourse is very modernist. It accepts the nuclear family and the modern systems of education and training as the basis of its alternative Islamic society" (p. 97). It is not that Hatem is wrong. But Gorkin and Othman by contrast show admirable restraint about reaching so confident a conclusion. For instance, they are more attuned to the tensions between Western modernity/secularism and Islam in matters having to do with the family.

The issue of women in Islam, and within the Muslim family, has been not only a provocative question for Western cultural theory but an emotionally fraught issue for women outside Western academe, as demonstrated by the 1994 United Nations' Population and Development Conference in Cairo and the 1995 United Nations' Fourth World Conference on Women in Beijing (see Haddad and Esposito, p. xi). Eschewing the contentiousness and emotionalism that sometimes accompanies representations of Islamic women on both sides of the cultural divide, this book offers a glimpse into everyday life informed by the kind of material specificity that a cultural ethnographer would see as indispensable.

Among the most striking observations to emerge from these pages is a sense of what one might call (after Paolo Freire's famous work, *The Pedagogy of the Oppressed*) the "conscientization" of the women, even some of the more traditional older women. The stories of the six women in the book make it clear that there is no turning back from the entry of women into the political fray. This politicization and increasing self-determination of women is a recent development in the tenor of everyday Palestinian life. Gorkin and Othman frequently observe that men are increasingly becoming open to the idea of political involvement for their wives, sisters, and mothers, even as the public role of women in society remains closely constrained within the dictates of the social codes of Islam and Muslim standards of propriety and modesty. As Gorkin notes, "what is striking is that not one of the six women in this study questions the *right* of women to be involved" although their "penchant for politics is quite varied" (p. 5).

The changing lives of the women capture on a small scale the struggles and the hopes of an emergent nation that is not yet universally recognized as a sovereign state, a nation in which the ordinary individual is often defined by his or her solidarity with Palestinian nationalism in a way that may be hard for an American or a British reader to grasp. The authors never let the reader forget the charged political backdrop of the ordinary stories they present. The absence of the state as a looming, disciplinary presence (leaving aside for the moment Yasser Arafat's authority) is a remarkable circumstance, because the Palestinians' sense of themselves as "a people," united by a culture and a future-orientedness as a people, comes not from a constitution or a government but from the ground up, from the everyday experience and political engagement of the ordinary person.

The authors recognize that in the struggle for political independence, many conflicts arise between traditional Muslim values and "modern" deomocratic exigencies, such as the conflict between Islam's respect for all life and armed activism. They are always alert to the possible tensions within families between so-called "Western" or "modern" values and "traditional" values, in matters personal and public. For example, they are conscious of the ambivalence experienced by each of the young women they interview in matters relating to finding a mate and starting a life independent of the parents. Indeed, what lends particular poignancy to the increased participation of Palestinian women in the secular, political struggle is often the implied or stated contrast with the importance of religion and tradition in their lives.

There is the story of Samira, for instance, who is caught reading Marxist literature by a very religious teacher. And there is the story of Umm Khaled who continues to believe in the power of faith and in the power of traditional faith healers, while at the same time expressing a strong objection to the intifada and a strong preference for a peaceful road to a reconciliation between the Israelis and the Arabs. In other words, the drama of the women's emergence into the public sphere is heightened by the complexity that emerges from these personal accounts.

Gorkin and Othman make no pretence of imposing any conceptual scaffolding on their subjects, and if Gorkin as a Jew has any bias toward or defensiveness about Israel, the reader would be hard pressed to see any evidence of it here. Both authors have the grace to let the subjects speak for themselves and in their own voices, respecting even the individual's colloquial style and judiciously allowing Arabic expressions to spice the translation.

The quiet tone of the authors' own prose and editorial commentary is a complement to the immediacy, and often the passion, of the six women's narratives. When they present their own views, the authors' personal candor matches that of their subjects. It is clear from his prefatory remarks, for instance, that Gorkin is aware of the unorthodox nature of a collaboration between a Jewish, "Western" male and an unmarried Arab woman doing ethnographic work on Palestinian women. And Othman is equally self-aware in her afterword to the book

that her role is precarious; sometimes she finds herself acting as a native informant and at other times as a "friend" among her subjects. She
acknowledges the difficult professional and personal position in which
she has placed herself. She knows she is vulnerable to the accusation of
"eib" or shame and notes that the support she receives from her understanding family in spite of all this is not something she could have
counted on. But both authors are also conscious that one of the charms
of this book is precisely this self-consciousness. And they know that one
of the reasons why this book will appeal to a student of contemporary
Cultural Studies is its self-referential ethnographic sophistication, so
that in a very understated way they allow themselves to become ethnographic subjects as well.

THE CONTEXT OF CULTURAL STUDIES

Gorkin is concerned to situate the book in the context of Cultural Studies. And one could say that the value of the book to Cultural Studies de-
rives primarily from the access the authors' "field work" provides to the
intensely private sphere of the Muslim family and even more significantly,
access to particular Muslim women's lives and psyches. And it is important to respect that particularity. After all, these six women are significantly different, and no easy generalizations can be made about the attitudes or outlook of "the Muslim woman," as though such a thing existed.
It has by now become a truism of Cultural Studies that one should not
conceptualize "the Muslim" any more than one should conceptualize "the
Oriental" or "the Black Man" as a homogeneous entity.

More generally, one of the key concerns for Cultural Studies is the
construction of subjectivity in a historicized context. Gorkin and
Othman are sensitive to this concern. They say that they are interested
not only in "highlight[ing] differences in generational experiences" but
in "captur[ing] something of the idiosyncratic and subjective nature of
storytelling itself" (p. 10). They go on to acknowledge too the inevi-

table effect of their editorial or filtering role: "the fact that we, as authors, choose to present some of these variations in perspective and not others, is a further subjectivity that cannot be overlooked" (p. 10).

Gorkin explicitly addresses the challenge posed to traditional ethnography by recent theoretical developments in Cultural Studies. He speaks, for instance, of the issues of accuracy and truth in the representation of the "informant's" life, issues addressed by what he calls a "new school of postmodern ethnography" (p. 9). According to this postmodern ethnography, informant and investigator both contribute to the construction of text and its meaning. This dialogical production of the informant's life, according to this new school of thought, should itself become part of the story, or at least the textual account should present itself as self-conscious about its dialogical nature and its "fragmentariness." Gorkin says he and Othman agree in principle "that both informant and investigator contribute to the creation of the text" and are conscious that their backgrounds as a white (Jewish) male outsider and a female (Muslim) insider certainly played a part in how the accounts of the six women's lives turned out. The interviews on which the narrative accounts are based would have been impossible or radically different had they tried to do the interviews alone. Had Gorkin attempted to interview the women by himself, for instance, they certainly would not have been as forthcoming as they evidently have been on intimate matters—matters having to do with the women's sexual lives and their emotions.

But Gorkin and Othman are not postmodernists. They place the emphasis on the informants, acknowledging but consciously minimizing any doubt about the verisimilitude or truth-value of the oral histories presented in these pages. The women are fully invested with authority over their own life stories. Gorkin and Othman attempt to suppress any conscious editorializing or distortion of the original histories, and as far as possible strive to maintain the objectivity of documentary recorders of authentic and unmediated experience. In any event, the reader is given to understand that all the cards are on the table, and at the same time that the book is not naively oblivious to recent issues in Cultural

Studies. It may be hoped therefore that the book will appeal not only to academic readers but to readers with a more general interest in cross-cultural understanding.

REFERENCES

Freire, Paolo. (1970). *The Pedagogy of the Oppressed.* Trans. M. B. Ramos. New York: Seabury.

Haddad, Yvonne Yazbeck, and Esposito, John L., eds. (1998). *Islam, Gender, and Social Change.* New York: Oxford University Press.

Hatem, Mervat. (1998). Secularist and Islamist discourses on modernity in Egypt and the evolution of the postcolonial nation-state. In *Islam, Gender, and Social Change*, ed. Y. Haddad and J. Esposito, pp. 85–99.

Umm Mahmud
and Marianne

(EAST JERUSALEM)

Umm Mahmud

Umm Mahmud (Adila)* is a short heavy-hipped woman who, at seventy-two years old, looks like—and is—the matriarch of a large family. Mother to thirteen adult children (ranging in age from twenty-seven to fifty-six years old) and grandmother to thirty-seven, she spends most of her time these days in the salon, kitchen, or veranda of her three-bedroom stone house where she likes to host her frequent visitors. Her husband, seventy-eight years old, a retired laborer, is generally somewhere around their yard tending his fruit trees, vegetable and herb garden, and rabbit hutches, or doing household repairs.

Married fifty-eight years, Umm and Abu Mahmud have lived fifty-four years in their hillside house in East Jerusalem, and all their children were raised here. From the veranda of their house there is a postcard-pretty view of the walled Old City and the golden-domed Qubat

---

* Only close family members might use a woman's given name; typically people refer to her as *umm* [mother] of her first son, hence, Umm Mahmud. Her husband is Abu Mahmud, father of Mahmud. Umm Mahmud often called her husband "Abu Mahmud" or, less frequently, "Hajj" or "our Hajj" (the honorific title for a man who has made the pilgrimage, the *hajj*, to Mecca). A woman who has made the *hajj* is known as "Hajja."

al-Sakhra, framed by the hills of southern Jerusalem that lead off to Bethlehem. Far less attractive, from Umm Mahmud's perspective, is the view directly behind the house: a Jewish housing complex that has recently been built.

Among the adult children only one unmarried daughter, Marianne, remains in the main house. A son, along with his family, lives in the basement apartment of the house; and twenty meters away, another daughter and her family have their home. Three more children and their families also live in East Jerusalem, while seven of the children and their families have emigrated (four to the United States, two to Kuwait, and one to Jordan).

We began interviewing Umm Mahmud in April 1994, shortly after we met Marianne. Marianne encouraged her mother to join her in the study, and the latter—to accommodate her daughter, it seemed—agreed to give it a try. A modest and traditional woman, Umm Mahmud was unaccustomed to talking about herself with strangers. And while she was quite adept at relating an incident or adventure, in the theatrical and semidiscursive way of women of her generation, she remained throughout our six interviews a somewhat reluctant subject.

All the interviews with Umm Mahmud took place in the comfortable veranda of their home. There, seated on the red velvet sofa, with the tape recorder lying beside two Korans on the wooden coffee table, we interviewed her—out of earshot of Abu Mahmud who, in any case, put up no resistance to his wife's or daughter's participation. Occasionally, one or another of the grandchildren would drop by out of curiosity, and at the end of the sessions Marianne would usually appear with coffee and something to eat. Once Rafiqa Othman did the interviewing alone: the occasion on which Umm Mahmud recalled the details of her wedding.

Born in 1921, as the British Mandate period was about to begin, Umm Mahmud spent her childhood and early adulthood in a turbulent period of Palestinian history. As a person with little interest in politics, the main thrust of her recollections and reflections concerns the private life of her family and herself. And yet, as a Palestinian living in East Jerusalem, her life was unavoidably affected by the political waves that engulfed the area. Below, then, are some of her memories of that period.

❧

I will start from the beginning. What I was told is that our family— my father's people- -have been living in this neighborhood for seven generations. Before that, they say, our people came from a village near Jaffa, on the coast. There were three brothers and for some reason they all went their own ways. One went to Egypt, one to Syria, and one came here to East Jerusalem. We are from that line. More than that, God alone knows.

My father's family, like almost everybody else, were *fellahin* [peasant farmers]. They had land a few kilometers from here. My father, though, was not a *fellah*. From the time I opened my eyes and could see the world around me, my father was a policeman- here, I'll show you his picture. [Umm Mahmud calls to Marianne in the other room, and the latter brings in an old black and white family portrait showing a mustachioed young man in a British police uniform standing above a seated young woman and a small girl, both in whitish floor-length dresses.] That was him in his handsome *sawari* [mounted police] uniform, which he wore while riding on his horse. He worked for the British until they left Palestine. And take a look at my mother! A beautiful woman, no? And look at that dress I'm wearing—this style is coming back just now. It's fine, don't you think? And the shoes are fine too. My father, God bless his memory, used to bring the shoemaker to our house to make us shoes. Aaah! I swear, those were good days, better than today, much better. [After a few minutes Marianne leaves the room. A nine-year-old granddaughter, Nabila, who had entered with Marianne, continues to sit on the sofa next to Umm Mahmud listening to her recollections.]

My father didn't work in the fields. We hired workers. And my mother worked too, especially at harvest time. We used to grow grains— wheat, corn, barley—and *kersana* [a legume] for feeding animals. We ourselves didn't raise sheep or goats. Just grains. My mother used to work very hard. She'd spend most of the day out in the fields when she worked, and she'd carry these huge loads around on her head. She'd help distribute the harvest to each of my father's brothers. Each brother had a special spot where he kept his harvest. We did too. More than that, I don't really know. I myself didn't work out there. What happened to our fields? Split in the inheritance among the brothers' children, and split again among their children—it's all divided now. No, I don't have any of it. I didn't inherit any of it.

In our family we were five boys and five girls. Seven of us are still alive. We used to live right over there, in that place with the blue shutters. [Umm Mahmud points to a house about two hundred meters away.] Two of my brothers and their families are living in it now. It's a good-sized place, comfortable. That's where I grew up. I'm the oldest child, the first. When you're the oldest daughter like I was, the way it was then is that you took care of the ones who came after you. You helped out your mother. When she was out in the fields I had to watch the children in the house, take care of the house—cleaning and washing up. Not cooking, though. My mother preferred to do all the cooking by herself. I never learned to cook until I got married and went to my mother-in-law's house. But I liked taking care of the house, doing the housework. That was alright with me. Except for one thing. I would have liked to go to school.

There were schools for girls in those days, oh yes. There was a very good one called the Islamic school, near al-Aqsa Mosque. It went up to ninth grade. It's still there, the same school. Some girls from our neighborhood were going there when I was a child. I'd see them go off with their school bags. I was so envious, I wanted to go too. One day I went to my mother and told her, "Tell father to let me go to school. Other girls are going." She answered me, "Alright, I'll ask him. When he comes home from work today." When my father came home she told him, but he immediately answered, "No, she's not going! What does she need school for? It will only make her strong-willed." My father—

blessed be his memory—he was an educated man. He knew how to read and write in Arabic and in English too. But he didn't want me to learn. He wanted me to fear him, to know that he was the strong one. My mother was a modest woman, respectful of my father. She couldn't press him. After he refused, she said to me, "Enough! Father says there's no school, so there's no school." Later, God be praised, she did press him to send my sisters and they got to go. Me, he left without schooling.

Now I have educated children myself, boys and girls. When they were younger sometimes they'd come to me with their homework. They would say, "Open the book. See if I've got this memorized right." And I would have to tell them I can't read. My husband, the same. Our Hajj was the son of a *fellah,* he spent his boyhood with his father growing chickpeas and lentils. He hardly went to school at all. A few simple things he can read—more than I can. But open up a newspaper and read it? No, no. Read the Koran? I can't, he can't . . . [Nabila leaning on her grandmother interrupts: "*Ya* grandmother, I will teach you. I will Arabic is easy, it's not like English."] May God bless you, sweetheart, but it's too late for me. My children, too, they wanted to teach me when they were going to school. Too late. When you're a girl, that's the time to learn. My father, blessed be his memory, didn't want me to learn. And that's the way it was.

So, while some of my friends were off at school, I was at home. There were others like me too—girls who stayed at home and did chores. One of the things I had to do was fetch water. I'd do this with other friends. There was a well up on the hill. We'd take jars on our heads and go up there two or three times a day, as much as was needed. Sometimes, if there was not enough rain that well didn't have water. Then we'd have to go all the way to Silwan [two kilometers away, to the south of the walled Old City]. There was always water down there. Sometimes the stream was so fast-flowing it was even dangerous. You could slip in and drown easily. I'd go down there with friends, like my neighbor across the way—she just died, God bless her memory. She'd come with a mule and we'd go together. My mother didn't like me riding this mule. But what, I was going to walk alongside a mule and not ride on top of him? I rode, of course. And then one day it happened. I was riding this mule, I slipped off and fell on my shoulder. I didn't dare say anything to my mother. That whole night I didn't sleep. "What's wrong?" she asked me in the morning. "I fell, mother, my arm and shoulder are hurting me." I didn't say anything about the mule. She didn't ask anything either. My mother made me a compress—back then you didn't go to a doctor for things like this. In the compress was a mixture of olive oil soap and raw eggs. She put it on my shoulder and it worked. Though, to this day my shoulder sometimes betrays me.

Besides that fall from the mule, another thing happened to me when I was a girl that I can still see as clearly as if it was before my eyes now, like on television. I was about thirteen years old at the time. My mother was out in the fields harvesting. I was in the house cleaning, and I wanted to be clever and do a real good job that day. We had very good furniture, like an old armoire with small sculpted camels on it and a wonderful old mirror. It was a piece of furniture from way back. I think my mother had it as part of her wedding gifts. Well, during the cleaning I took down the mirror and it fell from my hands and smashed on the floor. Half out of my mind, I ran to the fields where my mother was. "Mama, Mama!" I yelled as hard as I could. "What's wrong with you?" she yelled back. "What's happened? Did your brother fall into the well?" I answered her, "No, no. The mirror fell and broke." She said, "Oh God, let it be gone then. It's alright, go home and watch after your brother." I said, "But father is coming back from work soon. He'll beat me!" My mother tried to calm me down a little, and then she sent me home. Then my father came back, saying, "Who broke the mirror?" My mother, who was back from the fields by then, said to him, "Quiet. Not a word. Adila broke it when she was cleaning. Let it be." I was dying with fear, but my father didn't say one word to me.

Soon after that, I fell sick with something strange. I had a fever and my head felt all confused. People would talk to me and I wouldn't know how to answer. Someone would come to see me in the evening and I would say, "Good morning." I was half-crazy, I tell you. So my father decided to bring me to a doctor. The doctor looked me over and said I had an infection. He told my parents not to give me this to eat, and instead give me that. It didn't help, I stayed sick. Then my mother talked to this neighbor who told her what I needed was herbs. There was an old woman in our neighborhood who specialized in herbal cures. She cooked up this mixture of herbs and "sabbath eggs." That's what they were called—eggs laid on the sabbath. Don't ask me why "sabbath eggs," I have no idea. Anyway, they brought me this mixture, they surprised me with it. They came suddenly one day and said swallow it all down and leave nothing for anybody else. I did what I was told. And do you know what? I got better. Soon after that I was myself again.

I don't know if you believe in these things, but I do. I don't believe in faith healers or fortune-tellers—*haram*, forbidden. Those who pretend to know the past and the future are phonies. Only God knows what is written. *But,* traditional healers who use herbs, that's another thing. Some of their prescriptions *do* work like magic. That mixture they gave me, I've used it on others. Like with my son Tawfiq after his uncle Ahmad died. He was very close to him and he went into shock. For two years after that he went to this doctor or that. I didn't even know he was going to doctors until one day he told me. I said to him, "Tawfiq, I want you to try the cure they gave me." I took the same herbs—without the eggs—boiled them in water, and gave it to him for three days. I swear, it cured him. Really. Just like it cured me back then when I was in shock, and the doctors couldn't help me.

And that's the way it was. I remember those days just like it was yesterday. Things like that you can't forget. The good and the bad, *yom asal, yom basal* [days of honey, days of onion]—I remember, I remember. What else? Play? Sure, we played in those days. No, we didn't play with boys. My parents didn't approve of girls and boys playing together. *Haram!* I accepted it, and I'll tell you the truth, I have no regrets. I used to play with girls who lived nearby, cousins. We'd play house. We'd take old rags and make dolls out of them, and we'd take rocks and make the houses. For furniture, we'd use things like old sardine cans. And then we'd make up stories. That's the way we played usually. I liked it, sure. But there wasn't so much time for playing. There were lots of things to take care of around the house. And besides, by the time I was fourteen I was already out of my mother's house. I was married at fourteen. Who had time to play?

✐

My father chose my husband for me. What, the girl choose her own husband? It was arranged by my father—my mother talked with him about it—and I was told that I was going to be married to this man. I didn't know him at all at the time. But he knew me. My husband lived in the neighborhood and—he told me this after we were married—he'd had his eye on me. We are cousins, not close cousins, but from the same clan. He was about twenty then. His parents had wanted him to marry someone else but he refused. He let his parents know that he wanted me and they agreed. They came to my father and mother, and my father told them to wait and he would soon give them an answer. You see, my father respected their family and they knew that. My father had already married off his sister to my husband's older brother. But before he could agree to my marrying my husband, he had to make sure none of his brothers' sons, or a closer cousin, opposed it. A close cousin has the right to marry the girl—back then, anyway, that's the way it was. There was no opposition, so my father said yes.

My husband's parents then sent an old man in the neighborhood, a respected man, to arrange the *mahr* [bride price]. The *mahr* for me was a big one—forty Palestinian pounds pre-*mahr* and twenty Palestinian pounds post-*mahr.* You could buy a lot of things with it, and I did. I mean, my mother did. My mother went out and bought me about twenty

---

* The *mahr* or bride price (paid by the groom's family to the bride's family) was, and still is, typically divided into two parts: that paid before the wedding, the pre-*mahr,* and that paid in the case of divorce, the post-*mahr.*

pounds' worth of gold. Two gold bracelets, a gold chain, a gold earring, and four rings. I also got an armoire, a beautiful and expensive one—I wish I still had it. And I got a rug, sheets, six large pillows and two small ones, and four comforters that some Jew who called himself Abu Musa made for us. And some dresses, and other things which my mother, blessed be her memory, sewed for me. If I close my eyes I can see all these beautiful things before me. A pity I don't have them any-more. That's life, you're not thinking about it then, only later you realize you should have held onto them.

Anyway, that was what I did with the forty pounds that I got after they signed the *kitab* [marriage agreement]. The signing of the *kitab* almost didn't come off, though. I found this out later. When the *sheikh* [religious official] asked my father how old I was, my father stated the truth. "Fourteen," he said. The *sheikh* said he couldn't write the *kitab*, I wasn't legal age.* The men in my father's family quickly jumped in and said, "No, no. Her father has made a mistake. She's nineteen!" So the *sheikh* agreed and my father signed with my husband. And that was it. My fate was decided. Three months later we had the wedding.

Back in those days, the wedding was usually two days. The first night was *leilat al-henna* [night of the henna], and the second night was the wedding party. For me, the *leilat al-henna* was done the usual way. There was a party at my parents' house for the women of both families. The women in my husband's family brought the henna powder, and a woman who's an expert—they paid her to come—prepared the henna. She mixed it with some fragrance and made a paste out of it. Then she decorated my hands with all kinds of designs. Just my hands, not my face. While she was decorating me, the women stood around us singing things like, "Put out your hands / Open them so we can put on the

---

* According to British Mandate law at the time, a girl had to be sixteen years old to be married, that is, to have a *kitab* signed in her name. Now, as in 1948, the groom and the bride's representative, usually her father, sign the contract in the presence of a Muslim religious official, a *sheikh*.

henna / Beautiful decorations . . . " Something like that, I can't sing it so well. After the henna was put on they wrapped my hands in a cloth. I slept bandaged up like that, and the next morning when they brushed the soot away there were these beautiful decorations. Reddish-brown decorations. The next night, at the wedding party, as I danced my hands would show off these beautiful designs. You know, they don't do this anymore in our neighborhood or in the towns. Only in the villages have they kept the *leilat al-henna*. It's a fine custom though. I like it.

The big party was the next night, the wedding night. The whole neighborhood was invited, hundreds of people. The party is at the groom's house, you know. That's where the guests come and have the dinner. The custom then was that the night before, as the *leilat al-henna* is going on, the men in the groom's family slaughtered sheep. Ten, maybe twelve sheep—enough to feed everyone, and then some. They cooked the meat in a sauce in huge copper pots and served it with rice. There were also other things to eat. Okra and tomatoes, stuffed squash and eggplants, salads. The custom then was to send over some food to the bride's family. They ate separately along with close friends. The food that was sent over might be cooked or it might be the raw ingredients, sacks of rice and slabs of meat.

My mother preferred to do her own cooking. That was her way. She wanted to prepare a special meal. She roasted the lamb in the oven with potatoes. So delicious! Really, it was an even better meal than my mother-in-law served at her house. Yes, I ate it, why not? I ate with our guests, sure. Then, I got dressed—with help. There was a woman named *al-Mashta* [the comber], that was her nickname. She was an older woman, an expert at dressing and making up brides. I had many wedding dresses, as usual. My mother had chosen the patterns and a neighbor, an expert seamstress, made up the dresses. My mother had wonderful taste, she liked the finest things. "High, high" style. Beautiful dresses made of village silk and silk from India. Do you think they wear things like this today? No, not at all. They were floor-length dresses and magnificent. There was a white dress to wear when I was taken from my mother's house, and several others to shift into during the party. There was a blue one with half-sleeves and decorated with lace. Another was green streaked with a flower print. And there was a red one too. Oh, how I wish I still had them! I got rid of them when they became small on me. I used to have narrow hips, not like today—as you can see. What a pity I didn't save them!

So *al-Mashta* helped put me together in my white dress. It was delicate and sort of revealing up top. But no matter. I was covered —this was the custom—by an *abah* [a man's coat] so nobody could see my upper body or made-up face. That's the way I was when the men from my husband's family came to take me. He didn't come, of course. Just his father, brothers, and uncles. My father handed me over to them. How did I feel? Well, I'll tell you the truth, I didn't really understand it all. It's not easy for a girl to leave her parents' house, but I didn't realize the full meaning of it then. My husband's home was only a few houses from ours, so I figured I wasn't going far away. Still, when my mother and father began weeping, I wept too. But I was ignorant, I didn't understand the whole thing really.

We walked over to my husband's house. Usually, there's a *zaffu* [wedding procession], but we lived so close there was none. No horses either. Here the brides didn't ride, they walked. Unless the bride married someone from Silwan, or over in Lifta. Then, since it was a few kilometers away, she rode on a horse. Me, I walked. When I got there the guests had finished their meal. The men were sitting on straw mats and leaning on cushions out in the yard. They were sitting, talking, smoking. I went by them and into the house where the women were. Outside in the yard, a member of my husband's family was receiving gifts. Money. Not in envelopes the way they do it today, hidden and secret so nobody knows who gives what. Back then it was done openly, and with each gift they'd announce, "Abu So-and-so has given two pounds, or one pound, whatever. Thanks from God to you, Abu So-and-so." And it would be written down too. There was no shame in giving less. You gave according to your ability, and the groom's family used the money to cover expenses—the food, the musicians, the *mahr*. That's the way it was then. I swear, the old ways were sweeter, much sweeter.

So, anyway, I was taken inside the house with the women. The only man allowed inside was my husband. *Al-Mashta* stayed with me the whole time. I didn't know how to dance. She guided me, she even moved my hands for me. She put small lights on my fingernails and also on my body, lights that had batteries. When I danced, moving my hands with the henna decorations, my fingernails lit up. She also put a crown of flowers on my head. It was made out of jasmine flowers, so when I moved, the fragrance carried around the room. We danced and sang for hours, and every hour or so I'd shift into another of my dresses. *Al-Mashta* had brought along with her some old women who were experts in singing. They knew all the wedding songs. They sang and the guests sang along with them. Toward the end, as I was dancing slowly with *al-Mashta* guiding me, my husband came up to me. I was dancing with my eyes closed, and then, as I danced, my husband came and lifted the *tarha* [veil] I was wearing, and I opened my eyes to him. If I shut my eyes right now, I can see it all. Is this something a person can forget? I remember everything as if it were happening now.

And that was it. The party ended and I was married. Fourteen years old, and a bride. Sure, it was too young. I think a girl should be twenty years old when she marries, that's not too late. There's plenty of time to have children and the girl knows more at twenty. What did I know? I was ignorant, I had no idea what to expect. Did anyone tell me anything about the wedding night? No, nobody. My mother didn't say anything to me, nobody did. No friends, nobody. Talking about what took place on the wedding night was not something you did. It would have been too embarrassing. I was ignorant. I just figured that whatever happened to others would happen to me, that's all.

What happened the next morning? The usual, that's all. What was usual? Well, the usual was that the bride's family came in and washed off the bride. Usually it was the mother. My mother didn't wash me, though. My aunt, who was already living there, washed me. My husband went and washed himself. People had the idea back then that if the couple didn't wash they wouldn't have any children. They said the devil would get between them. So, my aunt washed me, and that was it. *Khalas*, finished.

The sheet? You want to know about that too? What can I tell you? The custom was that the bride's family would take the sheet with the blood on it and show it to people. With a girl whose reputation wasn't so good—I mean, there might be rumors about her—her father would take the sheet to the coffee house to prove everything was alright. With me, my mother took the sheet and went and washed it. People used to say that whoever washed the sheet, the food she cooked would be delicious. I have no idea why they said this, they just did. I tell you, I've never done anything like this with my daughters. No coming the next morning, no washing, no sheets, nothing. Today we don't do this, not here in our neighborhood.

Today, the young people know everything. Television, books. They read about these things, they know what's happening. They go off on a honeymoon by themselves and that's it. In my time there was no honeymoon. You got married, you spent a couple of days alone with your husband at your mother-in-law's house—they left you alone pretty much—and *khalas*, it was over. Your husband went back to work and you started to work at your mother-in-law's house. No, my young lady, no honeymoons back in those days. Not at all.

$$\text{❧}$$

Two days later I started my chores at my mother-in-law's house. I was part of their family now. She was a strong woman, my mother-in-law—strong like a man. But a good woman! God bless her memory. She taught me to cook and bake. I did the baking for her house, I made our bread. I swear, it was a good life in those days. Sweet, sweet as honey. We were three couples in the house. My husband's younger brother and his wife, along with his parents. Sometimes we ate together and sometimes separately. My mother-in-law, blessed be her memory, wanted us to be separate households. "Your husband is strong, he will provide for you," she told me. True, he was making enough for us. He was working as a stonemason in the Jewish graveyard on the Mount of Olives. Six years he worked there. His boss liked him, he's a hard worker, and he did fine. But really, I wanted us to be all together as one big household—share everything together. I got along well with my sister-in-law, so why not? My mother-in-law insisted we each look after ourselves, take responsibility for ourselves. That was her way. My mother had taught me to be obedient, so I went along. Sure I did.

I had my first child a year after I got married. When I got pregnant I didn't understand what was happening. I had no idea what it was like to give birth. My aunt was pregnant at the same time, so I figured I'll watch how she does it and I'll do the same. At the time, some women gave birth at the hospital and some at home. My parents wanted me to give birth in the hospital, not at home. I went to the hospital next to Maskubiya jail. I had the baby there. But he was born dead, I don't know why. The doctors turned to my father and said to him, "How did you marry her off so young? Was it so important for you to see her in a wedding dress?" My father wept. He blamed himself for the baby's death. My mother-in-law saw the baby. She told me later that he was so big and beautiful she couldn't forget him. Oh God protect us, his poor creatures! They buried my baby like he was an adult. They washed him, dressed him in white, prayed over him, and buried him in the graveyard. And that was it—my first one, gone.

After that my mother-in-law told me, "Enough, no more going to the hospital. It's your mother who wanted you to go to the hospital. From now on, you'll give birth at home. *Khalas!*" Two years later, I brought Mahmud at home. My mother-in-law helped me, along with the midwife. I tell you, I preferred it at home. More comfortable that way. In the end, I brought Tawfiq, Adel, Majda, and Marianne in the hospital. But really, I preferred it at home with a midwife. There was a good one in our area. She was an older woman. She didn't have any book learning, but she knew what she was doing. She'd come with her tools and help me give birth. Then she'd come each day for a week and keep coming back the first month. It depended. She's the one who taught me how to wash the baby, how to massage it at night with olive oil—you do it to make him strong. She'd put *kuhl* [ash] on his eyelids to keep the eyes healthy and she'd put powder under the armpits. From top to bottom she'd inspect the baby to make sure it was alright, no rash or infection or anything. She was very good. I'd pay her a half-pound every day she was with me, and besides that, each week I'd give her a present—a box of snuff, a scarf, some soap. Maybe my husband gave her some money too, I don't know.

And that's how I brought my children until the last four. I lost one after Mahmud, but then everything went alright. They came, sometimes one on the head of the other. Thanks to God, my children grew quickly and strong—because of breastfeeding. We didn't use anything artificial or cow's milk. If one of the babies was crying my mother-in-law would give it a pacifier which she made herself. She'd make it by taking a piece of cloth and putting some grapes in it, or a mixture of crushed almonds and molasses. We used these pacifiers when the baby got to three or four months, they'd sleep a couple of hours on it.

My husband usually didn't help me with the babies, no. Only when the twins came. Then he was so happy he helped me. I couldn't manage without it. I thank God for all our good fortune. Seven girls and six boys, I thank God for them all. Do I prefer boys to girls? No, I can't say that. Abu Mahmud and I love the girls the same as the boys. We don't prefer one over the other. It's God who decides, so we must love them both the same. When each was born we passed out chocolates and candies, the same for boys and girls. The thing we didn't do was an *aqiqa* [celebratory meal in honor of the birth]. Not for boys and not for girls. According to our religion, you know, we are supposed to slaughter a sheep, cook it, and invite the neighbors and family. Somehow, each time, we neglected this. I tell you, I'm afraid that God will take account of this, that we didn't do it. I wish we had, but we didn't. This is something I regret.

᠌

It was shortly after the twins came that the war broke out. That was 1948. We had six children then. We were living here in this house. It wasn't so huge as it is today, we were building it slowly, slowly. There were lots of disturbances at the time. Over in Dir Yasin* the Jews killed the people, destroyed their homes. People were afraid, very afraid. We didn't know what to think. Me, I hardly had any idea what was happening. We didn't have television, I couldn't read, my husband couldn't read—what did I know? I was busy with the children all the time, I didn't have time to sit and talk with people. I tell you, we were ignorant back then. We knew nothing.

My husband was working then in two jobs. He was a cook in one of the British government schools and he used to sell milk too. There was a Jew, Salem, who used to come over here on his bicycle to buy milk from my husband, and then he'd take it over to the western side of the city where the Jews mostly were living. We had contact with Jews, sure. I would shop at Jewish stores. Shoes—I remember buying wonderful shoes at this Jewish shop near the Damascus Gate. Very cheap and beautiful, with pretty designs on them. I can still see them if I close my eyes.

Why the war started I can't say. I'm not the one to ask about that. All I know is that one day the British people at the school came to my husband and said, "We're leaving. In another week everything will be alright." They gave him some money as a last payment and that was it. I don't know why they left. They just handed over the country and left. Do they come and tell the little people like us what they're going to do? No, they tell the big shots. I don't know why they left. It's the way of the world. There's life and death, and that's it.

* In Dir Yasin, an Arab village that was located on the western outskirts of Jerusalem, Jewish irregular forces massacred some 250 villagers on April 9, 1948.

The war didn't start all at once and then stop all at once. It kept starting and stopping. After Dir Yasin and some other things like that, I decided to store some supplies for us. Rice, flour, bulgur wheat, noodles, lentils, chickpeas, and sugar. I bought things like that. I prepared for the worst. There were people fleeing their homes all over the city. As the fighting got bad, the Arabs living over in West Jerusalem fled—from Ein Karem, Talbiya, Baqa. Here in the eastern part of the city, most people fled too. But unlike those others in the western part of the city, the people from here were able to come back to their homes because the Jews didn't succeed in conquering this part of the city.

We stayed put. There were attacks on and off. One time, during an attack with lots of explosions going on nearby, I took off with all the children. I grabbed the twins first, they were the youngest, and the rest just ran after me. I kept running until I came to where some Arab soldiers were. They took care of us, thanks to God. He who has luck lives, he who is fated to die dies.

There were many who got killed in this war. My sister's husband got killed and another three or four of our neighbors. They weren't fighting in the army, they just got caught between the Jews and Arabs shooting at each other. I almost got killed too—three times. I remember once sitting under a fig tree doing some wash. A dog was at my side. Suddenly a bullet flew by and grazed the dog. I was just lucky it didn't hit me. The second time I was visiting my sister, her husband had just been killed. Supposedly the UN soldiers were watching over things and it was safe to go out. I was walking up to my sister's when, I swear, a bullet struck behind me and then another in front of me. "Hey girl, get out of the street!" someone yelled. I took off. If it was my fate to die that day, I would have died. And the third time I almost died was right here when I was making bread outside in the *tabun* [clay oven]. Usually during the war I'd do my baking and cooking inside the house on a tin oven, so I didn't have to go outside when it was dangerous. That day I thought it was safe. I'd just finished patting down the dough, and I was leaning forward to place it in the *tabun* when a bullet flew by me. I heard it strike the tree. And sure enough, sometime later I found it stuck right in the tree. I was lucky again.

Our whole family was lucky. Nothing happened to us and nothing happened to our home. We didn't flee and we didn't return, we just stayed. Abu Mahmud was too old to be a soldier, and besides he had no interest in politics—never has. He sat through most of the war with me. Now and then he got some day work, doing a little stone work here and there. For a period he was working in the Old City doing some stone work in a church. A friend found him this work. It didn't pay much, almost nothing, but we were able to get by because we had rented out the upstairs of the house, where we live now. That kept us going, and also I kept things stored. So we made it through. God be praised, we made it through.

꙳

After the war, life went on. We kept renting out the upstairs of the house for a while, and Abu Mahmud found some construction work. There were hard times, and good times. If Abu Mahmud brought ten Jordanian dinars, I managed with that. If he brought a hundred dinars, I used that too. We managed. I'm a woman from the old times. The women of my time knew how to save money, how to use things—how to use old clothing and cook over a wood fire. We knew how to clean clothes without soap but with ash. That's right, you put the ash in a piece of cloth and then put it in with the dirty clothes into boiling water. The clothes come out brilliant, shining. Today's women have washing machines and detergent, and dishwashers, and sponges, and a mop for this and a mop for that, and still they get tired. Look, my daughter-in-law just today told me she bathed only one of her two children because she was feeling tired. I used to bathe ten children one right after the other. Can you imagine? My youngest daughter, Marianne, she's the same, running with this modern life. She'll get tired too. They have two, three children, and they're tired. They can barely manage.

Anyway, after the war I still had my six children with me. Then I had one, two . . . seven more. Thirteen. I admit though, it was one or two too many. I was getting too old to bring children. With Majda, my twelfth, I'll tell you the truth—I tried to stop it. I tried jumping up and down. I ran up and down the stairs. I worked extra hard around the house. None of this helped. I drank all kinds of liquids. Some women suggested onion water—water that had onions boiled in it. Some said to put a hot-water bottle on my stomach. Finally, I went to the midwife. She tried to help me by massaging my stomach hard with olive oil. It didn't work either. Nothing worked. The pregnancy went on, normal. Majda was born.

Alright, so that's it, I figured. No more. Then, six years later—what was I, forty-four years old?—I was pregnant again. I went to Abu Mahmud and told him I want to stop it. There was a doctor I learned about, a doctor who women went to to get rid of unwanted pregnancies. He charged ten dinars for this—a lot of money for us. Abu Mahmud gave me the money. He didn't go with me, he had to work that day. I was about two months pregnant then, maybe more. It was a rainy day in the winter. When I got to the doctor he told me he couldn't do it without the permission of my husband. Either my husband had to sign or my oldest son. Because of the heavy rain, the telephone wasn't working. The women in the clinic said to me, "Why get your son involved in this sin?" I went home, through the streets running with mud. It was a long walk. My son was there and he said to me, "What, ten dinars for this thing? Don't do it. Let's use the money and make a party instead." My sister's husband was there and he said the same: "Let's celebrate. Here, give me the ten dinars."

So that's what happened. They took the money, bought a sheep, and we made a party. Fate decreed that another child be born even though I didn't want another. So my thirteenth was born—a girl. I named her myself. Marianne, I called her.

Marianne

Marianne is the youngest of Umm Mahmud's thirteen children and the only one still living at home, in the house where she grew up. Although twenty-seven years old she seems younger, with a sense of playfulness, even mischievousness, about her. Unlike her mother, who wears the modest attire of traditional women (long dresses and a head scarf), Marianne prefers Western clothes (jeans, skirts, jerseys, and blouses) that accentuate her slim figure.

We met Marianne in April 1994. Rafiqa Othman vaguely knew her, and a mutual friend arranged the initial visit. Marianne agreed to participate, it seemed to us, primarily as a favor to this mutual friend. Once the interviewing was under way, she began to develop an interest in and curiosity about the project itself. For Marianne, more than for any of the other women, the interviews apparently had a cathartic effect, allowing her to air some of her conflicted feelings about her life, and particularly about her mother.

Most of our interviews with Marianne, as with Umm Mahmud, took place on the veranda of their house. Always gracious, Marianne would fix a snack or even a meal for us, and often while eating we would interview her. Her tone was animated and saucy; her words rushed forth, but in a less rambling manner than that of her mother. Though fluent only in Arabic, occasionally she peppered her speech with a phrase of English or Hebrew, most especially when discussing some provocative topic as her mother sat nearby.

Our interviews with Marianne continued for nine months, until January 1995. Most of what appears below was gathered in the first two or three sessions, when we asked her to recall some of her early memories, and her years at school.

❧

I was never supposed to be born. My mother told you about that, didn't she? She tried to abort me. But, as the expression goes, "A wild one always stays alive no matter what happens." The way I found out about all this was from two of my brothers. I must have been about three years old and they were teasing me. "Mama wanted to throw you away," they said. "She didn't want *you!*" I didn't know what they meant and I didn't want to say anything to my mother. Maybe she still wanted to throw me out. Then one day when she was hugging and kissing me, I started crying and I said to her, "Mother, how could you think of throwing me away? How?" She looked at me confused as I sat there on her lap. "Oh no, no, no," she said. "I never meant to throw you away like that. *Before* you were born, I meant, not *after.*" I couldn't really understand what she meant, only later I understood. But, at least, I felt better that now she wasn't going to throw me away.

You see, my mother and I—I'm not talking about now—but, back then, I didn't really feel she was my mother. I mean, I called her "Mother," I knew who she was, sure. But it was my older sister, Nuzha, who I called "Mommy." She's the one I felt closest to, the one who took care of me. I forget what number child Nuzha is—second I think, no, third. Being on the bottom of the pile of thirteen, you forget sometimes. Nuzha was the one I used to go to if I was unhappy, or if I just wanted something. I loved her more than my other sisters, more than anyone.

Then one day I heard that Nuzha was getting married. I think I was around six years old. I didn't really know what it meant, "getting married." Nobody explained anything to me. All I knew was that Nuzha was getting married and we were going to the wedding in Kuwait, wherever that was. And it wasn't just Nuzha getting married. Another sister was getting married at the same time. What it was, was that Nuzha and Fatma were both marrying men who worked in Kuwait, Palestinian men. These men weren't brothers, just some kind of relatives. I understood all this later. All I knew then—what was I, five or six or maybe seven?—all they told me was that we were leaving for Kuwait. Me, Nuzha, and Fatma, and my mother. Nobody else went.

I don't really remember a whole lot from that time, only a few things. We were there a while—two months, I know now. I remember the big house we lived in together with my sisters and their husbands, and I remember going for fish in restaurants along the sea where we lived. And sand, sand, sand, everywhere sand. And I also remember . . . wait, turn off the tape recorder and I'll tell you . . . Okay, okay. I'll say it on tape. I remember wanting to go into my sister Nuzha's bedroom, and each night for many nights knocking on their door. I wanted to sleep with Nuzha the way I always had at home. She used to put me to sleep each night, read me a story and then stay with me and sleep with me in the same bed. So, I kept calling to her through the door, "Why don't you open the door? What's going on in there?" My other sister and her husband, or someone, would come and take me away and we'd go out for a walk or visiting, even though it was night. In Kuwait, because it's so hot, you do a lot of going out at night. Anyway, that's the way it was for two months. After that me and my mother went back to Jerusalem. Nuzha and Fatma stayed on. Over the years, I only saw them a little. They're both in Jordan now with their families. They left Kuwait before the Gulf War, and now they can't go back. I've gone to Jordan to see them. Nuzha is still my favorite sister and I'm close to her children. She has four boys and two girls. I don't treat them like an aunt, I make no distance. I'm like a friend of theirs. And Nuzha and I are still very close.

But, going back to the time when we returned from Kuwait, I remember that more clearly. I later found out from my mother that she and my father were very worried about me: How was I going to manage without Nuzha? What I did—this I remember real well—I used to take a picture of Nuzha with me each day to school. I never showed it to anyone, I kept it in my school bag. This went on a long time. Then slowly, slowly, the picture began to get messed up. I wrote on the back of the picture, things like homework assignments or just scribblings. Finally, I stopped taking it. I returned to my real mother and she began more and more to take an interest in me. She became the one who put me to sleep at night. She didn't read me stories, she can't read. But she slept with me instead of Nuzha. And everything was fine, no problems.

And in school everything was fine too, no problems. The teachers used to like me. I was a real pretty girl and I'd dress up for school. Some of my older sisters knew how to sew, to make beautiful embroidered things. They made me this peasant dress once, with all the traditional embroidery on it, and the teachers loved it. These teachers weren't all so kind, though. They used to slap kids around, the ones who weren't paying attention. That's the way it was done, even in first and second grade. It's still done that way today sometimes. I got hit once or twice, too, but usually I was a good student and well behaved. Well behaved in school, I mean. At home, I was a little different, a little wild sometimes.

I had this "cousin," Muhsen. Actually, he was one of my sister's children. Back then, they lived in the apartment on the bottom floor of this house. Muhsen and I used to have this love-hate relationship. We were in the same school in first and second grade, it was a school for boys and girls. He was seven months older, but they put us in the same class so we could be together. We were very close, we played together all the time. Sometimes we even dressed for school in similar clothes— sweaters, say, that his mother made for us. Or, if Ibtisam made a birthday party for Muhsen, she'd make a party for me at the same time. But still, we fought all the time. As soon as the school bus dropped us off at the driveway below, we'd toss away our school bags and we'd go at it. Shouting, slapping, beating each other. Usually I'd win. Sometimes an adult would come out and stop us. His mother often stopped me from beating him up. My mother never intervened. I remember saying to her, "Mother, how come you never come and intervene, while Ibtisam always comes to protect Muhsen?" She answered, "He who plays with cats must suffer the scratches." I once also asked Ibtisam, "How come you always defend *him?*" After all, she was *my* sister even if she was his mother. You know what she said to me? "Marianne," she said, "Ever since you were born you were like a hyena with him. Even as a baby, it wasn't enough that you suckled at mother's breast, you'd come to my breast when I was feeding Muhsen and you'd push him away!" So she felt she had to defend him from me. Muhsen and I, we were like *ikhweh fi al-ridaah* [children who suckle at the same breast].

My mother, you see, never liked me to play with boys, even boy cousins. In her time they didn't do that, and she was against it. "Their games are crude and not for you," she would tell me. She used to go into these moods when she would force me to stay inside, like I was in jail, so I couldn't play with boys. Then the moods passed and she would let me go outside. My father never said anything, he stayed out of these things. He isn't a typical Arab father—you know, dominating and tough. He was easy on me and always nice to me. He never really hit me, just a light slap once in a while. And when he'd slap me, he'd always come immediately and make a *sulha* [peace agreement]. He'd bring me sacks of candies and tell me to keep them hidden in the closet and eat them slowly. He showed me where he kept money in his drawer and he told me when I need some change to go take it, even without asking. Really, he never stopped me from doing anything.

So, I used to play with the boys. Actually, it was either that or play alone. There were no girls my age in the houses around us then. Muhsen, me, and another boy—we used to play together a lot. We'd play cops and robbers. Or we'd play with a cart going full blast down our steep driveway. Sometimes I'd get real banged up. Or sometimes we would go up the hill, there were a lot of open fields in those days. Up there we'd pick this wild plant which looks like an onion growing, except if you rub just a little of it on your skin you get an awful itch. What we'd do is pick the plant and then stop some adult and ask for the time. The person naturally would expose his wrist as he looked at his watch, and one of us would quickly rub some of this plant on the person's wrist. And then we'd all run away as fast as we could. It was fun, I tell you, great fun—even if now it sounds a little stupid.

2

After that school I went to with Muhsen, the coed school, I went to another that was just for girls. It was a couple of kilometers away, in Beit Hanina. I went there from third grade right through high school. Girls there were from middle- or lower-class families. Upper-class families sent their girls elsewhere. What more can I tell you? It was routine, nothing unusual. I was a good student, so for me school was alright. In all the grades I did well—really, I'm not bragging. By the time I reached the high school years I had a reputation as someone who was really smart. I was excellent in things like math and physics, and also in religion and Arabic literature and language. I wasn't good in biology but I did well on the exams—because I always cheated. I would sit next to someone smart, someone who didn't mind because she knew I was good in other subjects. I think the biology teacher also knew what was going on but he turned a blind eye to it, maybe because he knew I was smart in other things too. With Arabic language I didn't have to cheat, I was outstanding. The teacher liked me. To this day, when I see her in the street, she stops me and says, "You haven't changed at all, you're as clever as always." My religion teacher used to like me too. I always had the courage to ask questions—not just learn things by rote—and he gave me the chance to ask what I wanted. He was a religious man. He's one of those the Israelis expelled to Lebanon a few years back. When they were filming those guys in Lebanon, I recognized him.

During this period, when I was a teenager, I no longer played with boys—oh no, *haram!* Just girls. I had lots of girlfriends. After school I'd go over to their houses. We'd sit together, sing, eat, laugh, talk about this teacher or that. I don't remember talking about boys, not then, that came later. Some of these girls are still my friends, we went to college together and we still see each other. What else? Well, if I wasn't visiting at one of my friends' houses, I stayed at home. I'd do my homework, or I'd help my mother in the kitchen. Nothing exciting. Sometimes I'd watch television, sure. I used to like watching these romantic films. Actually, I still like watching them. Films from Egypt or foreign films, like from Europe or India. Sometimes there were scenes in the films, scenes that, well, my mother would come in saying, "That's tasteless, *eib!* Turn it off!" I'd change it usually. Or sometimes I'd say, "Wait, wait, they'll finish soon!" The truth is, to this day sometimes there's a film I want to see and I know what's coming up is some scene, you know, tasteless stuff according to my mother. So, what I do is go into my bedroom where I have a small black and white television. I abandon the big color television and leave it to my parents—May they watch the news until they go dizzy from it! And I go watch what I want on that black and white television with its awful reception, all those lines on it, and the picture jumping up and down, but that's what I do. I tell you, I've got to save some money and get a decent television for my room!

I guess you've gathered that my mother is not exactly someone who you can talk to about certain things—about sexual things, I mean. *Eib, eib!* Rafiqa, remember the other day when you were asking her questions about her wedding? Oh yes, I heard. Most of it anyway. I caught it as I was going in and out of the veranda. When you left, she said to me, "Those questions of Rafiqa's—tasteless, completely tasteless." Don't feel bad, that's the way she talks, the way she thinks. Don't let it bother you. She answered you sort of, because you kept pressing her. But she was uncomfortable with it, that's for sure. Sometimes when I talk about subjects like that she tells me I'm a tasteless person, a person without shame. That's the way it's always been. When I was a girl I knew intuitively I better not say anything about these things to her. So I kept quiet. I never said anything. I remember when I got my period the first time. I kept it to myself, I didn't say a word for months. I hid the evidence from her, I burned the pads. While this was going on, one day a neighbor came by. This neighbor was the mother of a friend of mine. She asked my mother, "Did Marianne get her period yet?" And then she said, "My daughter just got hers, and she's so afraid." And do you know what my mother answered? She said, "Oh yes, she got it a while back. Afraid? Oh no, not Marianne. She wasn't afraid. She made nothing of it. She didn't even tell me about it." That's the way I found out that she knew.

And that's how it's always been in my family. With my sisters, I've never talked about sex, the wedding night, nothing. I don't ask and they don't say anything. Once in a while, these days, I do bring up a so-called tasteless subject with my mother. Not usually, but sometimes. Like recently, I told her about a friend of mine who got married. This friend is a little older than me, in her thirties maybe. I told my mother how this friend's father wanted to see the sheet after the wedding night, to make sure his daughter was a virgin. "He did?" my mother asked. "Well, I'll tell you, your friend's father must be crazy!" That's what she said.

Then she began to tell me about this incident. It's something that took place a while back, before 1948. There was this young woman who used to come and help my mother with the small children and with the house.

"Poor thing," my mother said. "Blessed be her memory."

"Passed away?" I asked, knowing there was more to it.

"Murdered. They killed her, the men in her family."

"Why?" I asked.

"Well, she got married, and right after that she was pregnant. The way they reckoned, it couldn't have been her husband. The child had to belong to another man."

I said, "Why couldn't they have gone to a doctor and checked it out?"

"Are you serious?" she said. "In those days they didn't go to the doctors for anything." And then she said, "Besides, she wasn't really a modest woman."

"If she wasn't a virgin, so they should slaughter her?" I answered.

My mother said, "So? To this day it goes on, no?"

"Then they're criminals," I told her. "That's what I think."

And no more was said. But tell me, they're not criminals? Look, you just don't go killing a woman because she's made a mistake—even a bad mistake like that. No?

⌐

Anyway, let's go on to something else. Where were we? High school. So I finished high school and then I went to college. No, I wasn't the first. Let's see, among my sisters three went up to sixth grade, one went to high school, and three of us went to college. Of the girls, I went the furthest. Among my brothers, three went to high school and three went to college. That's pretty good, don't you think? About half of us have college education. That's not bad if you consider that my father and mother, between them, never completed one year of school. That's the way it is now with Palestinians. Education, education. Everyone who can go to university, goes. Boys, and girls too.

For me, there was never any question about it. I never imagined for a minute that I'd finish high school and just sit around at home. What, I was going to stay here and clean and cook all day, and be a servant? No, no, that's not for me. I knew I was going, even if I wasn't very sure what I wanted to study. I was only seventeen then. When you're that age you don't know what you should do. Today, if I were choosing, I wouldn't become a teacher like I did. I mean, I like my work, but still I would probably choose something more challenging and where I could express myself—and make more money. Maybe law. I don't know, something else than teaching.

Back when I finished high school, I thought to go to Jordan and study like Majda and Khalil did. I had an 81 on the *tawjihi* [high school matriculation exam]. It's not bad, but it wasn't good enough to get me into the Jordanian colleges I applied to. Just for a moment I thought of college in Europe or America, but I got that out of my mind quickly since it's too expensive, and I didn't want to be a burden on my brothers in America. So that left me with some college or university here. This was before the Intifada, three or four years before. Still, there were lots of strikes going on at some of the West Bank universities, and they would be closed down for months on end. People advised me to go to Abu Dis College, just outside Jerusalem. It's a quiet place, they said, and I could finish in four years without losing time because of the strikes. *That* turned out to be wrong, way wrong. Once the Intifada started, every place had its shutdowns. But, at the time it seemed like good advice. Besides, Abu Dis College is a place that specializes in the sciences, and since I like science—math and physics—I figured it was a good place for me.

So I went to Abu Dis. They had dorms there, but being so close to my home there was no need for that. I went in the morning and came back in the afternoon. I can't say I really enjoyed it, not the way I later enjoyed Bethlehem University. It was a small place, quiet and serious. I made no new friends there. I was friendly with others, I spoke to everyone, but I hesitated to really talk to other students. I'm someone who, if I talk, I really like talking frankly and openly. I wasn't sure other students would accept that. Besides, when I was at Abu Dis I had to study very hard, there was not much time for friendships. The contacts I had were mostly with other students studying physics and math. More male students than female students. I found I liked that. I mean, I wasn't looking for love or anything like that—now, well, that's another story. The boys there were more like brothers to me. I liked that. Personally, I prefer to be friends with boys because girls are more jealous of each other. Girls don't help you with your homework or bring you a cup of coffee. Boys do. Boys would let me copy their homework. Not the girls. Many of the boys at Abu Dis were religious, observant. I was friendly with them, but none of these friendships remain. If I see one in town now we just nod or say hello, and then pass each other by. No more than that now.

The atmosphere at Abu Dis was religious. There were two mosques there, one for men and one for women. A lot of the students prayed—you know, the five daily prayers. I think because Abu Dis is a college of sciences a lot of religious students were there. Sounds strange? Not really.

I think, as a rule, those who study sciences are more observant. Maybe science causes them to be so, it makes you realize how much the world requires order to work, and so you see the need for God. Many students at Abu Dis used to discuss what the relationship is between science and religion. To me, science and religion are not opposed. If science opposes religion, then the problem is with science. Science is subservient to religion, science is about probabilities and religion is about certainties. There is no such thing as absolute certainty in science. Science comes from man, religion from God. I'm certain about this.

I'm a person who believes in religion, you see. I'm not as observant as I should be. I try to say my daily prayers, I fast on Ramadan, and like my parents, I expect to go on the *hajj* some day. But, well, I'm not an observant Muslim in the way I dress. A person can know something is wrong and still do it anyway. As they say, "God curses the part of oneself that leads him astray." Me, I just don't like wearing the religious garb—dresses that cover the arms and legs, head coverings. I like to wear skirts and short dresses. Don't get me wrong: I keep the hem below the knee and I would never wear a bathing suit. I don't even like to swim. Of course, maybe if I went to America or Europe I might raise the hem a tiny bit—up to here, just above the knee. I might, I know I might.

You see, there's a lot of conflicts in my personality. A person is always looking for the easy way. It's the nature of man to have a split between what he wants and what he knows is right. The Koran talks about this. Freud talked about it too—the superego and id, he called it. A person's character is determined by which of the opposing forces wins. Maybe when I get older I'll be closer to religion and that will give me inner peace. I know when I become a mother I'll be more careful, I don't want my children to be like me.

I have a niece, Nabila, she lives in the apartment below and she's always up here. She's nine. She asks me why I go out with makeup and why I wear the kind of clothes I wear. "Auntie," she tells me, "when I grow up I'm not going to be like you." She sees her mother and some of my sisters dressed modestly. Also, I think, children are more believing. They go through a stage in childhood when they are very religious. I remember when I was Nabila's age, we had a Greek Christian neighbor and I used to tell this boy, "You pray to a piece of wood!" And me and my friends would take these Christian kids by the arm and say to them, "Come with us, convert to Islam!" We were serious. Kids that age— nine, ten, eleven—they take religion seriously. I was more religious when I was younger than I am today. It also may be true that kids today are under more pressure to be religious. There's many adults my age who are very religious and they are raising their children to be like them. Maybe it's a good thing. I think it is.

I know my mother, and I guess my father too, doesn't feel I'm religious enough. But the way I see it, even if they're right, I *understand* religion better than they do. Where did my mother get her understanding of religion? From the mouths of others, she can't read. I've read the texts. My understanding is more precise. I'll give you just a small example. The other day we were listening to this *sheikh* on Jordanian TV and he started praising King Hussein, saying that the king is from the family of Prophet Muhammad. What's this all about? He's the king's man, that's all. Since when is King Hussein one of the Prophet's heirs? When I started ridiculing the *sheikh* my mother tried to hush me up, saying who am I to criticize the *sheikh*, that he's a doctor, a learned man, a man of religion. That's how she sees it, that's what she believes. Look, I'll give you another example. Sometimes we hear Arafat talking in religious phrases, and my parents believe that therefore he must be a religious man. Unlike them, I'm not willing to believe in his words alone. Maybe he's religious, maybe he's not. Sweet words of religion flowing from a person's lips don't make a person religious. I feel I'm a believer even if I'm not saying religious phrases all the time. I admit I make mistakes. I admit this to Nabila, I admit it to my mother. Maybe someday I'll change, God willing. And if not, I hope God will forgive me. God is merciful, so I believe he will.

I've gone off a bit on religion, haven't I? I was telling you about Abu Dis College. Well, I graduated. Seven years it took me because of the Intifada. Instead of finishing in 1988 as I expected, I graduated in 1991. Three years wasted! Abu Dis College was closed down for three years because of the Intifada. During that time we had some classes, but only a few. We'd meet in offices or houses or in a classroom someplace. The same teacher we had at the college taught the courses in these places. We finished some courses this way, but not nearly as many as if the college had stayed open. Some friends of mine went abroad—Jordan, Europe, wherever they could—in order to finish up. I thought of doing this too. Yet, it wasn't easy to arrange, and besides, we kept hearing that the college was about to begin again, next week or next month, soon. And so I waited.

While I was waiting, I worked in my brother Mahmud's office. Secretarial work, that type of thing. Mahmud was kind to me and he paid me good money too. He's a bit nervous, but very kind. He's my mother's favorite—the oldest son, and all that. Mahmud's always been like a father to me. Actually, back in those days when I thought of Nuzha as "Mommy," I felt Mahmud *was* my father. I thought he was married to my mother, and at the same time I thought of Nuzha as "Mommy." A little confused, I guess. Anyway, Mahmud was good to me during this period. Though, all the time, I kept feeling, "Marianne, you're wasting away your life. What are you accomplishing like this?"

In the end, praise God, I got my B. A. And then began a wonderful year. I got a scholarship to go to Bethlehem University and take courses for my teacher's certificate. Bethlehem was a fun place to go to. Oh yes, of course, the Intifada was going on, but it didn't disturb us that year. Bethlehem University wasn't all that involved in the Intifada. It's located way up on a hilltop where not many people live, and the Israeli army wasn't interested in the place. Some students would set tires on fire and they'd wait for the army to come. They'd wait and wait, and still the Israelis wouldn't come. They'd scream and curse, hoping the soldiers would hear them, and still they wouldn't come. Really, I swear, it was just like that.

So we had a quiet time of it. And a fun time. The courses weren't especially hard, and I had many more friends there than at Abu Dis. At Bethlehem University, the students in my area were older. A group of us became friends, six boys and four girls. Some were married, some single, and some were Christian and some Muslim. We used to hang around together and go on outings—to the woods or parks or on cookouts, things like that. Once in a while we'd go out in smaller groups, though not one girl and one boy, or even two and two. That was uncomfortable. I remember once we started off on a picnic or something, two and two, but we all felt uncomfortable. So on the way we stopped and found one of our girlfriends, and even though she didn't want to go we made her come anyway so that there would be no rumors.

Those were good times we had then. Two years ago, it was. Since then, we've all gone our own ways and don't see each other much. And me, well, now I have less time *and* less freedom to do such things. Work and come home, work and come home. My mother worries about me being out. "This is a bad time," she says. "Lots of bad things happening, lots of bad people going around." She wants me home before it gets dark. Really! Two days ago, I was out taking a driving lesson, but I got stuck in a traffic jam on the way home and was a half-hour late. She was all upset, angry and upset. What can I do? I'm living in her house, I've got to do it according to her way. You know, a friend of mine lost her mother a little while back. I went and paid a condolence call, and all the time as I was coming home I kept thinking what a hard thing it is when your mother dies. I came into our house and my mother was standing there. I went right to her, threw my arms around her, and told her, "Mama, I love you!" She hugged me back and then said, "Marianne, if you love me, then listen to my voice." And all I could say to her was, "Mother, I can't—not always. I just can't."

Umm Mahmud and Marianne: A Dialogue

An early decision we made while interviewing the women in this study was to speak to each mother and daughter separately. We were aware that our decision might arouse curiosity, even suspicion, in one of the two as to what the other might be saying. But the benefit was also obvious: alone, mother and daughter would be freer to talk about themselves, and especially about their relationship to each other. With two of the pairs this arrangement was easy enough to carry out: the mothers and daughters live in separate houses. But with Umm Mahmud and Marianne, who live together, it ran into problems. On occasion one of them—usually Umm Mahmud—would sit in for some minutes as we interviewed the other. And during the session reported below, Umm Mahmud came by at the beginning and remained through most of the meeting. What was to have been a session with Marianne alone became a dialogue between Marianne and Umm Mahmud; and even a trialogue, as one of us joined in.

It was probably not a coincidence that Umm Mahmud chose this particular day to enter Marianne's session for an extended period. Marianne had made it clear to us in the previous session that she was willing to reveal a secret, but only where she could not be overheard. Evidently, she had a secret boyfriend about whom her mother—she felt sure—knew nothing. We suggested to Marianne that we meet the next time in a café in West Jerusalem, and she readily agreed. Unfortunately, Umm Mahmud entered the veranda as we were making these arrangements, and she immediately indicated that a café was not her idea of a respectable place. It was not surprising, therefore, that a few days later we received a telephone call from an apologetic Marianne suggesting that we change the venue of the next session and instead meet in our usual place—at her home. Nor was it surprising, in light of all this, that the dialogue, or trialogue, took the direction it did. The following are excerpts from this session.

MICHAEL GORKIN: Marianne, you indicated in a previous session that while you were at college you lived at home, not in the college dormitories. Do other young women ever rent an apartment and live alone?

MARIANNE: Not as far as I know. No woman I know, did. It's not acceptable.

UMM MAHMUD: Go live by herself, leave her parents' house—why? Look, if the parents' house is far from the college, and the parents know there's a respectable family the girl can live with, well, that's fine. I've rented out the downstairs apartment at times to women students from Nablus and Gaza. I watched over them like they were my own daughters.

MARIANNE: I'd never go live by myself. Even if sometimes I feel like leaving here, still I wouldn't do it. If I did people would look at me suspiciously, there'd be a big question mark over my head. People would begin to ask, "What, her parents want no part of her?" I couldn't manage that.

UMM MAHMUD: Marianne is speaking weakly, I want to speak instead of her! Look, if a girl has her parents' home—impossible! It can't be! Our society knows right from wrong, we know the distinction. If my daughter goes the wrong way, I don't accept it. Our religion guides us, directs us as to the right path.

MARIANNE: Umm Mahmud* is right, she is. True, sometimes I feel I want to escape from here. I feel they're squeezing the life out of me and driving me crazy. But I can't get away, and really I don't want to. I like having my family around me.

UMM MAHMUD: The family never tries to squeeze the life out of anyone. No!

MARIANNE: No, I'd never live alone. I don't know anyone who's done it really.

RAFIQA OTHMAN: Let me change the subject slightly and ask you both another question along these lines. Mike and I have been going around together doing this book. As you see, I drive him in my car. My parents, my family, all know this. But, frankly, how do you view this—a single woman and a man going around and doing this work together?

UMM MAHMUD: I know the truth is you look at him as a brother, a friend, but someone else might not know this. Someone else might think, "Why is she going around with the foreigner, this foreign man?"

RAFIQA: Let me ask you this if I may: Would you allow Marianne to work on a book in this way?

UMM MAHMUD: If it were only me, well—but, you see, the question is what would others say?

MARIANNE: Mother, say what you think. Would you permit it or not?

UMM MAHMUD: I pay attention to what others think. Someone who doesn't take into account the opinion of others is not one of them. People say things behind that person's back, and she gets a bad reputation. Someone who follows the straight path is not gossiped about. If, God forbid, the girl goes wrong, people talk about the mother. "What, she's blind, she doesn't see what's been going on?" That's what they say. So. . . .

---

* This was the first time in our interviews with Marianne that she referred to her mother in this respectful (perhaps distancing) manner.

MARIANNE: [*Interrupting*] Mother—yes or no?

UMM MAHMUD: No.

RAFIQA: But look, is it possible that Marianne, who went to two colleges, never happened to sit alone someplace with a man?

UMM MAHMUD: That's different. There's a framework there, college is a place where people meet. Besides, there're professors there to watch over the students.

MARIANNE: You think the professors are sitting there watching over the students all the time? Maybe some of them are just *watching* the students—not exactly the way you think or would like?

UMM MAHMUD: Oh ho! Oh ho! Well, maybe. Yes, I watch television, I know what goes on some places. But look, my dear, I sent you to college to learn about life, to learn to choose good over bad. In the end, God will judge me if I chose the right way. In the end, we all die and we are all judged.

MARIANNE: I want to go back to the question you asked, Rafiqa. What I think about the two of you going around together is this: To me, there's nothing wrong with it. But you have to be able to put up with people's long tongues. Some may say horrible things, curse you. Others, maybe, may support you. In your place, Rafiqa—I'm speaking frankly—I wouldn't do it. You hear what my mother says. As long as I'm living under their roof, I've got to go along with their rules.

RAFIQA: And what if you marry—I want to speak frankly too—what if your husband has the same ideas as your parents?

MARIANNE: I'm hoping he'll be more enlightened.

UMM MAHMUD: You think so? You do? My daughter, our rules will seem easy compared to his, you'll see. Maybe the one you marry won't even let you go out alone to the grocery store down the street.

MARIANNE: You mean I'm going to pass from one jailer to another? [*Laughs*]

UMM MAHMUD: Go ahead, laugh. But you'll accept his ways, sure you will. That's the way it goes. You won't answer back the way you do with us.

MARIANNE: [*To Rafiqa*] I tell you, you're going to cause a war today in this house with all these questions.

UMM MAHMUD: May God watch over you young women!

RAFIQA: Alright, let's have a cease-fire right now, let's move on to something else.

⤳

[At this point we asked several questions of a benign, unthreatening sort. Umm Mahmud left the veranda to go to the kitchen—for five minutes or so. During that time Marianne picked up the thread of the conversation.]

MARIANNE: Rafiqa, I want to make a point that's been on my mind. We were talking before about how you're free to go around with Mike. What I want to say is—how should I say it?—that Palestinians here in East Jerusalem or the territories are a little different than those of you living among the Jews. That's what I think, what I've seen.

RAFIQA: In what way do you see the difference?

MARIANNE: Your thinking is different from ours. I mean, living among the Jews has made you change the way you see things and do things.

RAFIQA: For example?

MARIANNE: Well, for example, I think of some of the Arab women I know from the north of Israel. They're more open about things. At my school, some of the teachers are from northern Israel, in the Galilee. Now, if the principal of the school starts criticizing one of them, the teacher might defend herself, might even answer her back. Those of us from East Jerusalem would never answer back, we wouldn't say a word. The women from the north, they're not afraid.

RAFIQA: Any other examples?

MARIANNE: Yes—boys. With us, if a girl wants to know a guy, to start with him, she has no courage to do it. Those Arab girls I know from Israel, they do. Like, this one time I'd just begun working in the school and there was this colleague of mine from northern Israel. She was taking some courses at the same time at the Hebrew University, and there was a guy there who told her he wanted to meet a girl from East Jerusalem. She came to me and said straight out, "Marianne, you want to meet this guy?" She was going to fix me up with him. Well, nobody I know from East Jerusalem would do it that way—straight out, fix up. Here, to meet a guy is difficult, complicated. It has to be done secretly, roundabout. You just don't go meet a guy in some public place the way Arab women in Israel do it.

RAFIQA: It's not exactly that way for us.

MARIANNE: Look, I know an Arab woman from Israel who told me that this guy she was going out with was someone she had met like that in a public place. And you know what? Her parents knew about it, knew how she met him, and that was fine with them. My parents—they'd go along with something like that?

RAFIQA: What you're describing is more true about Christian Arabs than Muslims. And it's more like that for Arabs who come from the cities than the villages.

MARIANNE: Maybe. You know better than I do. I'm talking about just those I know, some friends of mine. The ones I know from northern Israel are Christian Arabs, that's true.

RAFIQA: The Arab women I know are not so free as you're saying, believe me....

[Umm Mahmud returned from the kitchen at this juncture, and the conversation halted momentarily as she announced that the food she was preparing would be ready in another ten minutes or so. She sat down and we then proceeded.]

MICHAEL: Marianne, could you continue in a more general way. Looking at Western culture generally—not just Israel—what do you see as the influence on Palestinians? And if there *is* an influence, is it positive or negative in your view?

MARIANNE: Speaking generally, my view is that the West has good things to offer and bad things too. Just as we do. What's wise for us is to take what is good from the West and leave the rest. For instance, in the West—I'm talking about Europe, America—they know how to get things done, to show up on time, to wait on line. We don't. And in many of these Western countries, they have a high standard of public sanitation. Their streets, neighborhoods—so clean. Here, everyone of us is interested in his own house and property, that's it. Also, people in the West are not given to boasting, they're modest. With us, that's rare. If one of us gets a doctorate or becomes rich, he makes a big show of it. Why shouldn't we take some of these good things from the West?

UMM MAHMUD: And the girls in the West—our girls should be like them? Look at the Israeli girls, girls on television. The way they dress, the way they act. . . .

MARIANNE: [*Interrupting*] I was about to say this. Some of our young people take the bad things from the West before the good. They have excessive freedom in the West, freedom without limits. The Western women's fashions go too far, their behavior is uncontrolled. Some of our girls, and boys, copy that. *That,* I'm against.

UMM MAHMUD: Maybe there are some girls here going around exposed like in the West, but not so many. Only a few. Most have known how to keep the traditional ways. That's what I do anyway, I don't need anyone else's ways.

MARIANNE: Umm Mahmud wants everyone to go along with *all* our traditional ways, and that's not good either. We have our own bad customs too.

UMM MAHMUD: Which ones? There's nothing bad.

MARIANNE: Millions of things, like I was just saying. Look, mother, you know this. Lots of families refuse to let their daughters study, go to college.

UMM MAHMUD: What, we don't let our daughters study?

MARIANNE: We do. But others don't.

UMM MAHMUD: Your sisters studied. *You* went to college, two colleges. You want to study more—fine. You get a scholarship to go to America and get your doctor degree—go! With my blessing—go!

MARIANNE: I don't know about a doctorate. Maybe. That's not what I'm talking about though. . . .

MICHAEL: Let me ask you this, Marianne. Who do you feel your models are—models for Palestinian women? From the West, or from here?

MARIANNE: Both, maybe. I can't say the American woman or the French woman is my model. Or the Arab woman either. No one type is perfect. I try to learn from all of them.

RAFIQA: What about Hanan Ashrawi?* What do you think of her?

MARIANNE: She *is* a good model and representative for us. She's educated, skilled. When she speaks with the Americans, she speaks in a good way, a million times better than Arafat. She makes a good impression for us. My brother in America told me that this American friend of his said to him, "If you've got a lot of Palestinian women like her, you're in good shape." I'm not like her though, not nearly so clever.

RAFIQA: And your view, Umm Mahmud?

UMM MAHMUD: She's fine. A good model, why not?

RAFIQA: Well, frankly, you don't mind seeing her on television giving Arafat a kiss on the cheek? You'd agree to Marianne doing that?

MARIANNE: I wouldn't agree!

UMM MAHMUD: I saw a Gaza woman on television who rushed up to Arafat and tried to kiss him. She's crazy, I think. When I was in America at my son's house, an American friend of his came by. He came up to me and wanted to give me a kiss. That's his customs, I guess. I told him, "No, no, keep back!" The others explained to him later that it's not our way.

MARIANNE: Rafiqa, when I say I take Hanan Ashrawi as a good model, I don't mean in everything! But look, if she wants to kiss Arafat, that's her business. She agrees, her husband agrees, Arafat's wife agrees—who am I to oppose it? No?

---

* Hanan Ashrawi was spokeswoman for the Palestinian delegation during the Arab-Israeli peace talks in both Washington, D.C., and Madrid, and is well known and respected among Palestinians.

UMM MAHMUD: Look, is nobody here ready to eat something? The food is ready I'm sure.

[Umm Mahmud and Marianne go to the kitchen and bring back some stuffed squash and tabbouleh, a bulgur wheat salad.]

MARIANNE: The tabbouleh, I made. The stuffed squash is my mother's. She's a real cook, I'm just an apprentice.

UMM MAHMUD: This is just a snack. God willing, you'll come some day for a real meal. Like *maqluba* [a chicken, rice, and eggplant dish], that's real food. Not like hot dogs or hamburgers or pizza. Someday you'll try my *maqluba,* God willing.

MARIANNE: Delicious. My mother really knows how to prepare it. . . .

Umm Mahmud

The dialogue that we recorded between Marianne and her mother had an unsettling effect on Umm Mahmud. In fact, it appeared for a while that she would no longer continue as part of our study; without the promptings of Marianne, we think it likely that she would have stopped. But after a couple of months she did agree to meet again, and thus we had another two interviews with her. For our part, we tried to steer away from subjects that might offend her—most especially, male-female relations. And with the exception of a few rough moments, when we inquired about her political views, our interviews with her proceeded on a smooth note.

What follows, then, are Umm Mahmud's further reflections—on the June 1967 War, politics, religion, her trips to Mecca and Washington, D.C., and also on her daughter Marianne.

✍

I'm the one who chose the name for my last daughter. Until then my mother-in-law chose the children's names. May God bless her memory. When Marianne was born my mother-in-law was sick, it was just before she died. So I chose the name. When I told my mother-in-law what it was she kept saying, "Tell me again, I can't catch it." Really, I don't know what brought the name Marianne to my tongue. I had never heard it before. People came to me and said, "How did you choose such a name? It's a Christian name." My husband didn't say anything. All the other names of our children are common Arab names. Why the name Marianne came to me, I have no idea. It just did. I liked it then and I still like it today.

2

A year after Marianne was born, I think it was, the war broke out. I brought her in 1966, yes, and the war came in 1967. This was a short war—only a few days. But it was a very cruel war, very dangerous. There was a lot of fighting all around us.

I remember very well when the war came. It began just before noon. We heard a siren on the radio and I asked, "What's going on?" Someone answered, "There's a war, the Jews have attacked and are coming our way." I hadn't expected a war. Not then, and not so suddenly. It wasn't like 1948 when you could feel it coming slowly. This time it started—bang!—and that was it.

I didn't have the time to prepare anything. Not like in 1948. I was caught empty-handed—almost. What happened is, just about the time when the sirens started, I was in the kitchen making *maqluba*. I was determined to get it done so at least we'd have something to eat. I fried up the chicken and put it in a pot. I was so scared and upset that I forgot to fry the eggplants too, I just put them in with the chicken and rice. It didn't come out well, I can tell you that.

When I looked outside people were fleeing their homes. Someone yelled at them, "What, are you going to do the same as in '48? Come back, don't flee!" I swear, nobody was listening, they were just taking off. These people, some of them walked all the way on foot to Amman. Some of my brothers and their wives, my sisters and their husbands, and one of my sisters and her mother-in-law—they all went on foot to Jordan. A lot did this, and some got killed on the way. Not my family—others. Oh God, those were hard days!

My husband poked his head outside, and what was there? One of our neighbors, killed. He had just gotten hit. My husband went to drag him inside when a Christian neighbor just down the way yelled to our Hajj, "*Ya* Hajj, what are you doing? You're going to get yourself killed too. The Jews are coming quickly. Gather your family and go to the church." There was a church nearby and we were on good terms with the Christians there. My husband turned to me and told me to gather the children. I said, "Why go? Let's stay. If it's our fate to live then we'll stay alive in our house." My husband silenced me. "Go, go, woman!" he said. "The Jews are coming quickly!" So I went. And as I went, sure thing, I could see people fleeing from houses nearby, and the Jewish soldiers going into their homes. It was terrible, like on the day the world comes to an end. All you could do is try to take care of your own. I grabbed the children, I grabbed the *maqluba,* and we ran to the church.

When we got to the church, we were not the only ones there. There must have been about eighty others. It was very crowded. I tried to arrange a spot for us the best I could in the corridor. There were adults and children all around us, sitting and lying there. But at least we had a place to be. We couldn't see anything, of course. We could only hear the sound of airplanes going overhead and the sound of gunfire—heavy guns, maybe tanks—all around. We didn't know what was going to happen to us. Only one person, the priest, had a radio. He kept coming in and out and telling us things, but who knew what would be the end?

We sat like that for five days. I think the war only went on for three days but we stayed five. The children were miserable, all of them. Marianne had a bad time of it. She was only one year old. I'd put her on the floor to sleep the first night—and what happens? My neighbor's daughter comes along and steps on her stomach. I swear, it was awful. The first day or two we were so scared nobody could eat. The men just smoked. After that, people ate what they had. By then my *maqluba,* which wasn't any good in the first place, was smelling bad and the rice was as sticky as glue. But never mind, people polished it off. Not me. I wouldn't touch it. I didn't eat until we got back to our house.

When we went back, we had a shock. Our house had been hit by several large bombs. There were holes all over. The refrigerator had been crushed, the stairs had been destroyed, and right in our bedroom there was an enormous hole from a bomb. But, God be praised, all of us were still alive. If we hadn't gone to the church, God knows what would have happened to us. The house, well, we had built it before from nothing, and we could build it again. It was still *our* house. We didn't flee, we still had it. Others, the ones who fled, what did they have? They were sitting in Jordan or God knows where, and they didn't know what their fate would be. Some people were saying then that the Jews would leave soon and they could come back. Others said, no, the Jews were not going to let them come back. Me, I didn't know. I had no opinion. Only now do we see what happened. What is it, twenty-five years later? Even more. The Jews are still here. God alone knows how much longer they'll be staying.

❧

You want to know what I think of—how's that?—"the Jewish presence" here? Look, I prefer not to talk about politics. I don't like politics. My husband doesn't like politics, he doesn't talk about it. Talking about politics just gives me a headache.

The Jewish buildings nearby—what's my opinion of them? I'll say it like this. If someone stole the shirt off your back, how would you feel? Five, seven years ago the Jews came here. They took this land, it used to belong to a family that left the area during the war in 1967. When the area was empty in those days, along came some Bedouin with their sheep and they took it over. Later, the Jews came and pushed the Bedouin off. The Jews claim that the owners in America leased it to them. People here say that what happened is that the main owner, a rich man, died. Even though some of the other owners are still here—one of them is living in the neighborhood—the rich man's wife leased it to the Jews. We, the people who still live here, say about those who give their property to the Jews, we say, "May God destroy their property!" I tell

you, this land is the best spot in the area. What a fine place! Years ago
we used to go there and sit under the trees. The air there plays freely
on you. Now who can go there anymore? We don't go near them and
they don't come near us. But look, let the Jews take what they want. If
the world is as it should be, in the end everyone will have their due.
Everything in its time, I say. Nobody takes anything with them when
they're dead. The Garden of Eden is only for those who have done justly.
There's a *sura* [chapter] in the Koran that says, "If God decrees something to be, so will it be." Can we do something against the will of
God? No, not possible.

Here, look at what happened a few years back to a neighbor of ours.
He was paying a visit to someone who was sick. He went to leave and
they told him, "It's too soon. Stay, drink some coffee." But he said to
them, "No, no, I'm in a hurry. I can't stay for coffee." He stepped out
the door and was run over by a car. Finished, just like that. It was his
fate, God decided his time had come. Am I right, or am I right? I'll tell
you another story. It happened to my brother-in-law's son. He was living
in Kuwait. *H-u-p-p y!* His pockets were overflowing with money. Rich,
rich. He did what he wanted, went where he wanted. One day in America, one day in Paris. All the time going here and there. Then comes
the war in Kuwait. He stays there until the last minute, escaping the
jaws of death at the last instant. He lived, yes. But now he's in Jordan
without a dinar. He's sick, almost dying from what's happened to him—
just forty-five years old. Before the war he took care of his brothers, now
they have to take care of him. The world turns. In the end there's only
death, and one must follow the right path. That's what I say. In the end
God decides the fate of us all.

What else can I tell you? The Intifada—what do I think of it? You're
asking me like I was Yasser Arafat. I don't know. Some people say it's a
good thing, that it has brought some good. The people who are leading
the Intifada say this. We got back Jericho and Gaza and we're getting
back more. So they say. God alone knows. Will everyone here be Muslims some day, or will the Jews make us all into Jews? God alone knows

what's coming. The way I see it, there's some people out of work with nothing to feed their children because of the Intifada. And lots of people from all over have sat in jail. The Intifada's good? I don't know. Me, all I want is that we live the same as the Jews are living, not one of us better than the other—the way it was before. Everyone should have their own life. God willing, it will happen. But I tell you, let's talk about something else. Politics gives me a headache.

❧

I'll tell you about my trip to America. *Trips* to America—I went twice. Once was thirteen years ago, I went for forty days. The second time was five years ago, I went for three months. I have three sons there in the Washington area. And I have a daughter in America, in some place that I forget the name of. I went both times to the Washington area.

I went without my husband. He didn't want to go. He told me, "If America was no further than the Bab al-Amud* I still wouldn't go." He's not interested in seeing new places, our Hajj. He can't sit still, he's always moving around—here in our yard. Planting, weeding, spraying. He has to be doing something. If he's not working, he's praying. He likes to pray. He stays in the mosque praying till late at night—especially during Ramadan. To the mosque, that's the only place he's willing to go. I can't even get him to eat out at anyone's house. He just likes my cooking. He's loyal to me, that's all. As our God said in the Koran, "A bad man gets a dishonest wife, a good man an honest one." And if I wasn't a good woman, I would have gotten a bad man. But, God be praised, the man I got has been halvah, sweet as halvah. He never raised his hand to me, never did anything to make me go home to my parents' house, never upset me in a big way. For more than fifty years we've been together and he's been like halvah. I swear, he has.

But traveling to America with me—no, no. My husband let me go

---

* Bab al-Amud, the Damascus Gate, is the large entrance on the northern side of the walled Old City.

alone. The first time I was a little scared. I prayed that there would be at least one person on the plane who spoke Arabic. No luck, I was the only one. One kind woman who spoke English tried speaking English to me, and then she spoke to me in sign language. God had mercy on me and brought me to New York. A stewardess who expected me, I guess, came and explained in Arabic that I should take a taxi someplace else and that I should give the taxi driver only three dollars even if he asked for twice that. I got into the taxi and sat next to the door ready to jump out if the driver did anything strange. Finally, when we got to another airport he said, in sign language, that I owed him six dollars. I started yelling at him in Arabic, "Three dollars is all you're getting — take it or leave it!" And I got out. A black man took my suitcases, and then suddenly my son was standing there. I felt saved. We got into another plane, a smaller one, and flew to Washington. I kept looking down, I was scared. But I believe in fate, and I figured if I was supposed to arrive I would.

I arrived. I stayed at my sons' houses—first one and then the other. I can't say I ever got used to America. Here in Jerusalem it's getting more and more like America, and it's hard to get used to it too. I had trouble in those big stores on the escalators. I kept falling off at the top. Then I figured it out. Once you take a big first step you're alright. And the American food—hamburgers, hot dogs, and other things I couldn't really eat.

The one good restaurant we went to was Mama Aisha's. It's a restaurant in Washington, or it was then—now Mama Aisha is dead. She died at ninety years old, or about that. She's a cousin of mine from here. She went to America when she was an older woman, just picked up and went. She went to be with relatives, but they didn't receive her well. She managed to find a husband and when he died he left her some money, and with this money she started the restaurant. Delicious! Food just like here. Stuffed grape leaves, stuffed squash, *melukhiya* [a spinach-like soup], and okra in sauce. Wonderful food. She wouldn't let me pay for it because I'm her cousin. She was a wealthy woman, made millions.

She even gave me the use of her car with her chauffeur. He drove me all around Washington to see the buildings. It was very kind of her.

Still, most of the time it was boring for me. Especially the second time when I went for three months. Most of the time I was left home alone by myself. The Americans work very hard. They have many conveniences, that's good. But how they work! They get up in the morning to drive to work and, I swear, they go off in their cars carrying their coffee and tea with them. Can you imagine it? For me it was boring, I tell you. My son wanted to cheer me up. He told me to go to a hairdresser and have my hair done up. He even told me I should wear pants. Maybe he wanted me to look like a young American woman, I don't know. I told him, "What, you think I've gone crazy? I'm wearing a *thawb* [a long, long-sleeved dress]." And that's what I did, same as here. A simple, flower-print *thawb* for the house and an embroidered black one for going out. I was not about to start dressing like some American woman just because I was over there.

I kept myself busy watching a little television—very little. And at Hatem's house it was less boring than at Khalil's. Hatem lives near the airport and there are four streets in front of his house. I used to sit on the porch and watch all the comings and goings, cars, planes, people. That was not so boring. And the food was better at Hatem's house. He knows how to cook and so does his wife. So we ate well there. Except once, the last meal when I was in America. It was the meal before I went to the airport. My grandchildren came running to me that day saying, "Grandma, you're going home and you've never tasted our pizza. You've got to have some!" My sons ran out and brought back this pizza. Me, I'm dreaming already of being back home, and they're dreaming of pizza. So just before we went to the airport we ate pizza. I've never eaten it again. Here in East Jerusalem they now have this American pizza. My son who lives in the apartment below brings it for his children. It's not for me. I like the Arab bread that looks like pizza, with olive oil and *zatar* [wild thyme]. Keep the American pizza away from me, thank you.

⚑

God has filled the world with his creations and I've had the chance to see some of them. Besides the trips to America, I've been to Kuwait and Jordan and Saudi Arabia. Saudi Arabia I went to for the *hajj*. Back in 1984. That was the trip that meant the most to me. God be praised, I lived long enough to make the *hajj*. My father and mother both went, and I hope my children will go too. It's an obligation, you know. Every Muslim who is able to make the *hajj* must do so.

A woman who makes the *hajj* cannot go by herself. She must go with a *mahram,* a man in her family who, if he's not the husband, is someone she can't marry. It can be a son or a brother. Me, I went with my husband. *That* is the one time he was willing to go further than the Bab al-Amud! He longed for this trip just as I did. Every believing Muslim longs for it.

We went in the summer. That's a hard time to go. Saudi Arabia is an oven in the summer. Our children, may God bless them, insisted that we go by plane. Really, I think by car is better. You see more and you're free to go and come back when you want. We went by bus to Jordan, crossing the Allenby Bridge, and then we flew to Saudi Arabia from Amman.

What can I tell you? We did what everyone did. The *hajj* has stages to it. Circling around the holy Kaba in Mecca seven times, standing all day at the plain of Arafat just as Ibrahim stood up to idolaters, stoning the devil at Mina, and then sacrificing sheep there because Ibrahim was willing to sacrifice his son Ismail. We did it all. My husband wanted us to rent a cart to go around the Kaba. That's permitted, but I said, "No, let's walk." I swear, I didn't feel tired. My strength came from God. Even a sick man would feel healthy at that time. My husband and I took care of each other. Really, *I* took care of *him.* At one point, we could have been trampled to death. We were on our way to throw stones at the devil, and there were enormous crowds. We were told not to go on a particular narrow street—it's called the Street of Death—because whoever falls while going there gets trampled to death by the crowds. "Never mind," my husband said, and he was about to enter this narrow place, but I yanked him to the side and we went the safer way. I may have saved us both. In the end we sacrificed four sheep, two each. I felt very good there. One feels very close to God during the *hajj*. Every year since then, when the time for the *hajj* comes around, my heart yearns for it again. God knows if I'll be able to do it again. Until now, the Israelis have only let us go once each, that's all.

The bad part of the trip was coming back by the Allenby Bridge. I tell you, the one good thing that *has* come out of the agreement between Israel and the Palestinians is that crossing the Allenby Bridge is no longer a nightmare for us. Now it goes smoothly. My daughter just came the other day to visit—no baggage searches, no body inspections, no humiliations. But back then it was terrible. Going to America alone in the airplane and not knowing where I was going was easy compared to crossing the Allenby Bridge. The Jews sure know how to humiliate us. Coming back from the *hajj,* they made us wait out in the sun. We all had to take off our shoes and leave them in one place. Go figure out later whose are whose. Naturally we wound up fighting among ourselves. Humiliating, absolutely humiliating. They make you go to an inspection room to search your body. Twice this young Jewish policewoman made me go into the room, and twice she sent me out without inspecting me. And both times she was screaming at me, "Get out of here, you get back out!" I thought Jews honor older people. At least if she didn't respect me as an Arab, then she ought to respect my age. I don't know why she chose to pick on me. To this day I blame myself for keeping quiet and not answering back. I shouldn't have allowed myself to be humiliated like that. But anyway, forget it. I tell you, nothing could spoil the *hajj* for us. I thank God that I had the strength to make the trip and that I and my husband, our Hajj, went together.

After the *hajj* I made some changes. Before then I never found the time to say my daily prayers. When I was a girl I used to perform the *salat* [five daily prayers]. Then when I got married and all the children came, I found myself too busy for it. My father used to scold me for having given it up. I told him, "Father, God willing, I'll return to it." Well, now I have. These days, if I miss even one of the five prayers during the day, I feel like I'm losing my direction, that I'm not a human being. Once you start praying for forty days in a row you get into the habit. It's hard for me to pray on my knees. They hurt. The doctor told me to lose weight, but that's not the reason. They just hurt. So I pray sitting or standing, that's what I do. What is important is that you pray.

Also, around the time I went on the *hajj* I started fasting again on Ramadan. I fast the whole month, it's an obligation. Actually, I do more than that now. I fast on Mondays and Thursdays too. The Prophet, may His name be blessed, used to fast on Mondays and Thursdays all year round. Now I fast these days too during the two months before Ramadan. It's not an obligation, but it's a good thing to do. That's what I tell my children. They all fast and they say their prayers. Khalil, my son in America, wasn't saying his daily prayers but now he does. He told me that he had a dream one night that the muezzin [prayer caller at the mosque] was calling him to pray. He had the same dream the second night, and he said to himself it must be a sign he should pray. So he washed himself and started to pray that very night, and he has continued. All my children in America are believers and pray. On Fridays the mosque there in Washington is as full as al-Aqsa is here. God be praised, my children have followed this path. The only one who doesn't say her daily prayers is Marianne. She fasts on Ramadan, but she doesn't say her prayers. She tells me, "Mother, God willing, I'll do it." I hope that she finds the way. Maybe she will just as I did.

What is this world and this life we have? A moment in eternity. The Day of Judgment is coming for all of us, and you must follow the right path. Just yesterday I went to my mother's grave. It's the first time in four years that I've been there. I was visiting a woman in the neighborhood and I decided to go. My mother, my dear mother—I look in the mirror these days and, I swear, I see her face. I look so much like she did when she was older, except she was prettier. She died at eighty-five years old, only a few years back. At her grave I recited the Fatiha [brief opening chapter of the Koran]. I recited it there, but no matter where you recite it, it benefits the one who has died and the one who says it. God shows mercy on you. I said to the dead ones there, "May the One who has helped you help us too. You arrived before us and we shall follow." This life is nothing but an instant, nothing more. I have tried to do what is right. God will judge me. Our Hajj and me, we've done what we could. God will judge us in the end. I hope, I believe, we have followed the right path.

❧

I don't know how much time I have left on this earth. I've lived a long life already. A good life. One of my sons said to me a while back, "Mother, you never got to do anything, you were always too busy with children." And I said to him, "My pleasure was in raising you, seeing you grow up. That's what I wanted from this life."

Right now, I have only one big worry—Marianne. I want to see her get married. Our Hajj, he doesn't worry. Never has. He's never worried a day in his life. He's taken care of us, made a living, and he leaves all the worrying about these things to me. He trusts me. Marianne's brothers don't get involved either. They don't try to arrange anything for her. She doesn't want them to do that. What she wants I'm not sure. A daughter should tell her mother everything that's going on in her life. That's the right way. But Marianne doesn't tell me about these things, so who knows?

These days young people have different ways. You know how some couples meet these days? By videocassettes! Someone in my daughter-in-law's family just found her husband with a cassette. She was dancing at a wedding and they took a videocassette of the dancing. The cassette was sent to someone in America—a person who has family here. And this man saw her on the cassette, and now he's married to her. Can you imagine it? I tell you, maybe we ought to make a cassette of Marianne and send it to America! Why not?

Seriously, I wouldn't mind if Marianne meets someone—a person from here—who wants to live there. Her brothers are there, they can watch over her. Why not? Up until now she has had many suitors. Some were uneducated and untrained. She didn't want any of them. She wants an educated man, someone like herself. Alright, let it be an educated man, that's fine with me. But, at twenty-seven years old, it's already time to choose someone. I want her to choose. I can't force her. *Haram!* You must not force a daughter to marry someone. But I want this settled. Settled while I'm still here. That's the one thing I'm still waiting to see. God willing, it will happen. *Fi idein Allah,* it's in God's hands.

Marianne

After the session with Marianne that turned into a dialogue with Umm Mahmud, the latter refrained from further interruptions. And for our part, we no longer suggested to Marianne that she meet us outside the house. The last three sessions were held on the veranda of their home as Umm Mahmud remained in the kitchen or salon, out of hearing distance.

It is important to note that during this time Marianne and Rafiqa became quite friendly. Now and then Marianne would telephone to discuss some personal problem she might be having with her mother, her boyfriend, or at work. This presented a dilemma for Rafiqa—a situation that often occurs when fieldwork is going well. Namely, one begins to ask, am I exploiting this friendship as a means of advancing the work? (Rafiqa discusses this problem in the epilogue). Suffice it to say here that an element of exploitation does appear unavoidable in such situations, no matter how scrupulous one attempts to be. In this instance, without the friendship it is unlikely that Marianne would have broached certain topics. In deciding what we could print, we followed one simple rule: only if Marianne agreed to tape-record her remarks did we feel free to print them.

Below, then, are some of Marianne's further reflections and rec-

ollections—on politics, Muslim fundamentalism, her work, and her boyfriend.

❧

Politics. I don't like politics, I try to stay as far away from it as I can.
Nobody in my family likes politics. Even talking about it is not
something I like. Politics leads to prison. I know that in Israel you get
put in prison for what you do, not for what you say. And East Jerusalem
is under Israeli law, I know. But, I stay away from it. I don't vote in the
Israeli elections—which I'm allowed to do as a Jerusalem resident. And
I stay out of the Intifada. Politics is not for me, not at all.

That doesn't mean I don't have views. Of course, I have. And things
that happen affect me, make me angry. I just try to keep these things to
myself. Look, okay, I'll tell you something. It's an incident that happened
just last week to a relative of mine. I don't want to say exactly who. What
happened is that this relative had his house demolished. Why? Because
he built it without permission. Forbidden—that's the law. The house was
next to the road leading to a Jewish neighborhood near here. I'm sure
the city has plans and, well, his house wasn't part of those plans. He had
a warning they were coming to demolish it, but he really didn't believe
they'd do it. The house was on his land, you see, land he'd inherited
from his father. When they came to destroy the house they didn't let
him take anything out, like sinks, doors, nothing. They didn't let him
remove any of it. He was extremely angry, beside himself with anger. It
was a beautiful house, it had cost him about 80,000 Jordanian dinars
[about $115,000]. They came to destroy it with a bulldozer. His wife
tried to speak with those who destroyed the house. Finally, she yelled at
them, "Do it! Do it quickly! Why are you destroying it slowly, stone by
stone? You're tiring yourselves out, you're tiring us out. Do it, get it over
with!" She finished yelling and she just collapsed, passed out. And that
was it. Now, they've moved into a rented place. He's a good man, the
best. He has four children, two boys and two girls. What they lost is a
life's savings, they can't replace it. *Khalas,* finished! It made me angry,

nily was furious—my mother, me, all of us. But, I tell
I wouldn't have taken the chance of building a house
. May God protect him. He never should have put him-
self in such a weak position. I feel terrible for him. But what can you do?

I admit that sometimes when the Israelis do things like this, or really,
other things that are much worse—like when the Israeli soldiers killed
lots of worshipers at al-Aqsa mosque—it makes me wish I *could* do
something. But what am I supposed to do? Throw stones? Throw
bombs? To throw bombs at soldiers and be willing to die, it takes a
person who's been so hurt by the Israelis that he hates them completely.
I'm not capable of killing a chicken in order to eat it. What, I'm going
to pick up a knife and go kill someone? No, no, never. *Haram,* forbidden. This kind of thing is not for me, not for my family.

In our family, nobody has been involved in the Intifada. Except one
cousin. Really, he wasn't involved—that's what they say. Israel accused
him of throwing a Molotov cocktail, and they put him in jail for three
and a half years. He says that he was going to the pharmacy to buy some
medicine for his grandmother, and that the army arrested him by mistake. Who knows? Anyway, he's the only one of my relatives who's been
in jail or involved in some way.

In the neighborhood next to ours there are a lot of teenage boys—not
like in our neighborhood. These boys have been involved in the Intifada.
They scream at us, the people in our neighborhood, because we haven't
been involved enough according to them. But look, okay, so these kids
have been busy throwing stones and making the Intifada. But what's
going to happen to them in the future? For several years these kids didn't
go to school, or they went and then came home early. This is the way
it is all over the West Bank, I'm telling you. There's a huge group of
young people that spent years not learning anything, and they're uneducated. What's going to happen to them? It's certain that they'll go on
hating Israel, but without education who are they going to serve? Israel,
that's who. They are going to be the simple workers, the cheap labor in
Israel's economy. We need educated people to build a Palestinian state.

If we try to build a state without educated people, it'll be a miserable state, that's all.

I don't mean to say by all this that I'm against the Intifada. In some ways I am, but in other ways I'm for it. There's no doubt that the Intifada has played a positive role in bringing people here together. People here have become closer, even more considerate of one another. Nobody these days would let a fellow Palestinian go hungry. Besides, without the Intifada I don't think anyone abroad would be caring about the Palestinian problem. The Israelis would go on occupying us. Nothing would have happened. Now, because of the Intifada something is happening. We are closer than ever before to having a Palestinian state. The question, though, is, what kind of state are we going to have? I don't think anybody knows the answer to that.

What kind of state would I like? Well, I'll tell you. I'm not sure you'll agree with me, but I'll tell you anyway. If I look at the possibilities—a state run by Arafat and Fatah, or a state run by the fundamentalists, Hamas—I prefer the religious state. I would support Hamas, but on one condition: the state they bring us is one that truly follows the principles of Islam. Within Islam, you see, everyone is permitted to express their own views. And in a state run according to true Islamic principles, women have their rights. I mean, the right to education, to work, to choose a husband. The fundamentalists here, Hamas, agree with this. They support women's right to get an education and work alongside men, on the condition that the women be dressed modestly and behave properly.

You see, Islam values women. More than Christianity or Judaism, I think. The phrase in the Koran that says God made man "superior" to women does not mean that men are better.* No, the word in Arabic is

* Michael Gorkin showed Marianne this phrase in the chapter "Women" (Sura 4:34) from the English translation of the Koran (*The Koran,* trans. N. J. Dawood [Harmondsworth: Penguin Books, 1974], 370) and asked her to comment on it.

qawamun and it means simply that men have greater capability. They're stronger, for instance. Men are also—the way I see it—more logical and less emotional than women. With women, emotions control them. Because men are stronger, they have the right to dominate—in the house, in the government. I support that. Ours is a male-dominated society. But, that doesn't mean men have more value than women. Women are just as valuable. Islam doesn't take away from women's value at all. True Islam, I mean.

[At this point, Rafiqa asked Marianne: "Do you think you can trust the fundamentalists to be supportive of women? You think they're going to let you go around dressed in your skirt and short-sleeve shirt, and do nothing to you?"]

Look, it's alright, I'll wear the *hejab* and the long dresses. So? Our problem is not what we wear, this or that dress. The important thing is what women's place will be in the society—honorable or not. It's not the fundamentalists who are forcing us to dress modestly. Islam demands that of us, it's part of the religion. But look, I know there are some fundamentalists who interpret Islam in an erroneous way. They use the religion to come down on women. Some of these fundamentalists are much too strict with women, always watching them to make sure their behavior is absolutely proper, always checking to make sure nobody is looking at the women. This is not the way to be. I'm against that type of thing.

Yet, the way I see it, the faults of the fundamentalists are fewer than the faults of other political parties. And so, if it comes to supporting a political group, I prefer them. There's going to be a struggle here in the Palestinian state, that's for sure. I don't know who'll win it. I do think, though, that Hamas is growing in popularity. I think a lot of people have said to themselves, "What have we achieved in life? We've lost everything—our country, even ourselves." They see a return to religion as a way of finding themselves again, of being stronger, and of regaining our country. It is written in the Koran that without our religion we are lost. I believe this. And I also believe that's one reason we lost our country. Regaining our religion *does* make us stronger. To me that's obvious. The Israelis, the Americans—you think they aren't afraid of the fundamentalists? Sure they are. The Americans want to go on dominating this area, exploiting all the kings and princes in the Gulf. If these kings and princes go, and people come into power who understand things, the Americans won't be able to go on dominating this region. So they're afraid—afraid of our becoming strong. I think a lot of people here, Palestinians, know this. Maybe I'm wrong, but I think the more time goes on, the more the fundamentalists are going to gain power. I hope so, anyway. My mother, too, she hopes for the same.

May God protect me, though, after telling you all this. But, okay, print it. I told you before that I try to keep as far from politics as I can. Politics gets you into trouble. What if the Israeli Ministry of Education doesn't like my views? As a teacher here in Jerusalem, I'm an Israeli government employee. They could decide not to renew my contract. I know a few people who can't get jobs because their politics has gotten them in trouble. It makes me worry a little. But go ahead. By the time the book comes out, who knows what will be?

2

I'm working this year as a math and science teacher in an elementary school here in East Jerusalem. I teach third graders. It's a school for girls only. Last year, I did substitute teaching, and this year they gave me a regular contract. How do I like it? The truth is, I do. There's too many kids in each class—thirty-five to forty. Still, I like the job. I love the kids, especially the clever ones who come to school looking so pretty and polished. I like teaching them and they like me too, no doubt about it. Of course, there are some kids who are difficult at times, and there are days when the girls are rowdy. And yes, once in a while I've had to give a girl a light slap—it's forbidden, I know—but a light slap to get someone's attention doesn't do any harm. It happened to me too at their age, and it caused me no harm.

Mostly, though, I don't have problems with these kids. My relationship to them is very good. Some days, if I'm feeling a little down, I'll say to them, "Help me by being good kids today." And they do help. When the lesson is over, some ask, "How was it, Miss? Did we disturb you or were we good?" Last year a woman supervisor from the Ministry of Education was about to come and sit in on my classes. Somehow the kids knew. They said to me, "Don't worry, let her come, that old lady. We'll show her. We swear we'll go through the lesson beautifully!" They did, too. Somehow they knew who this woman was, and they sized up the situation just right—including my worries about it. Just third graders, but clever, I'm telling you.

After class sometimes one girl or another will come to me and tell me her problems. At that age, eight or nine, they don't know how to keep secrets. If there's a problem at home—say, the parents are fighting—they tell me. One little girl recently started doing poorly on her exams and not bringing in her homework. We had a talk and it turned out she was being bounced back and forth between her two grandmothers' homes because the parents were getting a divorce. I talked to her, tried to comfort her, but there's not much you can do at these times. Just go a little easy on the girl, that's all.

They're sweet kids, really. Some of them write me little messages or notes. They write nice things like, "Miss, you're the prettiest teacher in the whole school," or "Miss, I like you." Sometimes they bring me presents. Once it was a flower vase. And once it was—how can I say it?—a sort of funny and sad gift. A pair of shoes. I think these shoes must have belonged to the girl's mother, and the girl had taken them without the mother's knowing it. The girl came when I was busy with another class and stood by the door. "Pssst! Pssst!" she whispered. "Come here, I've got something for you." When I went to the door she handed me this bag, saying, "Miss, I brought you this for Mother's Day." I looked at this old crumpled bag with two holes in it and high heels poking through. I opened it and I was shocked. The shoes were enormous, size 42. I thanked her and brought the bag back into the class. The girls had been watching all this, of course, and they immediately started urging me,

"Try them on, Miss." The shoes were scuffed up, dirty, and hideous looking. The last thing I wanted to do was put them on my feet. "Put them on, wear them," the girls began shouting. So I put them on. When the lesson was over and I was saying goodbye to the kids, a colleague came by and with a straight face said, "I hear you've been getting presents, haven't you?" Another colleague stood there laughing and laughing. In the end, I didn't give them back, but I didn't keep them either. I put them in a closet in the school, thinking maybe some poor person might use them someday. A few days later, the mother came to school for some reason or other. The teacher who saw her said to her, "You know, your daughter brought a colleague of mine a present—a pair of shoes." The mother didn't say they were hers, she just said, "May God curse that rascal of a daughter!" And the shoes, as far as I know, are still in that closet.

⌃

One of the good things about teaching at this school is that I like my colleagues. They're almost all women. Some are older, some are my age. Many are married and some are single. We joke around a lot in the teachers' room. Sometimes, though, if I come in and there are some teachers talking about their husbands, and maybe sex, they'll stop because I'm unmarried. "Once you're married you can sit with us, not now," they say. They tell me that in our school no single woman ever got married while she was working there. "But, by the end of the year," they say, "if you're not engaged, we're going to find you someone!" It's sort of a joke between us, but seriously it is a problem—meeting someone, I mean. It's not so easy for a single woman here in East Jerusalem.

The way many do it, is that their family looks around for them. But I want no part of that. I don't want my mother getting involved in this. Not my brothers or sisters either. And really, they've been good about it. They don't interfere in my life, my brothers and sisters. So, really it's up to me. I know best what kind of person I'm looking for, right? One thing I'll tell you for sure, I'd only marry a Muslim. Not a Christian. I know some girls who've done that, and it's not for me. He doesn't have to be an Arab. Let him come from Bosnia—you know, there's some Muslims who recently came to Israel from there—that's fine with me! I'm kind of joking, but about the Muslim point I'm serious. I'd only marry a Muslim man.

Actually all this is sort of theoretical because, well, because in a way I have met someone I like. A Muslim, yes. I've only known him a few months. The way I met him was through a teacher at work. She's a friend of mine, a married woman. I was visiting her at her house and Usama—that's his name—dropped by. I had no idea he was coming, she hadn't said anything to me. But, between them, they had arranged that he would come by. And that's how we met the first time.

What can I say about him? Really, I don't want to say too much. Perhaps he wouldn't appreciate it, and I don't want to offend him. What I can say is that he's an intelligent man, a professional person. He's a little older than me, and he lives alone with his brother here in East Jerusalem. No, no, I've never been there. Only at his sister's house have I seen him. There we can talk. Usually his sister and her children are there, but once in a while they leave the salon for a while and we are freer to talk with each other.

Once, only once, we met briefly in a public place. We were sitting there talking, and to tell the truth, I was so scared! I kept looking over my shoulder. It seemed to me that everyone was looking at me, and that everyone knew me and my family. Finally, I couldn't stand it anymore and I said, "I don't want this, meeting in public places is not for me!" You see, if anyone in my family saw us there, they'd make lots of problems. They'd say, "We trusted you and you betrayed us." They'd tell me, "We're a respectable family and you're going to ruin our reputation." They'd come down real hard on me, believe me. They'd tell me I had to leave my job, they'd say I have to stop seeing him, and they'd say if he comes to the house they'll break his legs. So, you see, there's no sense meeting in public places. I don't want to have any trouble, and really, I don't want to upset them. Sure, I'd like to be free to go out, and Usama would too. But, as I've told you, as long as I'm in my parents' house, I must live by their rules. And I do.

So, if we meet, we meet only at his sister's house. Mostly what we do is just talk on the telephone. I like the telephone. On the telephone you can say what you like, and besides, he has a nice voice. I like talking to him on the phone. We do it late at night. Our phone is connected to the phone downstairs in my brother's apartment, so I wait until ten or eleven o'clock, when people are sleeping. Then Usama and I talk. It's so nice, I'm much more relaxed this way. You can learn a lot about a person just talking on the phone. It may not be like going out, but this is what is permissible in our society and I accept it.

In Israel, in the West—so, they are free to go out. They are too free. Sex with this one and that one before marriage. I'm against that. *Haram!* Everything in its proper time, that's what I think. For us, once a boy and girl are engaged with the *kitab* written, then it is permissible to have sex. I don't mean everything, *l'al-akher* [all the way]. Kissing, hugging, it's perfectly alright. Even in my mother's time, some of this went on after the engagement. I once asked her and she admitted it. Actually, according to religious law, once the *kitab* is written the couple is married in a legal sense—so any sex is, according to our religion, permissible. But as far as social custom is concerned, "all the way"—that's such a stupid expression—is acceptable only after the wedding itself. I go along with this, and the women I know think the same. Having full sex before the wedding would be a mistake because during the engagement the two of them could wind up separating, and there's no Arab man who'll marry a woman if he knows she's not a virgin. Also, if she got pregnant, what would be the fate of the child? He'd be illegitimate, nobody would recognize him. That's a terrible thing. So I say, everything in its time. Sex and marriage, all in the proper time.

The teachers at school, they say to me that once I'm married they'll tell me all about sex. Really though, what do I need that for? If it's information I want, I can read or watch television. Something like sex, I think, is something I can only learn from experience. I have a friend who sometimes talks to me about her husband. But who knows, maybe her husband is different than my husband will be? I prefer to wait and find out. In our society, it's acceptable to wait until the wedding itself. Social acceptability is also part of religion. It's not right to go against what is socially acceptable.

ᕒ

It's hard to say what kind of marriage I want. A good one, of course. If I look at my parents, they have a good marriage. They're married almost sixty years, and they still respect and love each other. I can tell. No, I don't mean they hug and kiss in public, or even in the house in front of us—of course not. Alone, sure. Look, they have thirteen children, don't they? I agree with their way. I would be the same with my husband. No hugging or kissing in front of children.

I have no doubt, though, that my parents love each other. From what I can see they try to please each other. Especially my mother, she tries to please my father in everything. With his brothers and their families, even if he is annoyed with them, she always treats them kindly. And with my father, she's always good. If he says something that she doesn't agree with in front of company, she'll never contradict him. She always respects him. And look, just today we've been invited to lunch at my sister's house. My father doesn't like going, so before we all leave my mother will prepare him a cooked meal—instead of taking a day off from the kitchen. In my eyes, she's perfect with him, 100 percent.

About my father, I can't say the same. He loves her and respects her, I'm sure. When they're alone he's very kind to her. He'll bring her an apple and say to her, "Please, my woman, take it." Or he brings her a banana and peels it for her. He's kind to her. When they had twins—this I was told—he really helped her. He'd feed them and do lots of chores around the house. He still sometimes helps her with things, in the kitchen and that kind of thing. The neighbors know he does, and he doesn't mind. In these ways he's good. But, where he's not right is in front of company or in public. When they leave the house he'll say, "Follow me!" He walks in front of her, not by her side. She doesn't like this, but he insists on this way. And what is just as bad or worse, is the way he sometimes treats her in company. If she says something he doesn't agree with, he'll immediately contradict her in front of everyone. Especially in front of my sisters' husbands—then he's at his worst. Later, she'll say to him, "Be right with me. You're good to me when we're alone, when there's guests you're different." Sometimes it annoys me too and I'll say to him, "Father, why do you do that to mother? Why?" He doesn't answer. It's his way, that's all.

Men are like that, almost all of them. They like to show they're boss, that their wives don't understand, only they do. Almost all my friends' husbands are the same. It doesn't matter if they're educated or not—the same. My boyfriend? The same. So far that's mostly the way it's been. When we're alone at his sister's house, he's kind and considerate. But just let some guests come, he changes. He pretends he doesn't want to speak to me, like he isn't interested at all. What can you do? I have to swallow it. I'm not going to be able to change him. *Khalas,* that's the way men are. If we get married, I'll just have to put up with it—like my mother does.

One way I expect my marriage to be different than my parents', is in the matter of children. I'd never have so many like they did. I couldn't manage it. In their time, the idea was to bring many children and somehow God would provide. There was no use of contraception then—not like today. So kids came, one on the head of the other. I mean, that's alright if the mother can take care of them, and the father is a good man and has money to support them. Okay, let them have many. But me, I couldn't manage with lots of children.

If things happen the way I'd like, what I'll have is two or three. One boy and two girls, or the other way around. My husband will have money and I won't have to work. I'll be able to stay home and take care of the house and children. If I had to, I'd work. But I prefer it the other way. I don't want an enormous house. A small, well-furnished place is fine. Here in East Jerusalem, though not too close to my parents' house. I'd like each child to have his or her own room, and I'd have an office for myself where the kids can't disturb me. More than two or three kids would be too much. Children need time, energy, a big investment emotionally and physically. You have to send them to good schools, good colleges. No, I couldn't handle many kids, not at all.

And if I don't get married? Well, I've thought of that. I want to get married, for sure. But if I don't, what I would like to do is adopt children. One boy and one girl. I know this is not done much in our society. Yet, in ten years, say, I'll be more mature. And I'm free to do it if I want. My brothers wouldn't stop me. And our religion supports it. The Koran supports it. The Prophet himself adopted orphans. So, that's what I would do. I want very much to be a mother, to raise children in a different way than my parents did. I want them to grow up independent, able to see the world in an open way. I think I can raise children to be like that. I want the chance. But who knows? *Fi idein Allah,* it's in God's hands.

Umm Abdullah and Samira

(CAMP AIDA)

Samira

On the outskirts of Bethlehem, just off the main Jerusalem-Hebron road, sits Camp Aida—a Palestinian refugee camp built by UNRWA* in 1967. It's a small camp, about 2,300 people in all, and from the main road it appears less impoverished than the large camps in Gaza or elsewhere in the West Bank. Within Camp Aida, however, there are the usual telltale signs of a refugee camp: narrow dirt lanes, sewage flowing in open gutters, and small children darting to and fro.

It is here that Samira grew up along with her eight brothers and two sisters, and it is here that she got married and is raising her two children. Today, her house is a far more substantial place than the one-room (later, two-room) house where she was raised. It is a two-story concrete dwelling with a huge visitor's salon downstairs, and two bedrooms, a living room, and a kitchen upstairs. A television and videocassette recorder sit in one corner of the living room, and bookshelves (with many political books) sit in another corner. Hanging on the walls are some Palestinian-

* Even today the United Nations Relief Work Agency (UNRWA) assists Palestinians in Gaza and the West Bank, and provides various services in Camp Aida.

85

style embroidery and a large wedding photograph of her brother and his wife who, like Samira and her husband, paid a heavy price for their involvement in the Palestinian national struggle.

Today, at the age of thirty-one, Samira has little about her person to suggest that she has been a political activist for most of her life and spent three years in jail for throwing a Molotov cocktail at Israeli soldiers. Deferential in manner, she has a soft, even girlish voice; and when she speaks, there is an openness about her. Indeed, of all the women in this study, she was perhaps the most candid and self-critical.

Michael Gorkin had met Samira briefly at a workshop for Jewish and Arab mental health workers. A mutual friend who knew about the book suggested that Samira might be an appropriate subject for the study. As it turned out, Samira was our most enthusiastic participant. More than the others, she seemed to have a quick understanding of the nature of our project; in fact, she herself had read a number of books on Arab women and immediately agreed to talk to us.

We met with Samira eight times over a period of ten months. Every meeting was in the living room of her house, usually in the afternoons when she returned from her job as a social worker in a rehabilitation center. Typically her six-year-oid son and infant daughter were with her, while her husband—who fully supported her participation—was away. Two or three times Samira's mother came to sit with us for a short while. Yet she seldom joined in or engaged in dialogue with Samira. A mutual respect, and perhaps an element of distance, seemed to exist between them. And Samira made it quite clear that she preferred talking to us without her mother nearby.

In these excerpts from our first interviews with Samira, she recalls in her matter-of-fact style some of her early experiences as the daughter of refugee parents. She also reflects on how these experiences led to her early initiation as a political activist.

❧

I was born when my family was still living in Beit Jala, about a kilometer from where we are today. I'm the fourth child and the oldest daughter. I remember hardly anything from those years in Beit Jala. Only the house. It was a tiny house with one room and a kitchen. It was built below the level of the street that passed by, so from the street you couldn't see anyone was living there. I remember we had this German Christian woman as a neighbor, a very nice lady, and she would always bring me presents. I remember also that my mother used to stay up late at night sewing embroidery on dresses, beautiful peasant dresses, and for this she'd get paid. Much more than that I don't remember.

When I was five we moved to Camp Aida. By then I had another brother, Hatem, the one whose picture is on the wall here. And then my mother gave birth to my sister, Sarah, and then five more—Ismail, Fawaz, Mahmud, Maysun, and Jamil.

I remember those first years we moved to the camp but really I wish I could forget them. It was a hard time then and when I look back it seems even harder. Until I was eleven or twelve years old, our house was only one room and a kitchen—much too small for all of us. At night we'd sleep in the same room on the floor, except for some of my brothers who went to sleep at my grandmother's house in the camp. Each of us had our own place. Mine was in the corner beside Sarah. When my mother gave birth we'd all move into the kitchen. That happened a few times, and I can remember being very upset each time. We saw nothing, but we'd hear my mother moaning and crying out. Nobody ever said anything to us—it's a mistake, don't you think? I was frightened, I didn't say anything either.

Those years, and even later when we built another room onto the house, were very tough. My father hardly earned any money. He's a plasterer, that's his trade, but he didn't like to work. Even when he was a boy in his village he didn't work hard in the fields. That's what I was told. His oldest brother was the one who did the work. My father was lazy then and he didn't change even when he had children. This caused problems between him and my mother. She had to bring in money by sewing. Also my brothers worked. My oldest brother, Abdullah, dropped out of school when he was fourteen in order to help support the family. And my other brothers, when they were on vacation from school, they worked too.

We were barely able to manage. I mean, we actually didn't have enough to eat. What did we have? Well, in the mornings my mother would give us bread and tea. Sometimes there was some olive oil too. Next to our house there were some olive trees, and we'd get some of the harvest for watching over the trees. In the afternoons we'd always eat fried potatoes, and once in a while something else. In the evenings, if there was no food my mother would give us tea again. That was the usual fare. Maybe once a month or on holidays we'd have something special. My favorite was the chicken my mother made in our *tabun*. That was delicious! And I can remember having ice cream or candies every now and then. But most days we ate the usual—tea, bread, potatoes. Actually, I didn't know back then just how poor we were. Almost everyone I knew was living in the camp. All of us had pretty much the same harsh conditions. All my friends were like me. So I didn't really see the harshness of our situation the way I see it today.

The really hard thing back then for me was all the fighting between my mother and father. And a lot of this was brought on by my father's mother, my grandmother. She hated my mother. She was against their marriage, she never accepted my mother as her daughter-in-law. She used to whisper all kinds of things into my father's ear and then he'd go after my mother. The truth is, my grandmother was a difficult person. She used to live near the entrance of the camp and everyone knew her. She had run-ins with lots of people. She was tough, hard. Maybe because she was left a widow at a young age, thirty or so, and she had eight children to raise by herself. I don't know. I do know that my father admired her strength, and she had a lot of influence with him. I can remember in the later years of her life—she died fifteen years ago at the age of eighty—she was partially paralyzed and couldn't take care of herself. My brother Yusef and I used to go take care of her and sleep at her house. I had to clean and feed her, often in the middle of the night. This was when I was about fifteen years old. I did that for her and not once did she ever say thank you. I'd bring her food that my mother had cooked and she'd send me back with it—once, twice, three times. She wanted her son, my father, to bring it instead. Or my oldest brother, Abdullah, he was her favorite. She preferred boys to girls. She never loved me and I didn't love her either. The truth is, she was a bad person. She made our lives miserable, particularly my mother's life. As if we didn't have problems enough without all that!

2

Since I was the oldest daughter, I was given lots of responsibilities around the house. That's the way it goes, doesn't it? Whenever my mother left the house, went to the market or something like that, I was in charge of the younger children. I have a retarded brother, he didn't walk until he was five years old. I'd take care of him, clean him, dress him. Doing all this used to bother me. I was only ten at the time, it was too much for me. And doing housework—I couldn't stand it. I still can't stand it. Back then, I couldn't wait to get out of the house and play, to be free.

My father didn't stop me from going out and playing. A friend of mine, Samira—we had the same name—and another friend, Imtiyaz, used to go with me and we'd play five stones [a game like jacks], or we'd play with dolls that we'd make out of sticks. We'd dress these dolls up, make a house, and then play mother and children. Samira's father used to beat her for leaving her house to come play with us, but she was brave. She'd escape with us and just take her beatings. Besides playing with Samira and Imtiyaz, sometimes I'd play with boys. I'd play soccer with them. My father and mother didn't say anything about it. Not until I got a little older, anyway—like about ten years old. Although, really, I don't remember either of them ever saying, "No, it's an *eib!*" Nothing like that happened. It happened in a natural way. At about that age I just stopped playing with boys.

What I enjoyed also was going to school. It was another way of being outside the house and being with friends. I was a diligent student, smart. I wasn't the best, but one of the good ones. When I look back on it, though, I can't say that these schools were good ones, or that the teachers were good either. From first to ninth grade I went to UNRWA girls' schools. They were overcrowded, sometimes forty or fifty of us in classrooms that had no air in them and no heating. The teachers were tough on us, they'd hit us a lot on the hands and face. I can remember getting slapped in second grade, in math class, because I had left a blank page in my notebook. Can you imagine it? And we used to wear these uniforms to school, blue and white striped dresses. You can still see girls today going to school in these uniforms. Me, I was embarrassed by it because I had the same dress for years. It got so old that it had patches in the elbows, patches of a different color than the dress. I didn't have winter shoes. I used to yell at my mother, "Why don't you buy me a new dress, new shoes?" My mother used to sit there listening, not saying a word, just crying quietly to herself. Back then, I really couldn't understand what she was going through. Only later I realized.

My mother, she's illiterate. She always wanted to learn to read, but she never did. It's terribly embarrassing for her when she has to sign her name. All she is able to do is give a thumb print. When we were children some of us tried to teach her to read, but we didn't show her enough patience, so she never learned. My father can read. He went to school up through sixth grade, so he's able to read the newspaper, the Koran. He didn't think to teach her to read. Look, when I was in school and had problems with my homework, I didn't go to him for help either. It wouldn't have been comfortable asking for his help. And my brothers were all too busy. I learned early that if I was going to do well in school, it was up to me alone. I had to rely on myself.

From seventh grade on, I began to have some friends who came from outside the camp. We were going to the UNRWA junior high school here together, and it was through them that I began to get interested in politics. I started to write about my feelings—about poverty and suffering. My friends gave me political books to read, things about the Palestinian struggle, books on Marxism and class struggle. I was about thirteen then. I'd hide these books in with my school books so my father wouldn't see them. It was from these things that I began to understand about the Israeli Occupation, and about the national struggle against the Occupation —why we had to go on strike, demonstrate, and fight. Always though, when I was reading these books I was afraid of my father catching me. The truth is, I was more scared of him than of the Israelis! And he did catch me a few times. Then, he'd fly into a rage. He'd grab the books from me, tear them up and burn them. "*Haram! Haram!*" he'd scream. He's a religious man, and he thought my books were antireligious. He was also worried that I or my brothers might get politically involved, and he was afraid of what the Israelis might do to us. He tried to put a stop to it, but I wasn't about to let him.

In school, too, I had trouble with some of my teachers. In ninth grade I had this teacher who was very religious. He caught me reading some Marxist literature. He slapped me and accused me in front of the class of being a *kafer* [heretic]. He then told our class and several other classes too that we had to stay after school for a lecture on the danger of these kinds of books. I didn't stay, I knew what was coming. I was a stubborn kid, I was not about to listen to his criticizing me more. My girlfriends who did go to the lecture told me what he said and how he spoke about me in a humiliating way. I was very angry, furious. Though, I admit it, I wanted to get him annoyed. And after this humiliation, I was even more determined to rebel. It was the same with my father. The more he tried to stop me from reading books on Marxism or that kind of thing, the more I was determined to read them. I don't like to give in or be weak. It's a mistake, but that's the way I am.

I also was having trouble with the principal of that junior high school. My friends and I were going out on strike days then. This was before the Intifada, in the late 1970s. If there was a memorial day for some occasion—like Black September*—we'd go out on strike. Or sometimes, frankly, we'd go out on strike just for the fun of it because we didn't feel like going to school that day. The principal would then pounce on me and insist I bring my father to school. But I never brought him, since he might have yanked me out of school altogether. Instead, I'd bring in my older brother, Yusef. He may not have believed in what I was doing, but he loved me and so he never told my father.

By the time I got to high school, tenth through twelfth grades, I already had developed strong political opinions. More than that, I had begun to see that I wanted to fight for my views. I was reading all kinds of things—books by Victor Hugo, Maxim Gorky. And more political books. I remember one book that really excited me. It was called *Al-Fedaiyin* [The guerrillas]. It's a book that talked about the *fedaiyin* camps in Jordan, the training the fighters went through, and some of the actions they went on. I began to feel I wanted to be like them.

By that time I knew that our plight as refugees, our poverty, was the result of a great injustice that had been done to Palestinians. The Israelis had come as colonists, they forced us out of our villages, and they took our land. This same Israeli army that I saw every day in front of our camp had committed the injustices of 1948. My parents deserved to still be in their village, Al-Qabu. About this, my father and mother were in agreement with me, of course. What we should do about our situation— that was another story. But that *our* place was Al-Qabu—well, I'd heard stories about that all my life.

2

From the time I was old enough to sit and listen, both my parents used to tell us about Al-Qabu. They told us how in 1948 their families had

---

* In September 1970 the forces of King Hussein of Jordan attacked Palestinian *fedaiyin* [guerrillas] in their bases and refugee camps within Jordan. Several thousand Palestinians were killed during these attacks, and Palestinian resistance groups moved their main bases to Lebanon.

been forced to leave. But more than that, they used to talk about their lives there in the village. You only had to ask one question or say one word about the village, and my mother or father would talk for an hour about it. I used to enjoy hearing about Al-Qabu. If I wasn't angry at them on that particular day, I'd stay and listen. Especially I enjoyed listening to my father's memories of the village. He was older when they left—let's see, he must have been fifteen years old or so, and my mother was about nine. He remembered more. Besides, his memories were happier, more joyful. His family had eight children, my mother's had the same. But his family was a lot wealthier than my mother's family. His father was the *mukhtar* [village headman]. My mother's family was poor. Her father used to work far away in a stone quarry and he'd sleep there most of the time. So her mother and the children had to work the land they had. She would tell me how hard this was, and altogether I had the picture of how she suffered. It wasn't easy for me to listen to this.

But listening to my father I had the picture of a wonderful place. When I was little I used to like thinking about it. In my mind, I had this picture of a village up on a hill, and below were the fields and trees and a stream. Beautiful, no? My father remembered the village in clear detail, and I used to ask him all about their lives there. He never told me exactly how many dunams [about one-fourth of an acre] they had, he just said "a lot." They used to grow tomatoes, cucumbers, string beans, lentils, grains, and all kinds of fruit. They also raised animals— sheep, chickens, and rabbits. Some was for their own use and some was for the market. His father was known as a generous man, and since he was the *mukhtar* they were always having guests and slaughtering sheep to feed them. Not just on holidays, but regularly. It seemed like they had a good life there, they were rich and happy. I know that my father was never more fun to listen to than when he was talking about these things.

My father also told me about his oldest brother who fought along with al-Husseini in the 1936 revolt against the British Mandate government. He was a hero with the *fedaiyin*. And his mother used to help out this son in his fighting against the British. She'd bring him the ammunition.

She was able to sneak by the British soldiers because she was a woman. They never thought to stop her. My father wasn't a *fedai* himself, he was only a small boy while this was going on. But he admired his brother, and he admired his mother too. I used to ask all kinds of questions about these things, it was very fascinating to me. And also I wanted to know all about what happened in 1948—how we came to leave the village, where we went. I wanted to know exactly.

Later, when I was a teenager, we finally went back to visit the village. Al-Qabu is just across the green line,* not very far from here. Maybe it's five or ten kilometers. I've been there three times. When we were there my father talked and talked. My mother was mostly silent. I'm not sure what she was thinking then. Sometimes she'd just wander off by herself. I went around with my father. It was amazing to me how exact his memory was. The village is destroyed now, razed to the ground. The Israelis have made a picnic area out of much of it. My father, though, still knew where everything had been—his family's house, the mosque, their fields. I went walking out to these fields with him. Even though there were no walls to divide the fields, he remembered exactly where they were. They were terraced plots on the side of the hill. Each plot had its own name. He'd tell me the name and then he'd say, "It ended right here, and then so-and-so's plot began there." He showed me where their house was that the English destroyed, and he told me how they built it again. He showed me the place of their old mosque, and where his grandfather's grave was. And he showed me where they used to go swimming in the stream, and where they took their water. I would always take a drink of this water when we were there. It *was* good.

On all our visits to Al-Qabu, we'd bring back something from the

---

* On international maps from 1949 to 1967 the borderline between Israel and Jordan was colored green. Al-Qabu was just over the green line in Israel (see map), while Camp Aida was in Jordan. In 1967, when Israel defeated Jordan and conquered the West Bank, Samira's family—and of course others in the West Bank—could return for visits to their former villages.

village. My mother liked doing this. Each time she'd come back with a jerrican [about 5 gallons] of water. For her, it's a special water, different from any other water in the world. She'd also bring soil from the village. Once my uncle who lives in Jordan, my mother's brother, asked her to send him some and she did. Everyone in the family who used to live there is still very tied to the soil. They long for the village. They've always had the feeling that someday they will return. My mother told me that after they left Al-Qabu, when she was a child she would ask her parents for new clothes for the holidays, and her father would answer her that "the holidays" are back in the village. For them everything good and worthwhile is still back in Al-Qabu.

I can't say that I feel the same way. I understand my mother's and father's feelings, but I never lived there like they did. If you ask my mother she'll tell you, "One day we're going to live there again." I don't believe it. The Israelis committed a great injustice in forcing my parents to leave Al-Qabu, that's for sure. But realistically, there is no way they'll ever give it back—even though nobody is living there now.

Our struggle right now, the way I see it, is to get rid of the Israeli army that's occupying us here in the West Bank. I've lived all my life under this Occupation, and my struggle now, and from the time I got involved in politics, was against this Occupation. These were the injustices that were always before my eyes, and more than anything, this is why I got involved in the national struggle back when I was still a teenager.

2

In high school I got even more involved politically than I had been in junior high school. In tenth grade I was going to a high school in Bethlehem. It was a girl's school too, and I had five girlfriends who were very political like me. We went out on strikes whenever we could, and we encouraged other girls to join us on demonstrations. The principal was against this, she accused us of incitement and we got expelled. You see, back before the Intifada—this was in 1978—not so many students did things like this. It wasn't acceptable at all to go on strike or demonstrate. They came down hard on you. Only with the Intifada was overt political action more acceptable.

But that year, I not only got expelled from school for a while, I also got involved in something that caused me to go to jail. *That* was stupid. I mean, the thing I did was stupid. It was something here in the camp. We had this person in the camp who was collaborating with the Israelis. I was convinced of this. Several young people had been arrested here and I was sure he was the one doing the informing. So I decided to burn his car. I took a tire, went to his car, and was about to set it alight when he stepped out and caught me. He turned me over to the Israelis and they put me in jail for nine days. It was a silly mistake, an empty gesture, the kind of thing that kids do. I was only fifteen.

I was in Maskubiya jail for nine days. It was my first time in jail, I was very frightened. I didn't know what they would do to me or how I would react. When they called me to the room where they investigated you, I was scared stiff. There was an investigator there with the name of Abu Nehad. He wasn't an Arab, he was a Jew. All the investigators use Arab names. While he was asking me questions he moved very close to me, his chair touching mine. He put his hand on me. I tried to pull away or curl up. He kept putting his hand on me because he knew how insulting this is for women, especially Arab women, and he figured this was the way to get to me. I was scared as hell. He used filthy language and threatened to put me in a cell with women who were common criminals. If I didn't talk, he said, he'd put me in with these tough women, and he gave me to understand that they would hurt me or do God knows what to me. I wasn't beaten—not this first time I was in jail. In the end, they put me in a cell where there was an older woman, a huge woman from one of the villages near Hebron. She was half-mad. Her husband had been killed and she was wailing and tearing at her clothes. She scared me terribly, even more than the investigator or anyone else in the jail. I didn't dare say one word to her the whole time I was there.

At the end of nine days the Israelis let me go home. My parents were extremely angry. I hadn't seen them when I was in jail. My mother was angry more at what had happened *to* me. My father was angry *at* me. My brothers reacted as if it were just one of those things, part of life and nothing to make a fuss about. I was the first in our family to go to jail, and at that point, I was only the second girl in the camp who'd gone to jail. My father felt it was a shame and humiliation for the family, especially because I was a girl. He was furious at me. As a punishment, he yanked me out of school. He told me I was never going back, I was staying in the house. My mother was more sympathetic to me—not politically, but as a person. There was nothing she could do about this punishment, though. She stayed silent, I stayed silent, and then one day, finally, my father changed his mind and told me, "Alright, go back to school!"

I finished up high school in East Jerusalem. I went there to this top girl's school for eleventh and twelfth grades. I went on a scholarship. You see, I was actually a very good student, I had outstanding grades even with my political involvement. It was a good high school to attend if you wanted to go on to college. And I did. There were students in this school from Jerusalem's elite families and they had good teachers. But there was also a problem for me there. Not just for me, for others like me too. For the first time in my life, I was subjected to class discrimination on a regular basis. The girls from the elite families got to take special activities or courses in the school. A course in music, say—it was only for them. Besides this, the principal and many of the teachers related to the girls from the elite families in a special way. With them, they were sympathetic, kind, always polite. With those of us who were from poor families, they were nasty and insulting. The principal of the school made me feel that in her eyes I was someone inferior. She let me know that she considered me a troublemaker, the one who caused problems, the one whose hair was disheveled and whose clothes were of inferior quality. She told me once in her nasty way that she did not expect me to pass the *tawjihi,* and that I would never make it to college. I didn't answer her back or anything like that, but I was determined to prove her wrong. And I did. Out of the girls in my graduation class, I had the second highest score on the *tawjihi*. This was high enough for me to go to college and good enough for me to get a scholarship too.

That was fortunate. Without a scholarship I never could have afforded to go to college. My parents support the idea of education, but they didn't have money for that kind of thing. Five of us have gone to college in the West Bank—Yusef, me, Sarah, Ismail, Mahmud. Maysun is planning to go next year. In our family, education is respected as a way of advancing yourself, for girls too. But back when I wanted to go, in 1982, my parents had no money to pay for tuition. They gave me a little help in buying books, but that was all.

I had no idea what I wanted to study at college. I just knew I wanted someday to do something special, to make some special contribution to my people. Dreams, dreams, that's what I brought with me to college. I wound up studying English—don't ask me why. And the truth is, I wasn't very interested in my courses. I didn't even attend classes regularly. I was more interested in my friends and political involvement. Also, I met my husband that year, my freshman year. He was already a sophomore there at the University of Bethlehem and he was from Camp Aida too. And like me, he was very involved in politics. I met him in a straightforward, natural way. Before going to the university, I had hardly ever seen him in the camp. Then one day, Asam came over and introduced himself. We began to be friendly, nothing more than that at first. Then, after a few months, Asam said to me that he wanted a "serious" relationship with me. I was happy about this because I really liked him. He was a quiet type with a kind of personal courage, a person who had warm relationships with others on campus. Asam was from a different political group than mine, he was with the Communists. I was with Arafat's group, Fatah. Many boys who were with Fatah tried to make me break off my relationship with Asam. They said it was a mistake to get involved with someone from another political group. I paid no attention to them. I liked Asam, I was not about to break it off.

Outside the university it was difficult for us to see each other, especially here in the camp. But sometimes I would go visit Asam in his house anyway, without my family knowing. My parents would never have allowed it. If my father had known he would have gone crazy. Asam's mother was shocked that I visited him just like that. "How can this go on, a girl visiting a boy?" she'd say. I was scared she might tell my parents. But, because Asam is the oldest son, he was listened to and respected by his parents, and he made them keep the secret. Sometimes I would sit with Asam's family and sometimes I would sit just with him. He had his own room, his male friends used to visit him there, and so did I. We'd talk a lot about politics. Asam didn't always agree with me, nor I with him. But there was a mutual respect. He didn't pressure me to switch to his group and I didn't try to get him to switch to mine. We talked, we argued, but it never got unpleasant. And of course there were many things we agreed on completely. About the need for national struggle—for sure, we agreed. We also agreed on the need to take personal action. That's how we got into trouble, you know. Asam and I got arrested together. Did my mother tell you about that? Well, that's what happened. We went on this action, we and two others, and we got caught and put in jail. He was in for two and a half years, and I was in for three.

You have to understand that the period when we took this action was during the Lebanon War. The summer of 1982, it was. The Israelis had invaded Lebanon and were killing Palestinians—men, women, children. We were seeing this every night on our television screens, and it drove us crazy. My friends and I were burning with rage, and we felt we had to do something. Anything. We got together one day and decided to attack some Israeli soldiers. It was a kind of spontaneous thing, not planned out at all. We went up to the army checkpoint just outside the camp, Molotov cocktails in our hands, and we hurled them at a bus of soldiers and settlers. And we took off.

As I look back on it now, it was not a good thing to do. I mean, it was a foolish way to go about it. It was *not* wrong in the moral sense.

Look, I know the Jews see me as a "terrorist." If I were in their shoes, I'm sure I'd view me in the same way. But if someone could feel what it's like to be in our shoes, suffering from this Occupation on a daily basis, real suffering I mean, maybe then it would be understandable why we do what we do. There are some actions that are wrong to take. To kill women and children is, in my view and feeling, something I reject. If I were asked to do such things, I'd refuse. I love my children so much, how can I do this to someone else's child? Still, one has to understand what brings a person to do such things. For us, the Palestinians, it is a question of to be or not to be. And we want to exist as a people. We have this right, nobody can take it away from us. The Israelis try to deny us this right. They have no respect for us, they don't even treat us as fellow human beings. A person who struggles against the Occupation isn't a "terrorist" who has lost his humanity. He is fighting so his people can live their lives as human beings.

That's the way I see it. I don't reject the moral basis of what I did. I only feel, looking back at it now, that it was foolish to go about it the way we did. We were bound to get caught and we could easily have gotten ourselves killed. Which is what nearly happened. You see, once we had thrown the Molotov cocktails, the soldiers started running after us. Each of us had taken off in another direction. The soldiers were shooting all over, bullets flying all around, and I was running as fast as I could. I was just lucky I didn't get hit. None of us did—I found that out later. But they easily caught up with me, and when they did, they started beating the hell out of me with their rifles. They kept beating me until they got me back to their post. From there, they whisked me away to some other place, a place where they began investigating me.

The officer who did the investigating is someone who called himself Karim. He was very tough. A real nasty guy, filthy and evil. He started beating me with his hands and cursing me. He knew all about my family. He's the one who arrested my brother, Hatem, a couple of months earlier. Hatem was in jail then for throwing a Molotov cocktail, he was just starting to serve a three-year sentence. This guy Karim knew all about him, and about us, and was trying to pry me for information. But really, I had nothing to tell him. What I had done was a spontaneous act, that's all.

That same evening I was taken from this guy Karim to the Masku-biya jail. It's the same place where I had been three and a half years earlier. There, they tried to squeeze more information from me, but like I say, there was nothing to squeeze. They didn't torture me this time—only later did that happen, the third time I was in jail. They just held me there and then put me on trial. They had no problem making a case against me, they had caught me in the act. At the trial they said the Molotov cocktails we threw had damaged the bus, and one person had been seriously wounded. I have no idea if the Molotov cocktail I threw caused the damage. I had just thrown it and run. Anyway, they sentenced me to three years in jail. After a month, I was taken from Masku-biya and brought to Ramle jail. I spent the next three years there.

While I was there, my family came to visit. They were very loyal, they came whenever they were allowed, which was one visit every two weeks for a half-hour. In the beginning when they came, it was hard for me to see the pain in their eyes. They tried to be cheerful, but still I could see how troubled they were. Hatem and I were both in jail at the same time. It was hard for them to take. Also, what I didn't know during those first few visits—my parents hadn't said a word about it—was that ten days after I was arrested, the Israeli army destroyed our house. They bulldozed it into the ground. I only found this out later from the newspapers. When I read that, it hit me like a brick. From that moment on, I began to feel terribly guilty about how I had harmed my family, really harmed them. They had just added two new rooms onto that house before I was jailed, and now the whole place was destroyed. My father refused offers from others to live in their houses. He said he was staying right where his house was, no place else. They wound up having to live in a tent next to the destroyed house, and that winter was a terrible one. It was bitter cold, with lots of rain and snow. I knew how badly they must be suffering, even though they never said so and they just told me to take care of myself. It was the hardest thing for me about being in jail. I didn't really feel better until I heard they were rebuilding their house. Then I finally felt relieved, I knew they'd be alright. This was about ten months after I'd been in jail.

As for being in jail, it was nothing so unusual—at least it got to be that way. I was in a section with political prisoners, all Palestinian women. In the section next to ours were Jewish women, not political prisoners. These Jewish women were in for stealing, murder, drugs, or other crimes. We had contact with them, sure. We'd drink coffee and tea together and joke around. We just didn't talk politics, it would have caused problems. But we got along. In a way, we shared a common enemy—the guards and the police. And for them, like for us, the government was also their enemy. It didn't treat them right. Most of these girls were from the lower classes. They weren't our enemies, it was possible to sympathize with them. Most of them had good hearts, really. We managed fine together.

Of course, my real friends were among the Palestinian women. Some of these women I still see today. We visit each other or speak on the phone. Some of these women are great people. Nobody knows much about them, but some of them have the moral stature of a Nelson Mandela—at least I see it this way. They're special, no doubt about it. My contact with them helped me a great deal—to get through prison and to become a more mature person. When I entered prison I was only eighteen, still a kid. Some of these women took me under their wings, they guided me and helped me develop. In our section, there was a real camaraderie. There wasn't selfishness, but more a communal sense among us. What belonged to one, belonged to all. Even the guards had a certain respect for us. They could see how we were with each other.

The women in my section developed a study program that you could join if you wanted to. Some of these women were highly educated, they knew all sorts of subjects. I was glad to join and study. I made up my mind that I wouldn't waste time in prison, I'd do what I could to develop. I learned English there, mostly how to read. And I learned a lot about, I guess you could call it, international relations. We studied Japan, China, Algeria, Yemen—the political changes and revolutions there. And naturally we studied the Palestinian problem. The educated women who knew these subjects gave lectures from what they knew. We also had some books from the prison library. Other materials, which we needed but the prison authorities would not permit, we managed to smuggle in. We did this smuggling during family visits. The materials were printed in tiny handwriting on small pieces of paper and rolled up inside some plastic. We'd swallow it during the visits, and it would come out later in the toilet. We'd unwrap the plastic, quickly copy the materials in notebooks, and destroy the original. The guards caught on and we were discovered a number of times, but that didn't stop us. We went on doing it.

Anyway, besides attending study groups, I kept busy in prison by working. I who hate housework wound up working in the jail kitchen! I was there for a year until I was transferred to working outside in the fields, weeding, pulling out rocks, that kind of thing. This wasn't pleasant work, but it was worth doing. The rule in the prison was that if you didn't work, you'd only be let out of your cell for one hour a day. Those of us who worked were let out more. Some women were assigned to work in a sewing shop, and also a small factory that belonged to a major Israeli company. I didn't want to do these jobs. I was willing to cook for prisoners, pull weeds, but I didn't want to contribute anything to the Israeli economy. There were many of us who felt that way, and eventually it led to a big strike in the jail. We, the Palestinian prisoners, told the guards that we wouldn't work there, and what is more, we told them that from then on we would cook only for the prisoners and not for the guards. Up to then we'd been cooking for the guards too. The prison authorities responded harshly to all this. They retaliated by taking away our family visits and they closed down the library. *That* really got us angry. We started yelling and banging on the cell doors, and then they further retaliated by bringing in male guards who sprayed us with tear gas. After this, we went on a hunger strike. It lasted eight days and it got a lot of publicity. Some Jewish groups like Peace Now, and some women's groups, came to demonstrate for us. And finally the Israeli minister in charge of prisons, Haim Bar-Lev, showed up and we negotiated an agreement. We agreed that nobody had to work in factories or shops producing for the Israeli economy, and we no longer had to cook for the guards. They gave us back the library and family visits, too. And that was that. Life returned to normal.

From then on, until I got out, life was pretty much the same—work and study, like that. The fact is, I actually got a lot out of my time there. I mean, I learned a lot. More than I was to learn later at the university. The courses in prison were more interesting, for sure. But more than that, I would say that I learned about life there, about the important things. How to relate to people, how to stay loyal to your ideas, how to plan for the future. When I came out of prison, I was no longer the same kid who went in three years earlier.

The day I came out was strange. It was Asam who came to fetch me. We had stayed in contact throughout the time we both were in prison. We managed to get letters smuggled back and forth. And then when he got out, six months before me, he came to visit me twice. But the actual day I got out of prison, I didn't know he was coming. You see, I was supposed to be released on August 5, 1985. The prison authorities refused to let me go, they said I had to wait until August 28. Asam went and checked it out without telling my family or me, and he discovered that a mistake had been made. My release date actually should have been on August 5. The authorities claimed that my file had been misplaced, something like that. A few days later, it was August 13, I remember the guard coming to me and saying I was going to be released that day. I was caught by surprise and went a little crazy. I said I didn't want to get out that day. I wasn't emotionally ready for it right then. But they released me anyway. And when I stepped out of the prison, who was there? Asam. He and his friend. I tell you, I wasn't expecting to see him. It was a real shock for me.

Umm Abdullah

Just down the hard dirt lane from Samira's house, about fifty meters away, Umm Abdullah (Halima) has her house—the one that was rebuilt in 1982 after the original was bulldozed into the ground. The present structure is a simple, unimposing, single-story concrete building of four rooms, with a small patch for chickens out back and a garbage-strewn olive grove off to one side (where the family lived in a tent for ten months in 1982). Living in the house today along with Umm Abdullah and her husband are the remaining unmarried children, four sons and a daughter, all in their teens or early twenties.

Our initial interviews with Umm Abdullah did not take place in her house. There was some concern on everyone's part that her husband would not agree to her participation or, in any case, that it would annoy him; so we decided to meet her at Samira's house while she was away at work. Eventually, though, Umm Abdullah invited us to visit her at her home (while her husband was out). There in her salon—with photos of her husband and his stern-looking mother gazing down from the beige walls, and an old fan or kerosene heater humming or hissing off to the side depending on the season—we held the last three interviews.

At fifty-four years old, Umm Abdullah is still an attractive woman, with high cheekbones and light brown eyes and an electric, if infrequent, smile. Her hands, even with the three rings she wears, are the weather-beaten calloused hands of a *fellaha.* And in her embroidered black *thawb,* and white head scarf, she does look as if she is still a villager.

Loquacious by nature, Umm Abdullah seemed to look forward to the interviews. Like so many Palestinian women of her age or older, she has a deep feeling of anger—and pride—in having lived through, and endured, a hard history. *"Dhuqna, dhuqna* [we've drunk it all]," she often told us. She seemed to relish the opportunity to set down this story in a book for someone, somewhere, to read.

At times Umm Abdullah's story has the quality of a cri de coeur, most especially when she is relating political events. She keenly feels, and holds onto, her status as one of more than seven hundred thousand Palestinian refugees in the 1948 war. Also, the fact that five of her eleven children have served time in jail as political prisoners has clearly left its mark on her. When talking of these events she sometimes seemed not to be talking to us, but rather to the reader, somewhere out there.

In light of this, it is perhaps not surprising that Umm Abdullah is the only woman in the book who wanted us to use her real name. Her husband and family counseled otherwise, and in the end she reluctantly went along, although she insisted we call her by her eldest sister's name, Halima. And so we have.

In the excerpts that follow, taken from our initial interviews with her, Umm Abdullah recalls her life as a girl in the village of Al-Qabu, her family's uprooting in the 1948 war, and some of her ordinary-extraordinary experiences as a young Palestinian woman and refugee.

2

I am from the village of Al-Qabu, just ten minutes from here by car. Me, my husband, many others here in Camp Aida are from there. We even have some sheep here from Al-Qabu. That's right, these sheep are the offspring of those that came from Al-Qabu in 1948. We still keep them. But that's all we have. The rest is gone. Al-Qabu is in ruins now, the Jews razed it to the ground in 1948 after they took it. You can hardly recognize it now. Only we who lived there can recognize it and know how it once was.

I remember. I was nine years old when we left but I remember. I remember the war in 1948 too, sure I do. Oh God, tell me why did we leave? Why? To this day, we still ask ourselves this. If only we had stayed! We should have stayed—no matter what. But, people were afraid. I remember the adults talking. "War is coming here soon," they said. "What shall we do?" We could see the fires off in the distance. Al-Qabu is a village built on a hill. From there we could see all around. We could see the smoke coming from Ein Karem, Lifta, Al-Malha, Dir Yasin. We could hear the guns firing and the shelling. There were two villages not far from us. People from these villages came through here when they left [*hjiru*],* and some stayed for a while in Al-Qabu. And they sat around talking.

We were all afraid, very afraid. We heard about what the Jews had done in Dir Yasin, how they had massacred all the people there. We thought that might be our fate too. So it was better to leave than face that. That's what the men decided. Suddenly, one day they brought in some trucks. It was a cold rainy day. In October, it was. All of us were packed into these trucks. Me, my parents, all of the children. The whole village got into the trucks and we drove off to Beit Sahur, not far from where we are now. There in the fields, with no place to go, we got out. "What is going to happen to us?" we asked. Nobody knew then. Now we know.

Oh God, what a mistake! I swear, we should have stayed. Since that day all of us are blaming ourselves for leaving. If we stayed, the Jews might have slaughtered us. Or maybe not. There are Arab villages in

* A more precise translation of the verb Umm Abdullah uses here (from the infinitive *an uhajir*) is "migrated"; Palestinians often use it when referring to the manner in which they left/fled/were forced to flee their homes and become refugees in the 1948 war. Its noun form, *hijra,* traditionally describes the Prophet Muhammad's migration/flight from Mecca to Medina.

Israel where the people stayed—like Abu Ghosh. They kept their villages. If we had stayed, even if they slaughtered some of us, or most of us, the village could have survived. Some of us might have lived, and so Al-Qabu would still live. Instead, look what happened! We are left with nothing, living our lives in the camp. And Al-Qabu razed to the ground. Half of it the Jews turned into a forest, so they can go on picnics there! The rest is just rubble, the remains of what was. If you go there you'd never know what a beautiful place it was. Only those of us who lived there remember Al-Qabu as it really was, how it really looked. Who can forget? Not me.

2

It was a beautiful village. Really. Everyone said so. People used to come from all over to see the views from Al-Qabu. And the air, it used to blow from the west, clean and sweet—not like the air here in the camp, stinking with the smell of sewage. I swear, Al-Qabu was a Garden of Eden. A stream flowed in the valley below, and leading down to the stream on the side of the hills were terraced plots where we grew crops. In the spring, wild flowers would bloom on the hills and the fruit trees would blossom. Ah, the quince blossoms! They gave off a scent you could smell all over the village. Al-Qabu, it was a Garden of Eden, I swear it was.

My family were *fellahin,* like everybody else. We weren't rich and we weren't poor. My father and mother worked in the fields together. My mother was the one who worked the most. A lot of the time my father was away working at a rock quarry, and he'd sleep there. He'd leave my mother with the *baruda* [rifle] and she'd take care of us. She also took care of the crops. My mother could do the work of a man, and then some. She could plow behind the cow just like a man. And when it came to sowing the fields, she could do twice the work of my father. He would do twenty rows and she'd do forty. Oh yes, my mother was some worker! On market days she'd take a basket of vegetables in each hand, fifteen kilograms each, and she'd carry a small child on her back. Down the hill she'd go when it was still pitch dark. She'd catch the "Train"—that's what we called it, in English—it went by near the streambed, and in ten minutes or so she'd be in Jerusalem. She'd spend the day there selling and then return at night with good money. She was a clever merchant, very clever.

Usually we had good harvests, so there was enough for our family and also for the market. We grew lots of things. Wheat, barley, chickpeas, lentils, olives, cucumbers, onions, and all kinds of fruits—grapes, cactus fruit, quince, plums, apricots, and apples. I used to have my favorite apple tree. It was spread out on the bottom like an umbrella, and I'd just lie under it and the fruit would dangle down to me. And I had my own fig tree, a *qarawi* it was called. It bore light green figs that were reddish on the inside. We raised bees and they used to come to the flowers of my fig tree. The honey they gave had a special taste, a natural taste, not artificial. Besides this, we raised animals, of course. Chickens, goats, sheep. Every family had about a hundred head of sheep and goats. On holidays, or when guests came, we'd slaughter a sheep or two and have a real feast. There were no refrigerators. You ate the meat after you slaughtered, all in a few days. It was fresh and good-tasting, not like the stuff we get today. My father was a generous man. If guests came, he was always slaughtering a sheep and hosting them in a big way. My mother was a fine cook—her chicken in the *tabun* was known as the best in the village. I remember, yes I do. Those were the days in Al-Qabu!

We used to have fun back then. At the age of five, six, seven, I'd go out to the vineyards with my sisters and girl cousins. We'd watch over the grapes to make sure other kids didn't steal them. When we were out there we'd play. Sometimes we'd build houses of small rocks and make dolls out of rags. Or we'd play hide-and-seek, or five stones. Or we'd play backgammon just like the boys played. We'd play it on the ground with pebbles and holes. There was no girl who could beat me. Same with five stones. I was the best at that too.

I would have liked to go to school—like my daughters have. But back in those days there was no school for girls in our village. There wasn't a school for boys either, not when I was born. What there was, was a *kuttab,* where the boys would go and sit on straw mats on the floor and learn the Koran and maybe some other things. One of my brothers went to this *kuttab.* Later, they built a schoolroom and the smaller boys in our family went to that. Me and my sisters, though, we had nothing. A pity, really.

When I wasn't playing, I was working. A job I liked was taking care of the lambs. My father entrusted me with that. I'd take them off to the grassy areas and graze them. The lambs would get used to me and talk to me—baaah! baaah!—and they'd only go off with me. Afterwards, when they were fattened up, they'd be sold off or my father would slaughter them. That was hard on me. I'd miss the ones that were gone. I'd go over to the place where one was slaughtered and I'd think about the lamb, remembering how I took my jacket off in the winter and put it over the lamb to keep it warm. I'd say this to myself, not to anyone else. I loved those lambs.

Let's see, besides the work with the lambs, I'd also help my mother. Housework or in the fields—whatever she wanted. I was a good child, an obedient child. My mother would say to me, "Halima, go to the stream and fetch some water," and I'd go fetch some. And she'd say, "Halima, go find the goats," and I'd go find them. Or she'd say, "Go to the fields and bring back some onions," and I'd go and bring them. "Go pick the grapes," she'd say, and I'd go pick them. "Go pick some figs—the best ones high up on the tree," she'd say, and I'd go pick them. Yes, I worked, I worked.

But really, the one who worked harder than me was my oldest sister, the one whose name I want you to use for me in the book. She was eight years older and she had the hard work, in the house and the fields too. Poor thing! My father married her off at thirteen years old. In that time, they used to marry the girls off at twelve, thirteen or fourteen. She'd be used in the fields of her father-in-law as a worker. That's what happened to my sister. Her husband's family worked her hard and they beat her too. Four years after she was married my father went and took her back, he divorced her. There were no children, so her husband's family agreed. She came home and didn't get married again until she was thirty years old. She got a good husband this second time, and now she has three children. But she's had a hard life, my sister has.

My mother, too, had the same thing happen to her. She was married at eleven. *Haram!* The reason it happened to her was that her mother had died when she was two years old. Her father didn't have anyone to help raise her. He had a sister who was married in the village, and this sister had a son. So when my mother became eleven years old, her father arranged for her to be married to this cousin of hers—my father. The *sheikh* who agreed to write the *kitab* told them, "Don't let the wedding take place immediately. Wait another couple of years." My mother didn't want to get married, but back then you married when your father told you to marry. You didn't dare say anything. "I was still playing with the girls when they took me off," she once told me. After the *kitab* was written she went to live in her aunt's house. They all lived together in one room. Then, at fourteen years old, she had her wedding. At fifteen, she brought her first child, a daughter.

I swear, a woman had a hard life in those days. She worked in the house and the fields and she had to take care of her children. And do you think there was any mercy for her when she was pregnant? She'd have to go to the market carrying baskets on her head and in her hands, all while she was pregnant. She'd work in the fields too, right until she gave birth. One minute she'd be working with a hoe, the next minute she'd stop and give birth. Yes, right there in the fields. The other women would help her. Someone would go back to the village and get a scissors to cut the umbilical cord and bring a sheet or blanket to wrap the baby. Once I heard about a man who was alone with his wife in the fields and there were no women around to help her. He helped her by himself, but since he had no scissors he took two stones and cut the umbilical cord. He then went back to the village with her and the baby, she walking barefoot with the baby in her arms. Can you imagine? That's the way women had to do it. Two days later—yes, two days after she brought the child—she'd be back in the fields with a hoe, work as usual. It's not right but that's the way it was.

I tell you, sometimes I think God has brought the Palestinians to their fate now because of all the bad ways they've treated their women. Making women work all day in the fields, making them carry heavy loads on their heads, giving them only a few hours rest each night—I swear, it was cruel! I think my God has punished the Palestinians for that, taken away our villages. Really, that's what I think.

You know who treated our women well? The English. They did. I was only a child back then, during the period of the English, but I remember these things. If English soldiers saw a man beating his wife, they'd stop him and beat *him* instead. Also, in that time, if they saw a woman walking with a heavy load on her head and her husband walking behind her empty-handed, they'd take the load from the woman and give it to the man. Or even if they saw a donkey loaded up too heavy, they'd make the man take on part of it himself. And once when I was with my grandmother, who was blind, she was walking barefoot and an English officer helped lead her home, removing thorns and stones from her path. I remember these things, yes I do.

But look, there was another side to the English. I was told some of that. They destroyed my grandfather's house because there was a family member who fought against them as a *fedai*. I'm speaking about the period of the Arab revolt in the 1930s. My husband's family also had problems, lots of problems, with the English. His father was *mukhtar,* and my husband's older brother was a *fedai*. He got shot one time in both arms. His sister took him away to another village and hid him in a huge *tabun*. For forty days she put butterfat on his wounds until he healed. As soon as he was better, he went back with the *fedaiyin* to fight the English. My husband's mother used to help out her son. She'd bring ammunition to the *fedaiyin* by hiding bullets inside the bread as if it was a sandwich. Once the English came to her home searching for ammunition but she managed to hide it in time somewhere in the garbage.

She invited the English for lunch instead, and they never found the ammunition.

These are things I heard about the English. So I know they weren't just our friends. They fought against us, they caused us lots of problems. That's the other side of the English. Who can forget? Not me. I remember these things too.

&

What happened to us after we fled our village in '48? Everything, everything you can imagine. *Dhuqna, dhuqna.* In Beit Sahur we managed to find a corner inside a house to rent. In a second corner of that house was another family, and in a third corner was someone else. We had no water and were forced to go all over looking for some, and when we found any, clean or dirty, we'd take it. It was a hard time, believe me. Beit Sahur is a Christian community and . . . well, look, my husband told me to hold my tongue about these things. Today, these people are living like we are, they're occupied by the Israelis like all of us. In the 1967 war, when the Israelis took Beit Sahur and all the land around here, we reminded these people, "Now you're just like us. The same!" So look, what took place back in 1948, the way we refugees were treated in Beit Sahur—let's forget it. We managed to find water there, we found something to eat, we managed.

After about three years we moved to the town next door, Beit Jala. It's another Christian town. At least it was then, now it's half Muslim. We managed there too. I mean, it wasn't easy, but I don't want to go into that either. My husband told me, "Leave the past in Beit Jala alone, speak nicely." The mayor there *was* good to us. He helped get us a mosque in Beit Jala, he contributed to it himself. Those who were against us refugees, who were they? Not the good people of Beit Jala. Just drunks and Communists and other bad people. Maybe they were worried we'd take their land. I don't know. Let's just say that we managed with the help of some good people there. We managed as best we could.

We lived in Beit Jala most of the time from, let's see, about 1951 until we came over here to Camp Aida in 1967. But I was still young when we first moved to Beit Jala. I was about twelve years old. A young girl, really. About that time there was a family that came to my family to request me as a bride for one of their sons. I didn't want any part of getting married. I didn't want to be like my mother or sister. I wasn't ready to take care of a house, and I said so. Fortunately my parents listened. Besides, my father knew this family wanted to use me in the fields. They had a lot of land, and he didn't want them using me in this way. So my father refused.

But it didn't stop there. You see, I was a pretty girl then, very pretty you could say. I had rosy cheeks and was already, well, like someone a few years older. Not like now. Sadness has ruined my face. Take a look at Samira. She has my face, the way it was then. I used to look like her, real pretty.

What happened is that more men came to request me. When I was fourteen years old a Jordanian soldier came. The Jordanian soldiers liked Palestinian girls because of their good looks, their character, and the way they dress. Many Jordanian soldiers married Palestinian girls and then divorced them. This one who came for me was stationed up near the Iraq border, far from here. He was about thirty or thirty-five years old, and he already had a wife and some children. My parents met his wife and told me she was pretty, with blue eyes. He wanted me as a second wife. He told my father frankly that he would take me away and that I wouldn't be able to come back much for visits. My father didn't like that idea, so he refused. I was relieved.

Then when I was fifteen years old another man about thirty-five years old came. This one was from Syria. He had four children but no wife. He was widowed. He smoked twenty cigarettes each time he came. I think he really must have wanted me, but thanks to God, my father refused him. The man got very angry when he was turned down. He beseeched God to never let me marry another. He cursed me twice like this, he did. And right after that I began to get terrible pains in my arms and legs. The pains wouldn't go away, so my parents took me to a *sheikha* to remove the curse. First to one *sheikha,* then to another. Still the pains wouldn't go away. Finally, they took me to a doctor who said I had a case of "nerves." That's what he called it. And you know, to this day I still get these pains on and off, worse in the summer than in the winter. I'm sure I'll have them till my dying day.

While I was having these pains back then, still more suitors came to request me. Another Jordanian soldier who was stationed up on the hill in Beit Jala came by and requested me. My father turned him down. Then there were some Palestinian men who wanted me, refugee people like us. Again my father said "No." Finally, there came a family from our village, from Al-Qabu—the *mukhtar's* family. I was sixteen years old. My father said "Yes." I told him I didn't want to marry yet, but my father didn't listen to me. He had listened to me up to then, but now he said, "*Khalas,* you're marrying this one!" My father was a good man— blessed be his memory—he died just two and a half years ago. He was good, but he had a bad temper. He could go wild in rage sometimes. I didn't dare argue with him when he finally said, "This is it, no more saying 'No.'" So, *khalas,* it was over. I had to get married.

I was too young—of course, I was. I knew that back then, and I'm sure of it today. A girl shouldn't get married early. The older she is the more she understands life and the more she can understand her husband. At sixteen years old she's not ready. To take care of the house, and serve her husband, feed a baby, all this at the same time—I swear, by the time she's twenty years old she's wasted. She starts thinking, "Better I never got married at all!" A girl needs to wait until she's more than a teenager. And these days she needs even more time so she can finish her studies. At twenty-two or twenty-four years old she's ready. That's the way my daughters did it. Samira at twenty-four, Sarah at twenty-two. And May-sun, at eighteen, has refused many offers already—and I support her! Boys, too, should wait. At twenty years old they think they're ready, but they're not. They marry then and at twenty-six they already want a divorce. Better for the boy to wait until he's older too—say, twenty-six years old. That's my view. I'm sure I'm right.

But back then I had no choice. My father decided and I had to go along. I had never seen my husband. Only in the distance, walking here or there. I had never set eyes on his face. Oh no, no. *Eib!* Girls didn't have *any* contact with boys back then, they wouldn't dare look at them. If they did dare look at boys and got caught, they would be punished harshly. We all knew that. And if a girl dared to go off alone with a boy, God help her! They'd finish her off just like that. Poison her or cut her throat, *khalas.* Look, these things still happen sometimes now. Less maybe, but they happen. Fifteen years ago here in the camp, a man cut the throat of his *married* daughter when he heard she was having sex with some man besides her husband. He heard the rumor, didn't check it out, and killed her. He threw her dead body into the street. The police came and put him in jail, and then his family got a lawyer and got him out. Later he discovered that it had all been a false rumor, that's all. He repented but it was too late. Can you imagine?

Back when I was a girl it was even worse. If you were a girl, you didn't dare do anything that might cause someone to spread rumors about you. You didn't dare cast your eyes in the direction of a boy. God knows what might happen to you! So, of course, I never had a look at my husband. But he had seen me. He had been watching me going down to the stream and fetching water. He had had his eye on me and he had decided he wanted me. This I found out later. He went to his family—a boy could do that—and he told them I was the one he wanted. "Her?" they asked. "Why *her?*" They tried to talk him out of it. His mother was aware of my "nerves," I guess, and she said to him, "She's sick. She's like your sister, she'll never be able to bring you children." He answered, "No matter what, I want her anyway." And he began to weep. This I found out later. His sisters told me, and one time I asked him myself and he answered, "Yes, it's true. I wept."

So his family went along with him, even though they were against it.

They came one day and requested me. I didn't even know what was going on. They came, they left, and that evening my father agreed. My fate was decided. Soon after that they signed the *kitab,* and they agreed to have the wedding party four months later. *Khalas,* that was it. I was sixteen years old and my fate had been decided.

Between the signing of the *kitab* and the wedding, you know, the boy is allowed to come and visit the girl. It's not like today, of course. Today the boy and girl are allowed to sit and talk to each other. In my day, it was forbidden. My husband—this was in the four months before the wedding—came to visit and he'd sit and talk with my parents. He was six years older than me. I'd sit in the corner. I didn't dare look at him because of my father, I was scared of my father. But *he* was always stealing glances at me. I could feel it and it embarrassed me. When my parents were looking the other way I could feel him looking in my direction. It made me very uncomfortable. And one time, before the wedding this was, he came by looking for my father. I didn't know it was him and I opened the door. I quickly told him that my father was at the neighbor's. My brother's wife saw me speaking with him and immediately went and told my mother. My mother came shouting at me, "Girl, have you no shame! What's the matter with you?" She threatened me that if I spoke with him again she'd tell my father. Believe me, I didn't dare do it again. I was scared. The next time I spoke to him was the night of the wedding itself. Then it was alright.

2

The wedding was the usual kind they had back in those days. It went on two days, a *leilat al-henna* and the wedding itself. It wasn't like in the time of the village, like my mother's wedding, when the wedding went on for ten days. No, mine was two days, that's all. Before the wedding, I had bought a lot of things with the *mahr.* Some of these things I still have today. For me, the bride price was 110 dinars pre-*mahr,* and 20 dinars post-*mahr.* An educated girl used to get 180 dinars then, but I wasn't educated. Today an educated girl gets thousands. Samira could have gotten thousands but she didn't want a *mahr*. Her husband bought her some gold and things for the house, and that was it. Really, the *mahr* today has become much too much. The Prophet said the groom should give some kind of small present, a symbol. Today the groom goes broke paying the *mahr*.

Anyway, what I did with the *mahr* is buy gold. I got two bracelets for 22 dinars, today they're worth 300 dinars. I have these bracelets still. I keep them in my closet, I don't use them. I just wear rings today. And I also bought some *thawb*s, some nice ones. And I bought a few other things too.

The wedding was usual. It was in Beit Jala. There was a *zaffa,* with me and my mother and my sisters in a car. The men were singing and dancing the *debka* [a traditional Palestinian dance] in front of the car, and the women walked behind, singing and trilling. I wore a simple dress and scarf, and they covered me with a man's jacket. That was the custom. I hadn't gone to a hairdresser, and I didn't have all that make-up put on like they do nowadays. No, that wasn't our way. We did have a big dinner at my husband's house—they slaughtered some sheep. There was music and dancing, with the women inside the house, and the men outside. Everyone seemed to be having a good time. Even my mother-in-law looked happy. But she was only pretending. I didn't feel her hatred then, I was too young to recognize these things. Only later, I realized how unhappy she had been that night. She never accepted his choice to marry me.

After the wedding party, I moved into my husband's house along with his family. We were all living in one room. My husband and I had a corner of that room. We had no lamps, all we had was a tin can with a cloth soaked in kerosene, and when the family went to sleep they put that out and we were in the pitch dark. But the first night or two, the family didn't stay with us. They went over to the neighbor's. That was the custom. After a couple of days they came back and we all slept together in that one room.

What happened to me, though, is that the first night I was alright.

Then, on the second night, I got the shivers and terrible pains in my bladder. These are some of the pains I'd been having since I was fourteen years old. I got them again on that night, the second night. It was terrible. It got so bad that they had to take me to a doctor in Jerusalem. And do you know what he said? He said, "If you waited just two more days you would have died." He gave me medicine, but for the next nine days the pains continued. It was so bad that I kept beating myself, and I stopped peeing completely. Finally a woman from Beit Jala brought me this herb, it's called *rejl al-hamama* [the dove's leg]. She boiled it in water and I drank it, and immediately I was able to pee. I began to feel better. The pains went away for the time being. I mean, I still get some of these pains on and off—even today. I go to the doctor and get medicine for it, but when the medicine runs out the pains come back again. What can you do? I don't think it will ever stop.

꙳

It was not an easy life living together with my mother-in-law. She was a strong woman, strong-willed. Yes, that's her picture up on the wall. Not an easy person, believe me. Her husband died when she was still a young woman, and she had to raise the children by herself. She died fifteen years ago. God bless her memory. It's not good to talk about the bad things. She was my husband's mother and I say, God bless her memory.

My mother-in-law got her own place after we moved to the camp in 1967. But those years when we were in Beit Jala she lived with us. She helped me with the children once I started to bring them. Abdullah, Yusef, Ahmad, Samira, Hatem—they were all born in Beit Jala. And then when we moved to the camp, I brought six more—Sarah, Ismail, Fawaz, Mahmud, Maysun, Jamil.

I was seventeen years old when I brought the first. A son, Abdullah. I'm Umm Abdullah. It was a hard pregnancy, all my pregnancies were hard. I was sick, vomiting, the first four months with Abdullah, and with all the others too. I swear, if I hadn't gotten sick like that I would have brought more. Maybe fifteen or sixteen.

Abdullah—I brought him at the hospital. Most of my children were born in the hospital. I brought four at home with the help of a midwife, and I brought one in the clinic here in the camp. They're all fine, healthy, except for Fawaz who I brought at the clinic in the camp. He's retarded and lives with us still. He's a fine boy, all the same.

Actually, I liked giving birth at home. I liked having the midwife come and help me out. I had different midwives. One was from Beit Sahur, she had a license. Another came from Camp Deheisha and another was from here. Usually, the midwife would stay with me for a couple of days after the birth, or even a week if I needed her. I'd pay her for this, sure. I'd give her things from the grocery store, a little money. It wasn't much, but it was something.

With all my babies, I took care of them the village way, the way the women from the village used to do it. What's that way? Look, one thing I'd do is *kuhl* the baby's eyes. I'd make the *kuhl* by putting olive oil in a rag and then burn the rag. The leftover ash was *kuhl,* and I'd put it on the baby's eyelids for forty days. It helps the eyes grow strong and not get irritated or infected. I did this with all my children. I'd also massage and wrap the baby. What you do is each night you take some olive oil and mix a little salty water with it. You make a salve. You smear this all over the baby's body, massage it in good. It makes the skin so it won't peel, and when the baby grows up it doesn't smell. Then you wrap the baby in a tight cloth, roll him up in it. The baby sleeps like this and in the morning you take off the cloth and you wash the baby. Then you wrap him up again for the day. You keep doing this for four or five months, and that way the baby's bones grow strong and healthy.

I've told Samira about this, but she doesn't do it. These days I'm taking care of her baby daughter, Leila, but Samira won't let me do these things with Leila. She's wrong. She thinks that if you wrap the baby like I say, the arms and legs will be damaged, broken. She thinks that the salt will irritate the skin of the baby. But I tell you, it's a mistake not to do these things. Samira, and the women today, are making a mistake. Sure they are. The women of my generation, village women, know how to do it. What, our children didn't come out strong? Look at my children, look at Samira herself. She's not strong? And look at those of us who were born in the village—*we* had it the best! The air, the food, was healthiest back in the village. A mother breastfeeds her baby, but if she's not eating good food her milk isn't as good. Back in the village the mother's milk was good. Since we left the village there's not been the same good food for mothers to eat.

Me, I breastfed all my babies. But what happened with me is that none of my babies were ever filled by my milk. God alone knows why. So, I always would add some cow's milk. I always gave this cow's milk in a teaspoon, never a bottle, because if I gave it in a bottle they might stop breastfeeding. There's a lot of milk in a bottle and not much in a teaspoon, right? That's what I did with all eleven of them. I didn't want to stop breastfeeding—oh no! As soon as I stopped breastfeeding I'd always get pregnant. If I continued to breastfeed for two or three years, then I wouldn't get pregnant. The women around here told me about this, and it worked. Except once, with Sarah—I got pregnant with her while I was still breastfeeding Hatem. But usually it worked.

How was it when I gave birth to Samira? Well, I'll tell you the truth, it wasn't easy. It was like when I gave birth to my first, Abdullah. Maybe because Samira was a first too—the first daughter. I remember I wanted to give birth to her at home, but there was some problem, she wasn't coming out. They rushed me to the French Hospital. I remember I was yelling a lot, they gave me a shot, and then she came out. From the time she came out, I loved her. We all loved her, she was our first girl. It was me who gave her the name Samira. My husband had chosen the names of my first three sons. I named her Samira. I named her after a heroine who fought for Islam—a real brave fighter, she was. I had heard my husband and his friends talking about this Samira one time, when they

were telling stories from the Koran and about the Prophet. I decided
that's the name I want for my daughter. So that's what I called her,
Samira.*

She *is* a heroine too, don't you think? Samira has lived up to her
name. As a small child, maybe you couldn't see that one day she would
be so brave. She was always so sensitive, and a little nervous. More nervous than me. When I used to give birth at home, I could see in Samira's
eyes how scared she was. She never said a word, though. I'd put the
children in the kitchen, I wouldn't tell them what was happening. I
didn't want them to get scared. But Samira knew. I remember one time,
she looked very frightened afterwards. I tried to reassure her. I told her
that really there was only a little pain for a while and then it stopped. I
told her that I was ready to do it again, the next day. I don't know if
she stopped being frightened so much. I couldn't tell. She never asked
me a question about it, never said a thing. That's the way she is, Samira.

❧

I brought the first five children outside the camp, the last six here. A
little before we moved here my mother-in-law tried to get my husband
to marry another woman. She wanted him to take a second wife. This
happened when I was pregnant with my sixth, Sarah. She had never
wanted him to marry me at all, she had told him I'd never bring children. Now I had brought four sons and a daughter, and still she hated
me. She hated me so much that she prayed I would die. What can I say?
God bless her memory, that's all. She's my husband's mother. My husband, he wouldn't listen to her. She kept talking to him and he told her,
"No." He wanted just one wife—me. So my mother-in-law finally had
to stop pushing this thing with him.

She got her own place when we moved to the camp. We moved to

---

* We abbreviate Umm Abdullah's long anecdote about the heroine, "Samira,"
for the sake of her daughter's anonymity.

this spot. For a while our house had only one room and a kitchen. Then UNRWA helped us add another bedroom and a veranda. What can I tell you? We've managed, yes, we've managed. I'm a village woman, and we village women know how to manage. My husband worked some, he's a plasterer. Then my oldest son took up the trade and his brothers helped out too. Nowadays, my number two and three sons, Yusef and Ahmad, live in Saudi Arabia. They've done well there, they send us money. They tell us, "You've worked hard enough, rest." So we are fine now, we manage fine.

There were hard times too, of course there were. I think the hardest was back when they destroyed our house. The Jews destroyed it. It was back in 1982 when Samira went to jail. She must have told you about that, didn't she? Well, *that* was a hard time. We had been living in our UNRWA house, and we had just added two more rooms. We had water and electricity. We got that in 1978. Then Samira got arrested and they destroyed the house. It was the first time one of my children went to jail. Wait. . . . there was another time. Four years before that, Samira was in jail too—for a week. She was only fifteen years old then. Already she was involved in politics. There was someone here in the camp who was a collaborator with the Jews, and she decided to burn his truck. She got caught in the act. She was sent to Maskubiya jail and we weren't allowed to visit her. They investigated her, but she was clever. She never let on who was behind her action, who her friends were. She told them she did it on her own, she stood up to them. And so they let her go.

But four years later she was back in jail again. This time for throwing a Molotov cocktail at a bus full of soldiers. Ten days after she went into jail the Jews came here and demolished our house. They bulldozed it into the ground. Then, they offered us a tent to live in. We told them, "Keep it! After you destroy our house, you want to give us a *tent* to live in? Keep it!" We bought our own tent, a big one from Hebron, and we set it up in the olive grove next to us. We all moved in. It was a cold winter, lots of rain and snow, but we managed. We took an electrical cable and ran it from the *mukhtar*'s house to our tent. We had a refrigerator, an iron, even a television. We had lots of visitors too, they kept coming to visit us and support us.

We didn't tell Samira, though—not at first. When we visited her in jail we'd joke around and be lighthearted. We didn't want to worry her. Then she found out about it herself, she read it in the newspapers. She was all upset. But we told her, "Just take care of yourself. Don't worry about us." We told her, "We'll build a new house, a better one than the UNRWA house. When you get back you'll see!" And that's what we did. By the time she got out three years later we'd already rebuilt, and we were managing fine—just like I told her.

Samira

When Samira returned home from prison in 1985 she was twenty-two years old. Her political goals, and her life in general, had a clearer focus at this point. As she puts it, "Jail had crystallized my plans and hopes, I knew more what I wanted and how to go about it." Then in 1987 began the Intifada—the Palestinian uprising that swept more of her family into its fast flow and profoundly affected her own life, too.

In the section below, Samira recalls some of the events of these past ten years: her marriage, her giving birth to two children, her work as a social worker, and her continuing political involvement. She also recalls her return to jail for a month in 1991, during which time she was tortured. This experience was understandably the most difficult for her to relate (she had not done so before), and its impact on her life is, also understandably, still with her.

&

I remember that day I got out of jail, August 13, 1985, very well. How could I forget it? It was a shock to me. It was a shock to my parents too. They hadn't been expecting to see me home that day either. They thought it was going to be at the end of August. Then, suddenly, there was Asam bringing me home. They knew Asam of course, and they knew he was a friend of mine. My mother was aware that I liked him. My father wasn't aware of that, at least I don't think so. When Asam showed up with me they were angry. Instead of it being a joyful occasion for them, it was a big embarrassment. They felt it was an *eib*. How dare I, an unmarried girl, come in a car with a man? They felt I'd shamed them in front of the community, and they let me know it. I was hurt by their reaction, very hurt, but I should have expected it. Three years away in jail made no difference as far as that was concerned. Sad, but that's the way it is.

I, at any rate, *had* changed. I had grown up a lot. I knew more who I was. Jail had crystallized my plans and hopes, I knew more what I wanted and how to go about it. Asam—I knew I wanted him and I intended to go on with him, for sure. And I was sure he wanted me too. We both wanted to finish our studies at the university. He had already gone back, and I was determined now to continue my studies, not in English but as a social worker. In jail I decided that I wanted to work with people's problems in a direct way, and social work was a way of doing it. I intended to stay involved politically, but in a more organizational capacity. No more Molotov cocktails for me!

Asam and I soon decided that we wanted to get married. To do this, we needed to tell our parents and get their approval. His parents were no problem. The real problem was my father. He didn't want me to marry Asam. It wasn't a personal thing, it was just that he didn't want me marrying someone who was involved in politics. When Asam came to my father to request his permission, my father refused him. Asam waited a little and came again. My father refused again. This happened a few times. So Asam brought some respectable elders in the camp to plead on his behalf, but my father told them, "How can I give in now after having refused several times?" He's a stubborn man, my father is. He thinks he's the one who knows what's right and best for everyone. In the end, though, what happened is that I went to my brothers and convinced them that Asam was the man I wanted to marry. They agreed to go to my father, and finally they managed to convince him.

While all this was going on, I was seeing Asam of course. I wasn't about to stop. But I was scared like hell that my father would catch me. At least part of the time my mother was aware that we were seeing each other, but she kept it to herself. It was not easy for us to see each other, though. We were both still required to stay in the immediate area, and every day we had to go to the local police station and sign in as proof we hadn't left. So there weren't many places we could go alone. Sometimes, though, our friends would help us escape, they'd invite us on short trips—to Jerusalem or Jericho—and Asam and I would take the chance and go.

Even after we got engaged and the *kitab* was signed, my father still opposed Asam's and my being together in public—or at all. He wouldn't let me visit Asam's family, and when Asam came to visit me my father wouldn't let us sit together alone. I tell you, it was ridiculous. We had to deal with *two* Occupation authorities—the Israelis and my father! During that period, I was always scared of being caught by one or the other.

Not all fathers in our society are as strict as mine, things have loosened some, but still I have to say that our society is terribly repressed in this way. I managed, I did what I wanted. But still, a woman and man who love each other shouldn't be obliged to sneak around like we did. I believe a woman should be free to do what she wants with the man she loves. If she wants, she should be free to have sex with him. I don't mean in the way they do it in Israel and the West. I believe in freedom, but not in the extreme way. But look, I loved Asam, so why shouldn't I have been free to do what I wanted with him? It's my business, nobody else's. In our society, there's no support for the idea of having sex before marriage. A few do, they take the chance, but only a few. Me? I'll tell you the truth, with us it was Asam who's conservative in these things, not me. He didn't want to have full sex before marriage, he wanted to wait. I wouldn't be ashamed to tell you if we did, but we didn't. To me, whatever we did was perfectly alright. I have no guilt, no shame about anything. I tell you, in my view a lot of the problems that young people have in our society have to do with the fact that they are frustrated and repressed in this area. Our society is sick in this way, very sick. That's the way I see it.

⌒

We had a very nice wedding. It was done the usual way weddings are done here in the camp, but in a way it was special. I mean, naturally it was special for me, but it was also special for a lot of people here in the camp. Asam and I are both children of the camp, our families are well known here. And the fact that both of us had been so politically active, and in jail, gave people an extra reason to celebrate. Our *zaffa* through the camp—that's what you usually do, the bride and groom tour the camp with all the guests—was enormous. Guests came from all over the West Bank, and there were hundreds upon hundreds from the camp too. Many of our friends, like us, had been in jail, so it was a big procession of political activists. This gave it a special feeling. I was riding in a car and Asam was carried through the camp on his friends' shoulders. A friend of ours had a video camera that he just got from America, but he didn't know how to use it and nothing came out. All I have are some photos. Here . . . [Samira goes to the bookcase and brings a small framed photograph of herself and Asam standing together; she, elaborately made up and in a floor-length white bridal dress, and he in a black suit and tie.] We looked pretty good then, didn't we. A pity the video didn't come out!

Anyway, after we had toured the camp for a while, we then went to Asam's house for the wedding meal. In the camp these things are done very modestly. The guests don't take part in this meal, not even the bride's family does. Only the parents of the groom, and his brothers and sisters sometimes. The guests are given some sweets and soft drinks, but that's about it. The custom in the camp is that a neighbor of the groom's family makes a festive meal for the bride and groom. The way this happens is that a number of neighbors offer themselves as the one to make this meal. The neighbor who is most enthusiastic, or really the one who seems she's going to be most offended if she's turned down, is the one who's usually chosen. The groom's mother does the choosing. For us, a lot of neighbors wanted to do it, and Asam's mother chose a perfect one.

The meal this neighbor brought us was beautifully done, and the way she brought it was also beautiful. She put all the food—the salads, the meat and rice—on an enormous platter that she decorated with candles and red roses. She put this platter on her head, and she came dancing this way to Asam's house, dancing and singing and trilling. It was something special and the food was wonderful. She had really done a good job of it. It was a true gift from the heart.

It would have been nice to go away on a honeymoon, but for us that was out of the question. We had no money for this. Besides, we were not allowed by the Israeli military authorities to leave the camp. Every morning, I still had to go report to the police in Bethlehem. This made for a situation that was sort of funny. You see, the custom is that after the wedding the bride doesn't appear in public for several days. She's supposed to stay in the house. But, *I* had to go to the police each morning. So what I did is try to disguise myself. I wore jeans, a plain blouse, and I tied my long hair up, hoping people wouldn't recognize me. I left the house at seven-thirty in the morning. Still, some of the neighbors noticed me. I heard them saying to each other, "*That's* the new bride? What's going on here?" It was sort of funny for me to hear them. The whole situation was a bit ridiculous. Not the usual honeymoon, no?

Asam and I had our own apartment, just at the back of the camp. It was a place we rented, and we moved into it after the wedding. We had a bedroom, a kitchen, and a bathroom. This was very nice, a luxury for us. I was still going to Bethlehem University, studying social work. And Asam had just graduated with a major in Arabic literature and language. He hadn't found a job yet, but that was alright. We were feeling very good, glad to at last be in a place of our own.

But then Asam got arrested again. It was the beginning of the Intifada, and the Israelis rounded up a lot of people here. They put them in Atlit, a military prison. Asam was in for nine days and then they released him. Then, about a week later, they came back and arrested him again, what they call *maatsar minhali* [administrative detention]. He wasn't formally charged with anything, but they were holding him in jail for six months. During this period, they arrested some others from the Bethlehem area, a military group, and someone in this group said that Asam was the one giving them orders. So they put Asam on trial and sentenced him to five years in jail. He didn't get out until 1993.

For me this was awful. I was pregnant already when Asam was taken to jail. Two and a half months pregnant, something like that. I didn't want to stay alone in that rented apartment. The only other place I could go to was my parent's house. That was a bad feeling, but I figured I had no choice. So I went back. At the end of the year I gave birth to my son, Ali. I gave birth at Muqassed Hospital in East Jerusalem. My mother came with me. It was a difficult birth, lots of pain, but what was hardest was that Asam wasn't there. I didn't know when I'd see him again, or when we'd all be together.

As it happened, ten days after I gave birth I went to prison to see him. I went without Ali, I wasn't ready to bring him yet. I wanted to be there by myself. About two months later I brought Ali. Asam took a look at him and began crying. I was crying too, and so was Ali. All three of us. Asam looked terrible. His eyes were all red, his face was unshaven, he was thin, and his clothes were filthy. You could see they had been torturing him. Later I found out just how bad it was. They nearly killed him with all the torture. Asam had stayed silent, protecting his friends. You could see in his eyes the ordeal he'd been through. It was awful.

But, it was good for Asam, and me too, that I brought Ali. We were Asam's tie to life. I knew this. When you are in prison, these visits are what you have. You count the days between visits, they keep you going. So, I kept bringing Ali. As he got older, he looked forward to going, and unless he was sick I'd always bring him. The visits were only for forty-five minutes, and we had to talk to each other through an iron-mesh screen. You couldn't even hug, all you could do is shake fingers through the screen. But we went every two weeks. Ali used to ask me

why his father was in prison, and I explained it to him. He knows now
that the Israelis put us—his father, me, his uncles—in jail because we
are fighting for our country. He understands this. He's scared of the
Israeli soldiers. When he sees them with their rifles and tear-gas canis-
ters, he comes running home scared. He's also scared of our people, the
shabab [fellows] who cover their faces with head scarves. He's had a hard
time of it, Ali has. He's only six years old. I worry about him a lot. But
what can you do? That is our life.

⁂

While Asam was in jail, I continued going to Bethlehem University to
get my degree. It took me until 1991 to finally graduate because the
university was closed down for two years with the Intifada. We had to
take classes at people's homes. Mostly, we weren't able to study at all.
But I was very busy during these years with political work. There was
a lot to do. I was active in the Fatah student group, I was one of the
organizers in it. We planned demonstrations and strikes, and we kept
things stirred up. No, I didn't throw any more Molotov cocktails during
this time. Only a few stones here and there, that's all. Really, though, my
main work was more as an organizer, that's where I felt I could be most
effective.

I also became involved during this period with the Women's Committee for Social Work, working as an organizer of women in the villages and refugee camps in the Bethlehem area.* This was a new kind
of political work for me. Up to then I'd been involved in political work
as a student, together with men. I had never worked just with women.
But with the Intifada the Palestinian struggle had become a true mass
movement, and there was a need to involve women in a constructive way.

---

* The Women's Committee for Social Work is affiliated with Fatah, and is
one of four women's organizations operating in the territories under the umbrella
of the Palestine Liberation Organization (PLO) and representing different factions
within the PLO.

I'm talking about women from the villages and refugee camps, women who'd never been involved in political or social activism in their lives—women like my mother.

The way we did it is that we'd go to the villages and camps, and with a small group of women we'd get a committee going. At this point, almost every village and every camp has these women's committees. The kind of work we do is largely social and economic, but it also has a political impact. I'll give you an example. In almost all these places there have been no nursery schools or kindergartens for the children. These children have been neglected, they just stay at home with their mothers until they are six years old. So we bring in a lecturer to talk about the need for such facilities, and then we start to organize people to run the nursery or kindergarten. Sometimes we've been very successful, sometimes less so. Or I'll give you another example. We try to get the women active in something that will earn them some money, money they don't have to ask their husbands for. We help them produce things to sell—sewing, embroidery, or prepared foods like jams and pickles. We provide help in marketing these products, and this way the women make some cash. Even though the cash they earn in this way isn't much, it gets the women together and gives them a sense of accomplishment. All this has political results too. These women from the villages and camps who never before would have dared do anything political have wound up joining in demonstrations and strikes, and thus they've become part of the national struggle.

For me, this whole experience of working with women has been very meaningful. I'm now on the national steering committee of our Women's Committee for Social Work, but I still go to the villages sometimes. It's easy for me. Unlike some of my co-workers who are from the city, I'm very familiar with village women. Their families are like mine, the mothers are like my mother. When I go there now, I can see what a big change has taken place these last few years. It's amazing. I'm not saying that our committees are responsible for these changes—no, I don't mean that. I mean, there's been a social process that has taken place here, a lot of it due to the Intifada, and our work is part of all that.

These women in the villages and camps, just like my mother, have begun to free themselves from the domination of their husbands. If you want to know what's happened, you just look at my mother. She's still under my father's control a good deal. But now she goes out on demonstrations, on marches, and she doesn't ask his permission. Look, she's talking to you for the book. Most of the times you come, she doesn't even tell him you're coming. She does it because *she* wants to do it. She would never have been so free before. Before, she wouldn't speak up to him at all, now she does. She begins to understand that her views are worth something, that *she* herself has something to say and contribute to the society, not just to her family.

This is the big change that has come about since the Intifada. In a way the Intifada has contributed more to women than women have contributed to it. Under the cover of a national struggle, you could say, women have been able to leave their traditional places, their incarceration, in their homes. In many cases, when the husbands were jailed, the women have had to go out and work to support the family. When the Israelis closed down the schools in the villages and camps and cities, women organized classes in their houses. When their husbands and sons were put in jail, they went on demonstrations and hunger strikes for prisoners. And they've gotten involved directly in confrontations with soldiers—throwing stones or whatever. When all this first began to happen, the men opposed it. But gradually it became clear to the men that the Intifada is a people's war, and so women's participation has become acceptable. Before, the men looked upon women as weak. Now they've seen that women can stand up to soldiers, can face being wounded or martyred. Women have proved their ability to endure suffering, even more than men can if you ask me. All this has had its effect. Women have become freer now than they've ever been before.

The question we're asking ourselves now—me and other women involved in the national struggle—is where it's all going. We take a look at Algeria and we see what happened there. The Algerian women took a big part in the national struggle to rid the country of the French, and then they slipped back into traditional roles. Now the Muslim fundamentalists there are trying to take over the country. Is this our future? That's what we ask ourselves. And I'll tell you the truth, it worries me. Right now, the PLO has the support of most Palestinians. But if Arafat cannot succeed more in changing the real conditions of people's lives, if the Occupation continues despite all the negotiations, people will swing over to the Muslim fundamentalists, to Hamas. It's already been going on for a while. When people are desperate, they seek refuge in religion. Personally, I can't stand the religious extremists—not Jewish nor Christian nor Muslim. Religion for me is a private matter, and I respect that. I have friends who wear religious dress. Their way of dressing is their business, my way is mine. I fast during Ramadan. That's my business too. But, what would be intolerable to me is living in a state where I'm told I have to dress in a particular way or pray in a particular way. As a woman I couldn't tolerate living in a state run by Muslim fundamentalists. If it comes about, I'll leave, *khalas*. I don't know where I'd go, but I would leave. I haven't fought all these years, I haven't gone to jail, to wind up in a Muslim fundamentalist state. I swear, I'd leave.

⁂

Even though I was doing a lot of political organizing among women and students after the Intifada broke out, somehow I managed to stay out of jail. Some of my brothers got arrested during this period, and Asam was in serving five years, but the Israelis left me alone. Until 1991, I was alright. Then I got put back in jail for a month—this time for something that I wasn't involved in at all.

The reason it happened was this. My sister-in-law, Fatma—she's Hatem's wife—was martyred. That's her wedding picture on the wall. I really liked her. She was very active as a fighter. What she did this time was take a bomb to the Jewish market, Mahane Yehuda, with the intention of planting it, I think, in the toilet there. But the timing device must have misfired and it blew up on her instead. She was killed on the spot. Immediately after that my brother went into hiding, he knew they'd be coming after him. None of us knew where he was. The Israelis put a curfew on the entire camp, and they delivered Fatma's smashed-up body to the graveyard in a plastic bag. We weren't allowed to have a proper funeral for her. The Israelis only let eight family members attend. I wanted very much to be there, so I went. When I saw Fatma's face inside the plastic bag, her face all full of shrapnel holes, I about collapsed. It was awful. And then, as I was standing there looking at her, an Israeli Shabak* guy came up to me and grabbed me and put me under arrest.

This Israeli guy's name was Jad, that's what he called himself—an Arab name. I don't know why they all use Arab names, but they do. He took me to Maskubiya jail. They also took my sister, Sarah, there. Poor thing, she's a nurse, she's not political at all, but they arrested her too. Anyway, this Jad took me back to the same jail I'd been in twice before. As soon as we got there, he brought me to this yard—it's a very well known place—and in the yard there were several Palestinian fellows. They were all handcuffed or chained up, with their hands behind their backs or to a chair, and some of them were moaning and wailing. This Jad grabbed my arm and said, pointing, "Look, this one's been here twenty-five days, and that one ten days, and that one a month. If you don't cooperate, you're going out there too." It was January then, very cold. That night they put me out in the yard too. I was out there four days and nights, my hands chained behind my back, one reaching down behind my neck and the other up to it. After a while it hurts terribly. They didn't let me sleep at all, not a wink. And for three days they gave me nothing to eat. The only time they took off the chain was when they brought me in for interrogation. They questioned me about things which I knew nothing about. They knew I was in jail before and that I was

* Shabak is an acronym for Sherut Bitahon Klali, the Israeli internal security services.

still involved politically, so they thought I might know something. But, I swear, I knew nothing about what they were asking me, not a thing.

After four days they took me out of the yard and put me in a room. Not really a room, a shaft. This shaft was pitch black day and night, and not wide enough to sit in, and it was bitter cold. There's a cooling machine on top that blows cold air down on you. The prisoners call this shaft "the Refrigerator." The police call it "the Closet." In this shaft there's a half-chair made of stone, but the shaft is too narrow for a person to sit down on it. So you are standing almost all the time, or you put one or both your feet up on the stone chair. It's impossible to feel comfortable. They let you out only to interrogate you. The idea is to break you down so you'll talk easily. With me, during these interrogations, they cursed and threatened me constantly. They told me, "You're not going to get out of here alive." They kept threatening to strip me down naked in front of them. They never did strip me, though when I was in prison I heard stories about women who'd been tortured sexually. And I saw men there who'd gone crazy, and I knew of those who were trying to commit suicide.

But when I was in jail this time, in 1991, the torture methods they used were no longer so much physical as psychological. In the beginning of the Occupation—I know this for a fact—they'd take women and beat them like they were wild animals. They'd burn them with cigarettes, pull out their hair, and torture them sexually. I won't tell you they raped these women—though I've heard stories about that—but since I don't know this for sure I'm not saying they did this. They beat women on their sexual parts, this I know for sure. But the Shabak has since switched mostly to more psychological forms of torture. The brutal physical methods gave them a bad name outside. Everyone knew the Israelis were killing people in jail, beating them to death. But besides this, the Shabak realized that the psychological methods are often more effective. Depriving people of sleep, putting them outside in the cold or in "the Refrigerator," playing recordings of people screaming and crying—all this plays on a person's nerves and it destroys a person even more than the brutal physical methods. The body can get used to blows, sometimes. But the psychological methods break a person's mind eventually, and then the Shabak can get out of them what they want.

I want to tell you something. I understand that we are in a national struggle with the Israelis. But what I want to tell you is that the people that do this torturing, these Israeli interrogators, are not doing what they do out of nationalistic reasons. I don't believe it. These Shabak interrogators are doing it because they like it. I don't believe that most Israelis, most people anywhere, could imagine torturing others in these ways. But these interrogators are sadists. They like their work. I've come to know them up close, unfortunately, and I'm convinced of this.

Me, I survived it. I managed to be strong because I knew I had no information to give, nothing to hide. And I survived because of my son, Ali. I kept thinking all the time that I've got to stay strong and get back to him. He's my only child—he was then—and I love him so much, and I was determined not to break emotionally. What made things especially hard for me was that this period when I was in jail was during the Gulf War. January and February 1991. I kept saying to myself, "What will happen if Saddam bombs Israel with chemical weapons?" My poor son was without me or his father either. Asam was in jail then too. My mother was taking care of Ali. That whole month, twenty-five days, I kept thinking about Ali. When I did get sleep, I had nightmares. Like, I would dream that Ali was running on a roof and then suddenly he'd fall off and disappear. I'd wake up in a cold sweat, shaking. But, thinking of him is what kept me going and not breaking.

Another thing that helped me was that I had a wonderful lawyer. I love this woman. Leah Tsemel is her name, she's a Jewish woman. She's the only one who was allowed to visit me. Nobody from my family was allowed to come. Usually, Leah Tsemel doesn't have time to visit prisoners, but because of the Gulf War she had more time. In the beginning, they didn't let her visit either, but she appealed to the Supreme Court and won. She came several times, she passed messages from my mother, and she kept telling me to stay strong and she would get me out.

And she kept her word. At the end of twenty-five days I was freed. They let out my sister, Sarah, with me. She had been tortured too. When we got out, you couldn't have recognized us. We were filthy, we hadn't been allowed to bathe the whole time we were in jail. We were frightening to look at. We took a bus to the camp, and when we got there the Israeli soldiers at first refused to let us enter. There was a curfew on the camp that day. But they let us go home, and when we got there it was a surprise because nobody had been told we were getting out that day.

❧

I had told myself when I was in jail being tortured, that if I survive this, I'm going to quit political work and devote myself to my son and my family. *Khalas,* no more politics. Believe me, that's what I wanted to do. Just before I was jailed, I had bought this house. I had some money from the new job I'd taken, Asam's political group was giving some money while he was in jail, and I borrowed 2,000 dinars from a money lender I know in Bethlehem. I wanted my family to have a place of our own.

When I got out of jail, I continued to fix this place up. Slowly, slowly, I put it in order—I fixed up the two bedrooms, I put in a new kitchen and bath, and I bought some furniture. We moved in a year before Asam got out of jail. Ali and me. Also, Sarah stayed with us before she got married, and one of my brothers too. I'm proud of this place, really I am. But the pact I made with myself to stay away from politics, to just devote myself to my family, well, I wasn't able to keep it. I couldn't. The political situation hasn't changed, the struggle continues, and even though Asam has gotten out of jail, my brother, Hatem, is in now serving a life sentence. And we have friends still in jail too. So, I've continued with politics, the Women's Committee for Social Work especially. What can you do?

But now that Asam's out—it's been a year and a half—we *are* living a normal family life. We have a new baby, as you can see. Leila's her name. I always wanted a daughter. I want to raise her different than I was raised, to be free, free in every way. I'm trying, it's a hard job. Raising children is not easy. Right now, I'm not having another. I use contraception, of course. I couldn't handle another right now. In the future who knows, maybe I'll want one more. But not more than three. For sure, not eleven like my mother! Oh God, no! No way I'd do that. I couldn't manage with more than three, not at all. Even though, I will say, Asam's been a big help to me. He helps with the children and does a lot of the housework too. He's very liberal in this way. Even if his friends drop over while he's busy, say, washing the dishes, he goes right on in front of them. A lot of people around here consider this kind of helping one's wife as unusual, as if the husband is henpecked. Asam doesn't pay attention to it. Although once I gave him a load of wash to hang on the roof—that's where we have the clothesline—and he came running back down immediately with the wash in his hands. He said there were several old women watching him from their verandas, and he just couldn't go on. In front of his friends he's not embarrassed, but in front of these old ladies he was! I tell you, it made me laugh, really it did.

Anyway, these days the one who I'm really dependent on for help, especially with the baby, is my mother. I recently went back to my job after a maternity leave, and my mother takes care of Leila all day. I would have preferred to hire someone, but we couldn't afford it, and my mother insisted that she'd do it. So she takes care of my daughter all day, and my son too after school, if Asam or I aren't back from work. I can't say I agree with everything she does with my daughter. She has some old ways from the village. Like, after Leila was born my mother wanted me to massage her with salty water and wrap her up like a stick for a few months. I refused, and I didn't let her do it either. My mother tends to overprotect Leila and she overfeeds her too. The poor kid is fat as a football from this. But Leila is crazy about her, and my mother is crazy about Leila. And even though I feel guilty about the whole arrangement, it does let me go to work, and that I like—or at least I used to like my job. Lately, I'm beginning to think I've got to get a new job.

⌇

This job I have now, it's something I've been doing for about four years. Make that five years, as of this year. I'm a social worker at a rehabilitation center.* I started there when I was in my last year at Bethlehem University, in 1990. The director of the center is someone I knew at the university. I had pull with him. That's how things work in our society. You need pull. He hired people he knew, his friends, and I was one of them.

When I first started working there I really enjoyed it. I used to look forward to going to work each morning and being with my clients. The fact that I could talk to them and help them meant a lot to me. It still does, but in a way I think I've become burned-out. I feel overwhelmed a lot, and I can't stop thinking about the clients even after I come home. I tell you, I need a break from it.

You see, the majority of the clients we have at the center are Intifada victims. We have some people with handicaps due to birth defects, or illnesses like polio, but most of the clients are Intifada-related cases. We have an inpatient program and an outreach program. I'm working in the inpatient program, and I have about ten cases who I see once or twice a week. They're all young men who've been seriously wounded or tortured in jail or traumatized in some other way. The ones who come to us are the ones who can't cope with the trauma, they've broken down. Often their families have rejected them, their friends too, and they feel isolated and hopeless. Our job is to try to get them back on their feet. Job counseling, psychotherapy—that's what we offer them. And, if I look at it objectively, I'd say we do a pretty good job. We're able to help many of them.

For me the problem is—at least my supervisor thinks so and I agree with her—I overidentify with some of my clients. When I sit there listening to their stories, I find myself crying sometimes. It just gets to me,

* Samira requested that the name of the center not be used, and accordingly we omit it.

I can't help it. For example, I have this client from Gaza, a guy who received a head wound. The wound affected his speech and his memory, and his arm and leg are paralyzed. When he talks to me about his family's rejecting him, I find myself getting very upset. The tears start rolling down my cheeks, and I find it difficult to go on listening to him. I wanted to stop seeing him, but my supervisor encouraged me to stay in there, so I have.

Sometimes, also, I'll have a client who went through what I did. Torture, I mean. With one young man, he went through almost exactly the same—at the same jail and at the same time. Yes, he was there when I was. Usually, I don't tell my clients that I was in jail. I might say that someone in my family was in jail, but I don't talk about myself. I think it wouldn't be professional on my part, it would personalize my relationship to the client too much. But with this fellow, *he* knew I was there then, and he asked me about it. I acknowledged it, but I didn't go into details. Just acknowledging it was hard enough for me, I don't like remembering these things. Still, the fact that I was there built a special bond between us and enabled me to help him. Even now that he's no longer in the center, he still drops by to say hello and chat with me. I feel good about my work with him, sure I do.

But my work doesn't always go so well, there's lots of tough cases that I don't feel I helped much. One guy particularly is getting to me these days. In fact, this case has brought me to the point where I'm thinking I've got to get a new job, like I shouldn't go on there. What happened with this client is that just a couple of weeks ago he tried to kill me. Others stopped him and took the knife out of his hand, but if they hadn't, God knows what he would have done. He's not a client at the center now. He *was,* but the administration decided to send him home. He was causing too many problems, he almost burned down the center. I thought we dismissed him too quickly, too traumatically. He's a person who already was suffering from too much trauma and rejection. He'd been abused as a child, and in jail he was tortured by his fellow prisoners. They accused him of being a collaborator—which I don't think he was—and they tortured him. Now his family rejects him completely. He came to us, and what happened? We rejected him too. So he's gone crazy. For months after we sent him home he'd call me regularly, threatening me. He came twice and threatened me in person. I was scared, but what could I do? We have no guards or police protection. What are we going to do, call in the Israeli army? They wouldn't care anyway. So the situation just went on until a couple of weeks ago he came to the center with the knife and tried to get me. The janitor stopped him and very nearly got stabbed himself. I tell you, it was a horrible situation. I'm still shaken up from it. I don't feel safe going to work any more. I'm thinking seriously of quitting. I might.

You know, after this incident I stayed at home for a few days. My supervisor told me not to come in, to relax. I stayed at home with the children, I enjoyed it. I was able to relax some. During this time that I was at home, my mother told me I shouldn't go back to this job. I should get another job if I wanted to work, she said. She told me she had had a dream about my going back to the center, a bad dream. I gathered that in this dream, this nightmare, something had happened to me, maybe I got killed. I asked her, but she wouldn't tell me. She has this belief that if you reveal a dream, then it comes true. To this moment, she has refused to tell me. She just keeps saying that I've got to leave the center and find something else. Believe me, I'd like to. Maybe working with teenage girls, I think I'd like that. When I was a teenager I could have benefited from having someone to talk to. I think I could be good in this work. But right now, I'm stuck where I am. I can't afford to stop working. So, each morning I go off to the center scared. And my mother, she keeps telling me that I've got to stop soon. The sooner the better, she says.

Umm Abdullah

Her experience in the 1948 war and subsequent status as a refugee left their indelible mark on Umm Abdullah's political consciousness. Yet her shift into political actor is more recent. Women who had never acted on their political beliefs, among them many uneducated housewives like Umm Abdullah, were pulled into the wake of the Intifada. As the mothers watched their children enter the battle and suffer the consequences, they felt compelled to join them in some way. But for Umm Abdullah, Samira's imprisonment—which came in 1982, five years before the Intifada—was the spark that ignited her willingness, her determination, to confront Israeli soldiers.

And Samira was only the first of her children to be imprisoned. Four others have since been jailed, most during the Intifada. Her son Hatem is currently serving a life sentence in a maximum security prison. Hatem's house, located opposite Umm Abdullah's house, has been boarded up with the door welded shut by the Israeli army. Each morning as she steps outside her own house, she faces this reminder of her political fate, and as she puts it, "Each day my blood boils anew and my heart cries out for him."

In this section of Umm Abdullah's story, she recollects and reflects on some of her experiences, especially political experiences, in the last few years. She also recalls her "return" to Al-Qabu for several visits in the 1980s, and the impact this had on her.

2

After Samira went to jail and they destroyed our house, we lived in the tent for ten months. It was a big tent, I made it as comfortable as possible, but it was not an easy time for us. The winter was cold. At night all of us slept together in a row on the ground. We tried to keep warm. But there were some hard nights, rain coming through, everyone getting wet. What could we do? That was our fate. We endured it.

The Israeli soldiers kept coming by to check on us. They couldn't believe we were managing. Sometimes they started talking to us, nasty and rude. I remember once this Jewish officer started up. Haim was his name, I think. He asked my husband how many children he had. "Eleven," my husband answered. "All these are from *one* woman?" he asked. My husband nodded, and I jumped in, "I want to bring more!" This Haim gave me a nasty look. I repeated, "I swear, I'm going to bring more!" This time the Jew answered, "Oh yes? Go ahead, bring more." I looked him square in the eyes and started shouting, "I will! Sure I will!" And I began to curse him. My husband told me to shut up, but I went on cursing them and their fathers too. I swear, I did. It made me feel good to curse them. Sure it did.

Anyway, that's the way it was for ten months. Then we got permission to rebuild. Not from the Israelis, they didn't give us permission. We got our permission from the deputy mayor of Bethlehem. He told us to go ahead. He didn't write anything down but he said he'd take responsibility for it. Later, the Israelis caused us lots of problems because we didn't get permission from them. Many times they threatened to tear down the house again. But lately they're not bothering us, thanks to God. The money to rebuild came from my sons in Saudi Arabia. They could afford it. People came from all over to help us rebuild. You should have seen them working here. I cooked for all of them. In four days, four walls went up—room after room. In less than a month we were in our house. By the time Samira got out of jail in 1985, we had already been living in this new place two years.

Do I remember her coming home in 1985? Yes. Sure I do. We didn't know exactly when she was getting out, it wasn't clear. Then suddenly one day there she was! Her husband, Asam—he wasn't her husband then—brought her back along with a friend of his. We were happy, very happy. We began singing at the top of our voices and soon people came from here in the camp, from Beit Jala, from Camp Deheisha. It was a great joy for us. To have her back again, oh yes, a joy!

After she came home she returned to the university. She began her studies again to be a social worker. Asam was studying at Bethlehem University too. Soon after, they decided to get married. Did I approve? Yes, I was very glad. I knew they loved each other. Samira hadn't told me but I knew. People had told me that they went around together. And once when I was in Bethlehem, from a distance I saw them together. I pretended not to notice them though, and I never told my husband. To this day he doesn't know they were going around together before the wedding. But yes, I'm glad they got married. Asam is a good husband to her. Their relationship is wonderful, the very best. They're both educated, they're both nationalist and very involved in politics. She's a heroine and he's a hero. Asam's been back in jail since they got married. He was in for five more years. And Samira's been back in too, after Hatem's wife was martyred. What can I tell you? They have a good marriage, they support each other to the end. And you know Samira yourselves. Really, there's nobody like her. Look, a mother loves her daughter and the daughter loves her mother. When I'm sick, Samira's the one who takes me to the doctor, she forces me to go. When my husband and I went on the *hajj* a year and a half ago, she was the one who worried about us, and how we'd manage in the heat. Samira—she's got a warm heart. I'm proud of her and what she's done. I haven't been able to do what she's done, but if I could have I would. That's right. I would have lived my life like she has. Oh yes, I'm very proud of her.

I'm proud of all my children. The one's who've gone to jail for their beliefs, for their nationalism—I'm very proud of them. You see, just about everyone here in the camp has been involved since the Intifada began. If my children weren't involved, they'd be different from the others. That's the way it is. Because our children—Samira, Hatem, Ismail, Mahmud, and Sarah—have been in jail, our family is known as very active and nationalist. My husband is proud of them too. "What they've done is honorable," he says. You know, my husband is respected here in the camp because of our children. People treat him like a *qadi* [judge], they come to him for help in solving their problems. He's now like his father was back in Al-Qabu, a *mukhtar.*

❧

Since the Intifada began we've had one or another of our children in jail all the time. Mahmud was in for nine months. Ismail was in for four years. Hatem is serving a life term now. Sarah was in about a month with Samira. And Samira's been in three times, more than three years altogether.

The Israeli soldiers know our family by now, they like to arrest us. They know we're nationalist so they come after us. Sarah got arrested for nothing. She and Samira were taken in for interrogation during the time the Israelis were looking for Hatem. They both got tortured for doing nothing. And the time Mahmud got arrested and put in jail for nine months, he hadn't been doing anything at all.

That time with Mahmud, I tried to stop the Israeli soldiers from taking him. This happened about four years ago. Some boys from the camp were stoning settlers' cars up by the main road. The soldiers came into the camp chasing after them. They grabbed Mahmud. He hadn't been part of it, but no matter, they grabbed him anyway. I ran after them. I didn't have my shoes on, I was barefoot. People from here started shouting at me, "Go back, they'll shoot you!" But I tell you, I wasn't afraid. I just kept chasing them up to the main road where they had their outpost. They were cursing me and I was cursing them. There was a Jewish officer there who called himself Karim, and he said to me, "Get out of here!" I answered him, "*You* get out of here!" He didn't hit me, but I hit him. I pushed him. My blood was boiling, I didn't care what happened to me. I just didn't want them taking Mahmud. But I couldn't stop them, there were too many of them. They took him, they put him in jail, and he didn't get out for nine months.

That happened just a little before Hatem got arrested again—and got sentenced for life imprisonment. Ninety-nine years they gave him, it's the same thing. This is what has broken my heart. Mine and Abu Abdullah's too. We're both broken from this. I see Hatem's picture on the wall at Samira's house, his picture with his wife. It destroys me. I cry and cry and cry. Oh God, why? Tell me, why?

Hatem—he's broken now. They finally broke him. This last time he's been in jail the Israelis finished him. Hatem's twenty-eight now and he's been in and out of jail since he was sixteen. Six times. Let's see, the first time—three years. The second time—fourteen days. The third time—thirteen days. The fourth time—six months. The fifth time—two years. Now—life imprisonment. And this last time he didn't really do anything. He wanted to do something, yes. He was planning to attack a bus of settlers, but they caught him before he did it. What they put him in jail for is what Fatma, his wife, did. They wanted to finish them both off.

Fatma—she was martyred. Samira must have told you about that, no? She and Hatem had been married for only seventy days, that's all. They didn't even have time to enjoy their marriage. That picture on Samira's wall is of them on their wedding day. She was beautiful, a beautiful girl. And a fighter! Fatma was a real fighter. Earlier that year she had been involved in an action where she killed one and wounded nine. This was before they were married. Then she got involved in this thing that killed her. She was going to place a bomb in the Jewish *suq* [outdoor market] and it blew up on her. She was martyred.

As soon as that happened the Israelis came looking for Hatem. The Shabak came here and turned our house upside down and broke all sorts of things. They came several times, each time with fifteen or twenty men. They threatened to destroy our house. My husband said to them, turning his back on them, "Go ahead, do what you want!" I tell you, we weren't afraid. We were only afraid they'd catch Hatem and kill him. He had gone into hiding, we didn't know where he was. None of us did.

But what they did, the Shabak, is they hauled off Samira and Sarah for interrogation. They put them into separate cells and they tortured them, trying to get information. I kept thinking, "This time they'll kill Samira, and Sarah too." It was during the Gulf War. I was scared the whole time, scared also of the Scuds and the chemical gas that Saddam said he was going to use. I was taking care of Samira's son. Her husband was in jail then too. I was scared that we were all going to get killed this time. By Saddam, by the Israelis, by somebody.

After a month they let Samira and Sarah go. They knew nothing, so they let them out. And after forty days they caught up with Hatem. Collaborators must have tipped them off. How else could they have found him? They put him in jail and they broke him. They showed him pictures of Fatma's blown-up body and he fell apart. He began to say all kinds of things about himself. They got him to say whatever they wanted. And with that, they sentenced him to ninety-nine years. We visit him now in prison, Abu Abdullah and me. We're allowed to go there every fifteen days for a short visit, and we go every time. We never miss. Someone from the family always goes. As long as I'm alive, I'll go to him. Oh yes, I will. Our only chance that Hatem will get out is if there's peace and the new Palestinian government releases him. But who knows? Only God knows.

The Israeli army wanted to destroy our house again after they put Hatem in jail. But this time we got a good lawyer. A Jewish woman named Leah Tsemel. She's a very good person. She helped Samira and Sarah get out of jail. I wasn't able to visit them—the Israelis didn't let us—but Leah Tsemel did visit them, and she passed messages back and forth between us. Then she helped us save our house, this Leah Tsemel. She convinced the judge that Hatem was living in his own place, not ours, and that the army shouldn't be allowed to destroy our house again.

So instead the army boarded up his house and sealed the door shut. Hatem's house stands right across from our house. As I go out of my door each day I see it. Each day my blood boils anew and my heart cries out for him.

2

The Intifada has made big changes for women. It's gotten us moving. It's changed our lives. When we see soldiers beating our sons, we go wild inside. We have to do something to defend our sons. We do what we have to do without thinking, without fear. A woman who acts like this is respected by other women and they say she's a heroine. Not only the women say this. The men say it too. They say, "You women are stronger than we are. Courageous, real heroines, you are." That's right, the men sometimes talk about us this way now.

I remember one time these Israeli soldiers came into the camp chasing after some boys. These soldiers were cursing, cursing our religion. I came out and started yelling at them, "What are you doing to these children? Do they have stones and knives? They're just playing." The soldiers took these boys who they had caught and started beating them. They were beating them with batons, beating them so hard that they broke some of the batons on them. I swear, I jumped in to defend the boys. Even though my own sons weren't part of it, I couldn't watch them beating the boys. Some other women came to join me. A soldier grabbed me and pushed me against a wall. Another soldier said, "Shoot her!" One of them put his rifle in my face, but he didn't shoot. "I'm not afraid of you!" I shouted at him. "The day's coming when you people are going to get yours!" He cursed me and I cursed him right back. And you know, we stopped them from taking the boys. They left them there. But these boys were beaten so badly an ambulance had to come for some of them. Later, when I went into the house, my husband said to me, "Tell me, weren't you afraid?" He had stayed inside because he's a man, and if he had gone out they would have beaten him and arrested him. But, I swear, I wasn't afraid.

The Israeli soldiers—who are they? They're cowards, that's all. They've got frightening weapons, nothing more. Without their weapons they're nothing. I've stood up to them many times. When the *shabab* throw stones at settlers' cars up at the main road and then come running into the camp, I sometimes have gotten in the middle and directed them where to run. "Don't go that way, they're coming from that direction!" I tell them. "Here, go this way!" Sometimes the *shabab* have hidden in my house. I go out and see when it's safe for them to leave. I take their clothes and give them new ones so they won't be recognized. I tell them, "Calm down, relax, so it won't look like you've been running." These are things I can do. It's my way of helping, my way of joining the national struggle. It's all I can do. I don't have the time to join women's committees here in the camp. Samira does that kind of work, political work. I admire her. But I have to take care of my husband and my children, and sometimes Samira's children too. Sometimes I go on demonstrations or sit-ins at the Red Cross office or at the prison where Hatem is. I've gone, I've waved banners with Arafat's picture on it. But getting involved every week or month with a group of women, that's for Samira—not for me.

Together though, women of Samira's generation and women of my generation—we've done something. Sure we have! We're *samdin* [steadfast people]. We've learned to be steadfast, no matter what the Jews do to us. That's a new word, you know. *Sumud* [steadfastness]. We got that word from the PLO. There's even songs now about *samdin*, but don't ask me to sing them. Some people have named their children Samed. What it means is that the way we will win is by staying strong. *Lazem nusmud* [we have to be steadfast]. No matter how many martyrs we have, no matter how many are jailed, we have to stay strong. *Lazem nusmud!*

And we are strong! We Palestinians are a strong people. The strongest! There's nobody like us in the whole world. Wherever you go in the world there's Palestinians. In the Arab world, in Europe, in America—we are all over. And wherever a Palestinian is, he stays Palestinian. They can't manage without us in Jordan and Kuwait. Jordan was a desert before Palestinians came there. I've been in Amman. Who built all those houses and factories there? *We* did. In Kuwait, after the Gulf War, they threw Palestinians out. Now they're asking us to come back. They can't manage without us. And do you think Israel can manage without Palestinian workers? They can't. Our workers are stronger, more steady, and work for less. The Israeli government may not want us, but the Jewish bosses need us.

Oh yes, we Palestinians are a strong people. Sure we are. We are going to win in our struggle with the Jews. *Lazem nusmud,* that's all. There were many foreigners who came here and they all left. The Turks were here for hundreds of years before they left. The English came, and soon they left. And now the Jews are ruling Palestine, but they'll leave too. In the end, Palestine will be for the Palestinians. How long it'll take, I don't know. I'm not an expert on politics. But sooner or later, God willing, it will happen.

If you ask me who I'm for in politics, I'll tell you, it's like this. I'm for the PLO and Arafat. I want them to be in charge of the Palestinian state. That's what I prefer. But do you know who the Jews are most afraid of? Hamas, that's who. The Jews are more afraid of the religious Muslims than anyone else. Hamas says they want the Palestinian refugees from 1948 to be able to return to their homes. They don't want a compromise. *That* scares the Jews. Me, I want the refugees to be able to go back to their homes too. Of course, I do. And I'm religious, a believing Muslim. I pray, I fast on Ramadan, I've been on the *hajj*. That's the way I've educated my children. But I don't support the Muslim political party. I prefer the PLO, like Samira does. I think they have the best chance of getting a Palestinian state for us. They have the best chance of removing the Jews from around here. That's what I want. The sooner the better. We're fed up with the Jews, and I know they're fed up with us too. I've heard the Jews talking, here and on television. They don't want to be around us either. So let them go their way and we'll go ours. That's best. And then we'll see where it goes from there.

I don't know if in my lifetime I'll ever return to live in Al-Qabu. If you talk to Samira, she thinks there's no way we'll ever return. She says it's all over, *khalas*. But my sons, some of them, think differently. They think it'll take a hard fight, a real war, and then we'll all go back. Someday we'll live in Al-Qabu again. In twenty years or so, they say. Me, I don't know when it'll happen, but I believe it will. Maybe I won't live there, but God willing, my grandchildren will. That's what I think.

&

When they were small I used to talk a lot to my children about Al-Qabu. I'd tell them how our life was there—healthier, cleaner, better. I wanted them to know where they come from, where their village is. My sons, especially the younger boys, were very interested. Samira? Not so much. I don't know why, she was always too busy or had other things on her mind. She didn't seem so interested.

You know, here in the camp we still have sheep from Al-Qabu. When we left in 1948 a man brought some sheep with him. And today, more than forty years later, he has the offspring of these sheep. He holds onto them, he won't get rid of them. Some old men here in the camp say that if we lose those sheep we're all going to become ill. The man has to hold onto them, they say. And he does. He doesn't trade them away no matter what.

I've been back to visit Al-Qabu four times. After the 1967 war, when the Israelis conquered the West Bank, there was no longer a border separating us from Al-Qabu. You could go back and look around if you wanted to. Some people immediately went, but it wasn't safe. You could get shot by Israeli soldiers, by settlers. Really, some people who went back to see the village then were shot while they were there. Some were killed. It was dangerous, I tell you. It's the same today. Since the Intifada started, it's not safe to go there. The Israeli soldiers aren't the problem now, it's the settlers. The Jews have built settlements in that area, and those settlers are dangerous people. You could get shot easily these days. So we no longer take trips there.

But, back before the Intifada, our family went. The first time was twelve years ago. That was the hardest time. It had been more than thirty years since I had been in Al-Qabu. When I got there, I could see that the place was destroyed. The houses were bombed. I went up to where our house had been. I looked inside. I could see the spot where I used to sleep, and the spot where my mother gave birth to one of my brothers. I could see the spot where my grandmother used to sit, and the spot where the *tabun* was. The *tabun* was still there. I remembered my mother baking and cooking in it. I called my brother over, and I said to him, "Take a look over here, the *zatar* you planted is still here!" And then we saw at the side of the house the carob tree he had planted. We started crying, crying hard. "Oh God," I said, "Why did you force us to flee our village? We and all the others too from all the other villages—why?"

I went over to the old well we had in Al-Qabu. Some of my sons came with me. An underground spring flows into this well, and you can walk down steps into it. Before we came back to Al-Qabu I had made a vow that if I ever got back there, I would bathe myself in this well. And I did. I had my sons sit around as guards. You see, Israeli soldiers were nearby and you could see they'd been bathing in the well too. So my sons guarded me and I went down and washed myself again in Al-Qabu's waters. I swear, there're no waters like them in the world—sweet, sweet like ice cream.

The rest of my family, my husband, were resting under some trees down by the stream. Some of the children were playing. We had brought some food for a picnic—chicken, stuffed squash. But what kind of picnic could you have then? Right opposite us were Jewish soldiers and Jewish tourists having a picnic too. They were cooking out on fires by our old stream. The area by the stream had been turned into a picnic ground by the Jews. They've planted trees all over the place. I couldn't sit still, I had to walk around. My husband said to the children, "Your mother is lost in memories."

I wandered off by myself. I went out to where our land was. I went to the "floor plot." That's what we used to call it. Each of our plots had its own special name. I could see that some of our trees are still standing. The almond trees, the grapevines, the fig trees were still there. My fig tree, my *qarawi,* was still there too, it was still bearing fruit. I swear it was. But other trees, the apricot and plum trees, were finished. Nobody had cared for them and they had died. The olive trees were gone too. Uprooted. The Jews had uprooted them, and other trees were planted in their place.

I kept walking and looking and talking to myself. I had a headache, my head was killing me from all this. I swear, anyone who goes back to his village is going to get a headache—for sure. I've heard of people who died when they went back to their villages. They died of sadness, they got heart attacks and died on the spot. Me, I just kept thinking and asking myself, "Why? Why?" If we had nothing to eat but the soil, we still should have stayed in Al-Qabu. I tell you, we who left our villages can never forgive ourselves for leaving.

After that first time in Al-Qabu, we went back three more times. Not all of us went each time. Sometimes we'd go with the neighbors and we'd visit their villages too. Ras Abu Ammar, Dir al-Hawa, nearby villages that had been lost too. Once or twice we brought along food to cook on the fire. We'd go out to our old vineyard, and we'd have our picnic there alone, away from the others.

Each time we went to Al-Qabu I'd come back with things from there. I'd bring back water from our well so that those who didn't go with us could drink. I'd bring back soil. Once my brother who lives in Jordan asked me to get him some, and I did. I'd also bring back whatever was growing. Cactus fruit, almonds, figs. One time I brought back a couple of branches from my fig tree. I planted these branches next to our house in the camp and they took real well. But a neighbor's goat got to them and finished them off.

Each time I went back to Al-Qabu I got a headache. But still it was good to go. I wanted my children to see it. I wanted them to know it's still there, even if it's in ruins now. God willing, the day will come when we can leave this camp and return there. We have land there. My husband's father was the *mukhtar,* half the land in Al-Qabu belongs to his family. Yes, God willing, we'll sell our house here and build a new one there. That's what I would like. God willing, one day it will happen.

Umm Khaled and Leila

(VILLAGE OF ABU GHOSH)

Umm Khaled

Twelve kilometers west of Jerusalem, nestled in the Judaean hills, is the village of Abu Ghosh. It is an uncrowded, attractive place, with its five thousand inhabitants, almost all of whom are Muslims, living in spacious one- and two-story stone houses that sprawl along the valley and up the hillside. At the base of the village are freshwater springs and, in a distinctive architectural arrangement, both the village mosque and a nearby twelfth-century church are built over the springs. This church, and the monks who tend to it (and live in an adjacent monastery), have played a crucial role in the recent history of Abu Ghosh. In no small measure they have been responsible for another of the village's distinctive features: it was the only Arab village to survive when Israel conquered the area in the 1948 war.

Umm Khaled (Amina), at seventy-two years old, is one who lived through this recent turbulent period in the history of Abu Ghosh. It is here, as a citizen of Israel, that she raised her family of sixteen children. Today all of these children are grown, and most continue to live in the village. Umm Khaled, now a widow, lives with the youngest of her daughters in a hilltop house. A thin woman in somewhat frail health, she spends most of her time at home these days, visited frequently by her children and "hundred or so" grandchildren.

Living not too far from Umm Khaled is one of the writers of this study, Rafiqa Othman. Though Rafiqa had never visited Umm Khaled before we began this book, each one knew of the other, and so it was relatively easy to arrange for an initial meeting in December 1994. As it turned out, Umm Khaled was most receptive to being interviewed for a book on Palestinian women—a receptivity that would have disappeared had Rafiqa not gone alone. (Indeed, when it was suggested that her coauthor pay a courtesy call at the completion of the interviews, Umm Khaled stated that she would not be comfortable with "a man from the outside" in her home, now that her husband was no longer there.)

With Rafiqa, Umm Khaled was both forthcoming and hospitable, plying her visitor with stories and food in equal measure. Seated in her flower-filled salon, with a photograph of Abu Khaled on the wall across from her, she carried on tirelessly despite her asthma and raspy throat. Occasionally her youngest daughter, Nafuz, would come by to listen to her mother's reminiscences. But most often the interviews were conducted when Umm Khaled was alone.

As with the other older women in this study, Umm Khaled's narrative style was at times discursive and repetitious. We keep some of this quality, but in the interest of readability we pare various digressions. In the section below, then, are some of Umm Khaled's recollections of her childhood spent in Jerusalem in the 1920s, her return to Abu Ghosh to get married in the mid-1930s, and her family's struggle to survive in the village during the 1948 war.

2

Look all around us, we're the only Arab village that survived in 1948. All the other Arab villages in this area are gone. Al-Qastal, Suba, Qaluniya—gone, destroyed. We alone survived. Do you think this was an accident? It wasn't. We survived because our village has always had a special fate. Abu Ghosh is a place that has had God's blessing. It goes way back, from the time this village began, as far back as anyone can remember.

I can't say I know all this history. Others know it better. What I know, I heard from my grandmother and mother and my aunts and mother-in-law. They told me how Abu Ghosh came to be. It started far back, they say, before the time of the Turks. One day a holy man was traveling through this area. He was tired, so he stopped. He tied up his donkey and he lay down. He had some bread and grapes with him, and he placed them at his side. Just before dozing off he prayed to God. He prayed that this wonderful place would some day be a wealthy village inhabited by many people. The holy man slept and slept—for forty years he slept. When he woke he found the same bread and grapes and donkey by his side, and all around him was a wealthy village with its vineyards. The name of this village was Qaryat al-Enab [village of the grapes].

This is what our village was called for many years, maybe hundreds of years. Some people here, you know, still prefer this name and call our village Qaryat al-Enab. But to most of us, it's Abu Ghosh, the village of Abu Ghosh. That's the name it got back in the time of the Turks. The way the name came about was this. A powerful *sheikh* from far away, a place called the Caucasus, came here and became the ruler. He had a loud voice, a booming voice, and when he talked in the religious courts there was this loud echo. That's why they called him Abu Ghosh, because of his voice.* He used to dress in elegant clothes—silk robes and a turban—and he walked with a fine, decorated cane. He was an important man. In his time he was the head of Abu Ghosh and he controlled all the villages from Jerusalem to the sea. He also had enemies, people from other villages who didn't want him to be so powerful. One day, it happened that the men from another village came with their

---

* The Arabic *ghosh*—from the letters *ghein, waw, shin*—is the root of a verb that means "to dispute, to argue loudly."

swords to make war on Abu Ghosh. There was a great battle, many men fell, but *sheikh* Abu Ghosh managed to survive. And so did his three sons. The way the sons survived is that Abu Ghosh's wife sent two away, one to Egypt and one to Syria. And the third she hid here in the village with a holy man. This third son's name was Issa and he went on living with the holy man.

When Issa came of age, they had to find him the right wife, a good woman. Fate brought him Wafa. Wafa was the daughter of a special woman, a woman blessed by God. Years before, when Wafa was a girl, her mother had been praying on *leilat al-qadr.*[*] While she was reciting the Koran, suddenly the sky opened up to her. So, she requested that God grant her daughter the best of the best in life—honor and wealth and sons who would be good, strong, and generous men. And her request was granted. I tell you, ever since I heard this story, I've been praying that on *leilat al-qadr* the sky will open up to me too, so I can request that me and my family will all enter the Garden of Eden when our time comes. But so far, it hasn't opened. Anyway, for Wafa's mother it did open, and Wafa herself was blessed. She married Issa, the good, religious son of Abu Ghosh. They had four sons—one called Othman, another called Ibrahim, another Abd al-Rahman, and another Jaber. Each of these sons had their own offspring, and so on. And today the village of Abu Ghosh has four clans, each named for one of the four sons of Issa and Wafa. We are a good village with generous people, as you know. And we survived, while all other villages around us were destroyed. Only we survived the 1948 war. Why? Because of Wafa's mother, who had the sky open to her on *leilat al-qadr,* and because God granted her wish. That's what I believe.

---

[*] *Leilat al-qadr,* or Night of Power, falls on the twenty-seventh night of the holy month of Ramadan; on this night Muhammad is said to have received a divine revelation—the first in a chain of revelations that were later transcribed as the Koran.

2

I was born here in Abu Ghosh, the third one of ten children, and my father always told me that my birth was special. Right after I was born, he got the job with the English as a policeman, and he always believed I was the one who brought him this luck. That's what he said. So, because he got this job I didn't grow up here in Abu Ghosh. I only moved back when I got married at fourteen years old. Most of my childhood I spent in Jerusalem, where we moved after my father became a policeman. In my childhood, I wasn't a *fellaha*. I was a daughter of the city, which is something much different.

In Jerusalem we had a very good style of living. I really enjoyed it there. My father got a big salary, five pounds a month. With that you could eat meat every day, wear nice clothes, go to the Turkish bath— really, we lived well. We lived inside the Old City walls, in Harat al-Sadiya [a neighborhood of the Old City]. We rented a house there, a fine place. My father would travel around with the police, and my mother and the children would be at home. My older brothers, Muhammad and Amir, went to school. The best of the best. My father spared no expense to educate them. Muhammad learned to read and write in Arabic and English, he was brilliant. And Amir too, he was clever in Arabic calligraphy. For my brothers, my father was willing to spend on education. For me and my sisters, no. I went a year to a school near al-Aqsa Mosque. I learned to read a little, but I don't remember now. Today I can read two words, "head" and "heads," that's all. My father took me out of school after the first grade. He bought me a sewing machine. How did I feel about that? Well, it wasn't my fate to learn. Back then they didn't encourage girls to learn, not like today. My father said it was better for me to learn to sew, so that's what I did. It was fine with me. I didn't know any other girls at the school, so it was good to be home with my younger sisters and brothers.

Since I was the oldest daughter, I was given a lot of responsibilities. My father really trusted me. From the time I was about eight my father would give me part of his salary each month to use for shopping in the *suq*. A grocery owner told my father once, "This daughter of yours is worth ten sons!" I'd do the buying for our family. My mother would tell me what to get and I'd go from place to place to get it. Back then, with hardly any money you could fill up a couple of baskets with vegetables. And meat—for one agora you'd get four kilos! I'm telling you, we ate like kings. My mother would prepare wonderful dishes. If they needed to be baked in an oven—meat dishes or cakes—I'd bring the pan with the food to the baker's, right near our house. He'd bake it in his wood-burning oven. Or sometimes, when my mother was too tired to cook, we'd bring in food from the restaurant near us. We'd bring in hummus, kabab, fried eggplants, salads. Also *tisikya,* that was my favorite. It's small pieces of bread soaked in hummus, with spices and pine nuts. Oh, that was delicious! I'm telling you, we ate well back then.

But we worked too, sure we did. We didn't have water in the houses. We'd have to go down to the stream outside the Old City walls and fetch it. That's drinking water, I'm talking about. Water for washing clothes, we'd get from a well near the house. My mother used to have a woman come in to help her with the wash, and of course I and my sisters helped too. I was given the most responsibility, though, since I was the oldest. I remember this one time, my father came home with his uniform dirty and he said that the next day they were having an inspection. "Something has to be done quickly," he said, and turned to me. "Don't worry, I'll take care of it, father," I told him. I took the pants, cleaned them *really* well, but since I didn't have an iron I folded them at the seams and put them under my mattress that night to press them. I cleaned his jacket, polished the buttons till they shone, and the boots too. The next day when he came home, he said that the commander had complimented him on how he looked. My father said to me, "My daughter, you have whitened my face!" I felt very good about this, I knew my father was proud of me. I think I was about ten years old at the time.

Once a month, when my father got his salary, we'd go to the Turkish bath. My father went by himself, and my older brothers went together.

It was open to the men in the afternoons and evenings, and the women in the mornings. I'd go with my mother and all the children. It was an enormous place called Hamam al-Ein. It wasn't far from our house. My mother would take soap and towels and a fresh change of clothes for each of us. She put us under the spout where heated water came out, and she'd scrub and scrub and scrub, till our skin was peeling. Our faces would be all red when she finished with us. We'd then go to this corner in the bathhouse where you could cool down by drinking cold sodas and eating oranges. Sometimes we'd stay for hours. You could stay as long as you wanted, nobody would bother you. Brides would sometimes be there with their families, just before the wedding. It was a fine thing to do, going to the Hamam. I looked forward to it. It was like a family outing.

Besides this, we'd also go out on weekends, on Sundays especially. That was my father's day off. My mother would prepare a picnic basket and we'd go to the stream in Silwan, or over to the grounds near al-Aqsa Mosque. My sisters and I would jump rope or play five stones. We had a good time in those days, I remember them well. Also, sometimes, during the Little and Big Feasts,* we'd go back to Abu Ghosh. We'd take a bus from Jerusalem and go there for a few days. We'd stay there at the house of my aunt, my father's sister. Yes, my aunt Khadija, who became my mother-in-law when I married her son. Her husband was dead, she was raising the three children by herself, so we stayed with them. My father was close to her, he was helping to support them, and their house was big enough for all of us.

I liked visiting Abu Ghosh on these trips, it was a big change from the city. Clean air to breathe, not stuffy like in Jerusalem. And you could sit under a fig tree all day, resting and doing nothing. No, it wasn't in my mind then that I would be coming back to live in the village. My cousin—oh no, I had no idea that someday he'd be my husband. I swear,

---

* Umm Khaled is referring here to *id al-fitr* [feast of the fast-breaking after Ramadan], and *id al-adha* [feast of the sacrifice that occurs annually during the *hajj* period].

no. I never even talked to him then, not one word. *Eib!* He was eight years older than me, I was only a girl and he was almost grown up. He went off early each morning to his job at the monastery, he worked on the land there. I had nothing to do with him. I stayed with my sisters and his sisters when we were there on those trips. Later, when my father decided that I would marry my cousin, I was surprised. I didn't expect that at all.

ﻉ

The way it came about that I married him was this. My husband—I didn't know this then, I found it out later—wanted to marry another girl, a stranger.* His mother didn't want her, she wanted a different stranger. He refused. There was a disagreement between them. My uncle, my father's older brother, got into it. My uncle was a strong man in our family, everyone listened to his voice. He told my aunt and my husband that he should marry me. "Take Amina and forget about the strangers," he said. "Take our brother's daughter. She's the one for you." My uncle's word carried great weight. He decided it.

One day I was told that my aunt and my cousin were coming to visit us in Jerusalem in order to request me. When I heard this, I ran outside the house. I ran over to an uncle's house. I didn't want anything to do with this request business. Marriage, what's that? I didn't want any part of it. I was only thirteen years old at the time. I had never sat before with guests when they visited. If people came to the house, it wasn't permitted for girls to sit with grown-ups. A single girl wouldn't sit with married women. She'd serve coffee and then leave. I didn't want to be there when my cousin came, oh no! I didn't want to live outside our house. I was used to my family, I wanted to stay with them. But my

---

* Umm Mahmud used the word *ghariba* [stranger], by which she means here that the girl was from outside their clan, which commonly includes all descendants of a great-great-grandfather.

uncle's wife convinced me that I should go back to the house. So I did, and that was it. I was told that I was going to be married to my cousin.

The wedding didn't happen right away, though. This is because a terrible thing happened in our family. My two older brothers died around then, one right after the other. Nobody could even think of weddings anymore. Muhammad was eighteen and he had just started his job as a policeman, like my father. He caught typhoid fever, went to the hospital, and was dead eighteen days later. Then my father got Amir into the police and right after that he died too. Amir was handling his *baruda* and it misfired. He was shot straight through the chest. My family, my father and mother, all of us—we didn't know what to do with ourselves, we were in shock. Not just us. The whole clan in Abu Ghosh, everyone. We were all in mourning. Nobody got married then, there was no taste for it. It went on like this for a year and a half, there were no marriages in Abu Ghosh, not in our clan and not in the others either. The other clans respected our family's grief. It wasn't like today, where after forty days, the mourning period is over, you're free to do what you want. Back then death had a real meaning. People mourned for a long time. So a lot of girls in the village who were engaged during that time had to put off their weddings for a year or so. Me too, of course. Then finally my father said that we had to go through with my wedding. Even though there was still no taste in our family for a wedding, my father said, "We must start, so the others will be free to follow." So that's what we did. We let it be known that we were going to have a wedding, and then others felt free to have theirs too.

But my wedding wasn't a real wedding. Other girls in the village had usual weddings then. They wore white bridal dresses, they went on a *zaffa,* there was music and dancing. I had none of this. There was no wedding party, and instead of a white wedding dress it was decided that I wear a black one. My husband was kind. He agreed that the *mahr* I got was twice the usual amount. He felt bad for me. But still, all the new clothes I bought as part of my wedding gifts were in dark shades—navy blue, brown, dark green. I didn't buy anything light or bright—no reds or pinks or yellows. My husband also dressed for the wedding day in dark clothing, a *jalabiya* and a jacket in dark colors. When his family came to bring me from my parent's house back to Abu Ghosh, my mother was so sad she couldn't speak. And my father, all he could say was, "My daughter is leaving my home, it's like losing my sons—they all go." And that was it. I left my parents in East Jerusalem and went to Abu Ghosh to live with my husband and his family.

Going to live in the village was not easy. By then, I was a city girl, not a *fellaha*. To visit the village, fine. To come live here, that was something else. I'm not going to lie to you. It took me quite a while to get used to being in Abu Ghosh. I had to work much harder here than in Jerusalem. There was no primus stove to cook on here, and no bakery to buy bread. And do you think I liked fetching wood to make a fire? Or cleaning clothes without soap, but with ash? No, no. I didn't like it. I was spoiled some from the city life. I was used to restaurant food once a week and meat almost every day. Meat in Abu Ghosh? Hardly ever. My mother-in-law used eggs instead of meat in her cooking. And we ate vegetables, just vegetables. My husband brought them from the monastery where he was working as a *fellah* on the monastery's grounds. They were fresh and tasty, but I missed the city food, my mother's food.

My father knew how hard it was for me coming back to Abu Ghosh. I was his favorite daughter, he loved me very much. So, once every few weeks he used to come back to the village with a present for me. Some sweets from Jerusalem, and pistachios and peanuts and other things he knew I liked. Then—it was about three years after I was married—he decided to move back to Abu Ghosh with the whole family. Slowly, slowly, he had been building a new house here. He made a good salary as a policeman, and with this money he paid some *fellahin* to build him the house. The English had a police station just outside the village—it's still there today, the Jews took it in 1948—and he got assigned there. The English gave him this beautiful horse. He used to ride on patrol all over the area, from village to village. Oh, I remember that horse! You'll never see one so beautiful, a reddish brown horse with white spots. My father used to fit her out so well and brush her like she was a bride. When there was a wedding in the village, they'd ask to borrow the horse for the *zaffa*. People in the village loved this horse. My father had her for a long time, until 1948. Then, when the war broke out and he went over to Jordan, he sold it. Oh, I'm telling you, such a horse I've never seen again. To this day, when I watch television and see horses, I look for one like her. But I've never seen one her equal, not even on television.

***

So, I was telling you about what it was like to come live at my mother-in-law's house. Well, I got used to it slowly, slowly. My mother-in-law was the only one in the house. She had her room, we had ours. My husband's two sisters had both gotten married just two days before us, so they were gone. I got along well with my mother-in-law, it helped that she was my aunt. The ones who got into arguments, really, were my husband and my mother-in-law. But I stayed out of it. My uncle, the one who decided we should marry, had told me, "When the two of them have their fights, don't get drawn into it. Let them settle it themselves." I took his advice, it was good advice.

My husband and mother-in-law were close, though, very close. My husband's father had died when he was seven, he was *yatim al-ab.*[*] He was going to school then—not a real school, just a *sheikh* that boys went to to learn how to read. He stopped going so he could support his family. Someone had told him that his mother was going to remarry and he went half-crazy, screaming and crying and jumping up and down. He insisted on going out to work. He found a job in the monastery, they took him to work in the fields they owned. He was a good worker and all the monks liked him. When they prayed, he went and prayed too at

---

[*] For a child whose parent has died, Arabic distinguishes *yatim al-ab* [orphan without a father] from *yatim al-umm* [orphan without a mother].

the mosque next door. The monks were proud of him. He was serious and even-tempered like them, and religious. On his way back and forth from work he would read the Koran. He had learned to read the letters in school, and his mother had taught him to read the Koran. She, herself, couldn't read, but she had learned the Koran by heart from her father. That way, when my husband first started to read the Koran, she corrected him and after a while he could read all of it. So, back and forth he'd go from work reading to himself. That's the way he was. A religious man, calm and quiet. Not like me. I'm the one who gets excited and temperamental sometimes, and who likes to talk. My husband, he was a man of few words.

In the beginning of our marriage, I tell you, we hardly talked at all. Only a little when we were alone and nobody else was around. In public, even in front of my mother-in-law, we never exchanged words. My husband preferred it that way. Also, the custom of the time was that husbands and wives didn't talk to each other in public. I mean, if they were outside the house, they didn't say anything to each other. Today, wives not only talk to their husbands in public, they'll argue with them openly. Take some of my daughters, take Leila—if she doesn't agree with her husband she'll speak right up. Her eyes are not ashamed in front of men. If you ask me, this is not a good thing. The women of today—most of my daughters, Leila too—go around with their heads uncovered. This is right? Maybe you don't want to hear me say so, but I don't think it's right. I couldn't do it. Back when I was married, and until maybe twenty-five years ago, I used to wear a *mandil* [delicate veil] over my face whenever I left the house and went to the *suq,* or clinic, or anywhere. One time I remember, it was shortly after I was married, I passed my husband in the street here in Abu Ghosh. I was going to take the bus to Jerusalem. My face was veiled and he didn't even recognize me. But even if he had recognized me he wouldn't have said a word. You didn't talk in public in those days. Not if you were modest, you didn't. Oh, no. *Ya* Rafiqa, things have changed here in our village since then, I swear, things have changed!

2

So that's the way it was back then, my dear. Abu Ghosh before you were born, before your time. What else can I tell you? About my children, giving birth? Alright. I had twenty-one stomachs,* you know that, no? Well, I did. But, it took me a while before I brought my first. I was only fourteen years old when I got married, and I didn't bring Khawla until I was sixteen. My mother-in-law was worried those first two years. My husband was her only son, she wanted to have heirs. But what was I supposed to do— take one from my parents' house? Finally, though, I pleased her. I got a stomach. All the women in the village who saw me said I was going to have a son. They looked at my stomach and said it was sitting nicely, easily, it had to be a boy. I wasn't very old, I figured they knew what they were talking about. I was sure I was going to bring a son. When my time came I went to the hospital, an English hospital. After many hours finally I gave birth. The nurse told me, "Congratulations, you have a baby daughter!" I answered her, "No, mine's a son!" She told me again that it was a daughter, and I repeated that it was a son. Back and forth it went. When my mother and family came to visit me, my mother asked, "What did you bring?" I answered, "I brought a son, but the nurse is telling me it's a daughter." My mother laughed and laughed.

Once I saw my baby, I was happy with her. She was healthy and well formed, that's what mattered. My mother-in-law was happy too, really. And my husband seemed happy. He passed out sweets and was smiling at everybody. That's how he was when the girls were born. With boys, he'd put on a serious face, no smiling. He wasn't a man to show his true feelings, he hid them. Years later, after I'd brought all the children, one day we were sitting and talking, and then he admitted it. He admitted that each time I was pregnant he'd go to mosque and pray for a son.

* Umm Khaled and other village women occasionally refer to pregnancies as "stomachs."

But when a son came he'd hide his happiness, and when a daughter came he'd pretend to be happier than he was. That's how he was, Abu Khaled, he wasn't one to let on to his true feelings.

Well, it took until the third time for me to make him truly happy. I brought Khaled. My husband named him after his own father, who'd died when he was a boy. Despite his serious face, I knew he was happy with Khaled. After that I brought three more sons in a row—Issa, Ibrahim, Muhsen. My mother-in-law was very satisfied with me. I'd brought her heirs. She helped me out with all of them, feeding and washing and wrapping them. We worked together side by side. I couldn't have managed without her, God bless her memory.

In the beginning, though, the doctor told me I shouldn't bring too many children. He said it wasn't good for my health. I have asthma, since I was seven or eight I've had it. I'm always coughing and my throat is sore a lot of the time. When I was young, my parents once took me to this woman in Jerusalem who treated me by burning my throat on the outside with a hot fork. It didn't help. Nothing helped. Herbs, medicines, nothing. So I've been sick with this throat and asthma all my life. When I started to bring children, the doctor warned me that I should wait four years between pregnancies. My mother-in-law was with me that day and she said to the doctor, "*Ya* doctor! Listen, my son is the only one I have. If she can't bring enough children, my son will take another wife along with her." She was serious, yes. Later she told me that according to our religion, he had a right to four wives. I didn't want that, of course. *Al-durra murra* [the second wife is bitter]. Did you ever hear of a good second wife? So I kept on bringing children. What else could I do? There was no other way.

The hardest birth, no doubt about it, was the time I brought Muhsen. What made this one so hard is that after I got my stomach, the war came. This was 1948. Almost everyone had fled the village. My mother-in-law was gone, my mother was gone, my sisters—all gone over to the Arab side. Only a few of us stayed in the village, and most of us were hiding out in the monastery. The monks were very kind to our family, maybe because my husband had been working all those years with them. They gave us their reception room to live in. But when my time came, my husband said, "It won't be good to bring the baby here, go back to our house." It was a quiet time during the war, so I went back there alone. Our house then was near the monastery, in the center of the village. Nobody came with me. What I did is put a plastic cover over the bed so I wouldn't bleed on the bedcovers, and I lay down. I twined a sheet like a rope, tied it to the iron poster of the bed, and held on. When the hard contractions came, as I lay on my back I pulled the sheet. That helped. I was scared, very scared. I prayed to God that I would bring this baby and return to my other children. And God answered my prayers. The baby came out healthy. I had no way of cutting the umbilical cord, though. Finally, my daughter came with this woman. She helped clean me up, but she refused to cut the umbilical cord. She believed that if she cut it—this was the way some women thought then—afterwards she wouldn't be able to have any children. My husband, who arrived by then, said to her, "Cut it, do it! Go ahead!" But she refused. She left me there hanging between the heavens and the earth, with my poor son tied to me. A half-hour or so later, finally my husband found another woman who agreed to cut it. Everything was alright. I stayed there in the house with Muhsen, that's what we called him. And the other children and my husband came back too. Thanks to God we were alright, even though the war was still going on. We stayed there in the house then, although the Jews started giving those of us who stayed a lot of troubles. But we survived. We didn't flee and didn't return, we just stayed in our house.

❧

When I think back to the war in 1948, I think it was a miracle that we survived. God protected us. God protected Abu Ghosh. Even though almost everyone fled, we managed to keep our village. Ours is the only village in the whole area that wasn't destroyed, thanks to God. We were very fortunate.

We knew a war was coming, but nobody knew when. People started getting very scared. The English were still here, but there was fighting going on in villages all around us. Many people in Abu Ghosh decided to leave, they went over to the Jordanian side. They took a few suitcases like they were going on vacation, hoping they'd come back in a few weeks or a month. My mother-in-law left with her two daughters and their families, and my two married sisters and their husbands left too. One of my sisters, Jalila, was married to the *mukhtar* of the village, Hammad R. The English gave him ten rifles to defend the whole village. Can you imagine, *ten* rifles for all of us? Hammad R. knew we didn't stand a chance. And really what happened is that as soon as the English left, the Jews swooped right down on us easily. My parents had left with my two unmarried sisters just before that happened. My father had gone to Jerusalem to get his salary. The way back was closed off, so they had to stay over there on the Jordanian side. My husband had wanted me to go with my parents and take the children with me. He gave me 100 pounds. "I just sold our cow," he said. "Take this money and go with your family." I told him, "It's not enough money, it won't last. I'm staying here, no matter what happens. If you die, I'll die with you. If you live, I'll live." My husband didn't argue with me, he let me stay.

We hid out in the monastery. There weren't so many of us left in the village, but those who were still here hid with the monks. We were all there on the day the English left the area, and the Jews came swooping down on us. There were a lot of shots for a while, like chickpeas popping in a pan, and then there was silence. The Jews came to the monastery and made all of us go to the center of the village. We thought they were going to shoot us all. We heard some of their soldiers say, "Let's shoot them." For hours we were out there in the sun, not knowing what they were going to do with us. Some of the soldiers stood guard and others went through the village, house to house. Then, they got some orders to leave us alone, and as quickly as they'd come, they then left. We knew they'd be back though, and we were scared.

After they'd gone my husband and I went up to our house. The whole place had been turned upside down. They'd opened the closets and thrown things out. I immediately went to the mirror on the closet door. Behind it, between the glass and the wood backing, I'd hidden the 100 pounds my husband gave me when he sold the cow. He knew the money was there too, we were the only ones who knew. But when I took apart the mirror the money was gone. My husband immediately began accusing me. He said, "What did you do with that money? You gave it to your parents, didn't you?" I was shocked to hear him talk to me like this, and besides I knew it wasn't true. It made me stop and think, and I said to him, "Your mother is over there, and you're asking me what *I* did with the money?" He got real mad. We started arguing harder and harder. Both of us were convinced the other was lying. It left an awful feeling between us.

The whole thing didn't really get solved until months later. This was after I gave birth to Muhsen, and we had moved back into our house. The Jews still came around on raids. They'd come at night or in the day, you never knew when. There'd be the sound of their boots marching up the steps. I swear, it used to make me tremble. To this day, if I see a Jewish soldier or policeman, even in the distance, the chills run through me. When they'd come on these raids, you never knew what would happen. Always, they were looking for someone or something. Well, this one time they came knocking on the door, demanding we open up. I was shaking, shaking, shaking. They came in and started turning things upside down. One soldier said to me, "Where's the key to the closet?" Before I said anything, this other soldier—his name was Moshe, he was always in on the raids—he turned a table upside down and found the key. He opened the closet and went straight to the mirror and began taking it apart. There was nothing there this time, we had nothing left. But then my husband and I both knew what had happened to our 100 pounds. When the soldiers left, my husband said to me, "Now

I know how the money disappeared." His heart relaxed. Mine, too. The bad feeling that had been with us all the time finally was gone. We knew who had taken the money.

Because we were back in our house, we didn't have anything else stolen from us. But all the others who had left the village had their homes emptied. The Jews came with trucks, they broke into the houses and took everything they could. Couches, armoires, chairs and tables, silver and copper platters, pitchers and glasses—everything. They came in broad daylight. They loaded up and left and then came back and loaded up and left again. We couldn't do anything about it. Some Jews also came with their horses and donkeys and went out to the fields and carried off boxes and boxes of vegetables and fruits. Tomatoes, cucumbers, almonds, and grapes—they took it all. What could we do? We had no way of stopping them.

Later, after the war, they took the land too. The Israeli government confiscated land from this one, that one, from whoever they wanted. We had three dunams in the village in my husband's name. *That* they didn't take. But we also had ninety dunams in my husband's name down by the village of Emwas.* We still have the papers proving that it's ours. That's flat land down there, good for growing wheat and corn and sesame. Many people in Abu Ghosh had land down there. We would sharecrop it out. The people who worked it gave us part of the harvest and kept part of it themselves. In 1948 the Israeli army conquered that land, and we never got it back. I told my husband, "We didn't flee, that land

* Emwas, an Arab village about fifteen kilometers from Abu Ghosh, after 1948 wound up on the Jordanian side of the border. But many of the fields around the village—including those of Umm Khaled's husband—remained on the Israeli side of the border. Before 1948 farmers in hill villages like Abu Ghosh often owned land on the plains and either worked it themselves or rented it out. In the 1967 war the village of Emwas was captured by Israel from Jordan and was later razed to the ground.

is ours. Go claim it!" Abu Khaled answered me, "Their army is sitting on it. The most they'll do is offer me a few agorot for it, so forget it. It's gone." Today, I understand—I've never seen it, only my husband went back—the Jews are farming it. They're growing guavas there, he once told me. But I still have the papers that show the land is ours, it belongs to us.

After the 1948 war, or sometime during it—the war kept going on for a long time after the Jews first entered the village—the Jews came one day and announced that they were giving us identity cards. Anyone who was living in the village and wanted a card could have one. The card meant you were an Israeli citizen. It meant you could stay in the village, they wouldn't throw you out. We all went and got our cards. The Jews themselves appointed us a new *mukhtar,* Marwan S. He replaced my sister's husband, Hammad R. But who was this new *mukhtar?* An illiterate man, that's all. He wasn't educated like Hammad R. The Jews wanted someone who they could control, so they appointed him. I don't know how much he helped them or what. I know he sold vegetables to them and made good money that way. More than that I couldn't say.

During this period there were a lot of people from Abu Ghosh who had gone over to Jordan and who now wanted to return. Some had already sneaked back before the identity cards were passed out, and they managed to get their cards. I have some cousins who succeeded in this way. Others tried after the cards were given out, and they had problems. My mother and father tried when it was too late. My aunts and uncles too. If you had connections with the Jews, or you were able to make connections, then you could get an identity card and stay. If not, the Jews would sooner or later catch you on one of their raids, and they'd dump you across the border again. They'd come in trucks, they'd load you up and dump you in Jordan. My parents got dumped this way twice. No, my father got caught twice and my mother once. The second time my mother managed to stay here a while, but then she heard that my father was thinking of taking another wife. So, she didn't wait any longer in

Abu Ghosh, she went back to the other side to join my father. They stayed there until 1965, until we managed to get the papers so they could return to the village.

In the beginning, right after the war, it wasn't so hard to sneak back and forth across the border. I mean, you might get shot at while trying it—but mostly you could make it across. There were infiltrators* who knew the good routes and you could pay them to help you across. The infiltrators were mostly young men from Abu Ghosh. I had some cousins who were doing this work. They'd go over the mountains at night, hiding out in caves when they had to. They not only brought people over, they also brought money and food and clothes. Some of the villagers who fled from here in 1948 took lots of money with them, and they sent back some to their relatives who stayed. The money was simple to hide, but if your relatives sent you food or clothes, you could easily get caught. When the Jews came around on raids they were looking for these things.

One time my sister Jalila, who married Hammad R., sent me and my husband some shoes and slippers, along with other things. The Jews came by here on a raid and my husband greeted them at the door. They looked at his shoes and said, "The infiltrators brought you these, they're not from here. What else have you got?" They turned the house upside down, but all they found were my slippers. They were the most beautiful slippers I'd ever owned. They took them too, along with the shoes. I was furious. But nothing else happened to us. We weren't hiding any infiltrators, we weren't doing anything else against them, and we had our identity cards. So they left us alone.

After the war was over, two years or so after, it was very hard to sneak over. You had to come back with your papers in order, otherwise it was very risky. My two sisters managed to get back with their families this way. Actually, what happened was that my sister Hamda's husband man-

---

 * Umm Khaled referred to these individuals as *mutasallelin* (sing., *mutasallel*), which is commonly translated as "infiltrators." In this context the Arabic term does not carry a pejorative meaning, as does the English term "infiltrator."

aged to get across through some connections he had. He then arranged for Jalila and the *mukhtar,* Hammad R., to get their papers too. So both families and all their children came back to Abu Ghosh. This was a little after I had brought Leila, it must have been 1953 or 1954.

For Jalila and her husband, coming back to Abu Ghosh was a hard thing. It was very hard on the *mukhtar,* he came back with nothing. Whatever money they had taken with them in 1948 was gone. They had spent those years living in the Bethlehem area. Hammad R. was treated there like a traitor. When he arrived in 1948 they cursed him and said to him, "How did you turn your village over to the Jews?" They humili-ated him, and they even attacked him physically. For five years he lived there in disgrace, and then he managed to come back here with my sister and their children. Yet what happened to him here? The people in the village still respected him. We still thought of him as the real *mukhtar* even though the Jews had appointed someone else. But Hammad R. came back with nothing—nothing above him and nothing below him. The Jews had taken his land, and even his house had been emptied out by thieves. He didn't have one agora to support his family. So he had to go to work as a common laborer, along with boys from the village. This same Hammad R. who once was *mukhtar* of *mukhtar*s, the most re-spected man in the area, the one who made a *sulha* between families and was always hosting guests and slaughtering sheep for them—who was he now? Nobody. That's the way he saw it, anyway. He felt so hu-miliated by all this that he prayed to God to hurry his end. That's what my sister told me. Hammad R. didn't want to live anymore. And one day God answered his prayers. He came home from work that day car-rying his tools with him, his hammer in his hand. When he got off the bus in the village center, it was raining hard and there was thunder and lightning. A lightning bolt struck his hammer and Hammad R. was burned like a stick. God had ended his humiliation. My sister was still a young woman then and she had small children to raise herself. What a life she's had! Poor thing. I suppose you know that one of her sons, Walid, is married to Leila. That's right. Leila's husband, Walid, is the son of Hammad R. And Walid, you know, is a respected man in the village now, his father's good name still clings to him. My sister, she spends a lot of time over there with them, though she still lives in her own house, Hammad R.'s house. She's an old lady like me now, both of us are widows now. Time sure goes by, doesn't it?

Leila

Leila is Umm Khaled's eighth child and fourth daughter. She is a plump-ish, pleasant-looking woman of forty-two who, like her mother, speaks in a rush of words and is open about her views and sentiments. Unlike her mother, however, she has a modern, fashionable look to her: she wears makeup, she does not cover her long brown hair with a head scarf, and she prefers blouses and dresses bought in the department stores of Tel Aviv.

Leila and her husband, Walid, were both raised in Abu Ghosh and chose to remain there to raise their seven children. Today, they live in the valley of the village, about a hundred meters from the mosque and monastery. Reflecting Walid's success as a building contractor, they are converting their house from a modest five-room place to an expansive two-story building with ten rooms and a majestic veranda, a house fit—one is tempted to say—for a son of the former *mukhtar.*

All seven sessions with Leila took place at her house, either in the salon or the kitchen. At times it was possible to interview Leila alone, but just as often someone else was hovering nearby—her mother-in-law, her married daughter, or one of the younger children. Her husband, Walid, was seldom there, although Leila did apprise him of her partici-pation in the project.

Before this study Leila and Rafiqa Othman had not visited each other, but Leila was receptive to being interviewed because like Umm Khaled she was familiar with Rafiqa's family; in fact, she had gone to school with Rafiqa's older sister. Leila was even willing to have Michael Gorkin participate in the interviews, but since we had interviewed her mother alone, we decided to interview the daughter this way also.* Michael made a social visit only at the end of the interviews.

Born four years after the creation of Israel, Leila is the one woman in the book who has lived all her life in a Jewish state. Her experiences in school, at work, and as a mother raising children all reflect this fact. Indeed, when asked how she would describe herself, contrary to others in the book she did not refer to herself as a "Palestinian" but rather as an "Israeli Arab." (Umm Khaled, by comparison, said, "I'm a Palestinian with an Israeli identity card—a Palestinian Israeli.")

The material below, excerpted from the interviews with Leila, covers her entire life—her childhood, schooling, marriage, work experience—as it unfolded in the village of Abu Ghosh.

ﺯ

W here do I start? I don't know how to do this. What, just talk about myself? Alright, fine. Let's see, the first thing I want to say is that, like you, I'm from here. All my life I've lived in Abu Ghosh, and I expect to be here the rest of my life. I love the village, it's a fine place—good people, right? All my sisters and brothers are here still, except for Muna and Nadia who are over in East Jerusalem. And Walid's family too, they're all here. That's the way it is with our village. People stay here usually, they marry someone from here. Abu Ghosh is a good place to live.

How do I remember my childhood? Well, I can't say I remember much. Not before school, anyway. We didn't do much as kids then.

---

* As we indicated in the introduction (see note 10), we were concerned about potential opposition to the study from Leila's brothers.

There was no nursery school or kindergarten in the village back then. You stayed at home, or went to your cousin's house, or you went to the grocery store to get something for your mother. That was it, a different kind of day for kids than today.

Our house was in the center of the village near the monastery where my father worked. Today, my brother Muhsen lives in it—he was born there during the 1948 war—and part of it, the downstairs, is rented out now to the village as a nursery school. What I remember is that back when we were living there, we had three bedrooms. One for my parents, who had a real bed. And a bedroom for the boys, and a bedroom for the girls. We slept on floor mattresses in rows, one next to the other according to age. I slept next to Rana, my older sister. Oh God, how we used to fight! She'd pull my hair, I'd pull hers. Over the least thing, we'd be at each other. That's how it is with *rusiya,* * isn't it? Each envies the other. Today, we're friends, all that's gone. She has ten children, and we get along fine. No problems.

Back then, if we got into fights we'd have to straighten it out with each other. Or maybe one of my older sisters, Khawla or Zahira, might get into it. They helped out my mother. My mother, herself, was too busy for things like that. She was always working—cleaning, washing, cooking. With fifteen or sixteen kids, she had no time to get involved with one or two of us. I mean, it wasn't like today where you sit and talk with the child. They didn't do it that way then.

I remember when my brother Khaled died. Nobody came and talked to me about it. Not my mother, not my father, nobody. I was five years old. I remember Khaled was pale, but I didn't know how sick he was. He was my oldest brother, tall and handsome with blond hair and honey-colored eyes, and with this pale skin. Then one day there was a lot of crying and yelling, and someone said Khaled's gone, dead. Death, what's that? I didn't understand what it meant. Nobody came to explain it to

* In Arabic, *rusiya* refers to two siblings close in age: one child is born on the "head" [*ras*] of the other.

me, I had to understand it myself. The truth is, I didn't understand it till much later, when I was a schoolgirl. At five years old, who knows what death is?

❧

The thing I really liked as a child was going to school. The school was only a few steps from our house, in the center of the village. I went there from first to eighth grade. That's all we had in the village then, there was no high school. I would have liked to go to high school like your sister did. I wanted to study more, to be a nurse maybe. But my parents didn't agree to my leaving the village and going to Jerusalem to high school, the way your sister did it. So when school stopped here, I had to stop too.

I was proud to go to school, I used to like going off each morning with my book bag. We'd wear these school dresses and blouses, light blue things with the school emblem, Abu Ghosh School, and a bunch of grapes embroidered on the blouse. That's how you had to dress. You couldn't wear pants if you were a girl, only if you were a boy. And if you were fourteen years or older, you were expected to cover your hair with a head scarf. That was the custom then, it changed later.

In the classrooms—there were eight, one for each grade—we were together with boys. They sat in their section and we sat in ours. But we'd talk together, joke around, and we were friends. They were like brothers to us. If you ask me, it's good to have boys and girls in the same classroom, nothing wrong with it. Of course, after school we didn't go play with boys—oh no! Our parents wouldn't have allowed that. School was one thing, after school was another.

Me, I liked being there in school. I liked learning things, new things. Which subjects? I liked English, that was my favorite, I think. And Hebrew, we learned that too, starting in fifth grade. I used to speak it fairly well, but now I've forgotten most of it. Walid, he's the one who can really speak, he's fluent like the Jews even though he only went to eighth grade. And, let's see, what else did we learn? Oh, math—that was the hardest for me, for sure. And then there was religion, geography, and history. And Arabic. We studied our own language too, from first grade on.

With Arabic, there were some problems. This was because our teachers were not from here, they weren't Arabs. They were Jews from Arab countries, mostly from Iraq. You see, when I was going to school there were hardly any Arab teachers. Not until the seventh grade—then, we suddenly had a change. A new principal came, an Arab man, and also a lot of Arab teachers from up north who had finished college. Until then—this was 1965 or 1966—we were taught by Iraqi Jews. These Iraqi Jews spoke fluent Arabic, but it was different from ours, much harsher. They said the *dh* and the *q* from deep in the throat, not softly like we do. So what happened is that all of us were speaking like Iraqi Jews, at least in the school. When the new principal and teachers came they got very angry at us. They wanted us to speak right, like from here. I remember the principal came one time to our class to see if we were making progress with our accents, and every student who was still speaking the Iraqi way got hit on the hand. I got hit too, yes I did. I remember it to this day.

Other things also changed at the school shortly after this new principal came. He was a strong man, a good man, I think. He cared about the students. He brought about some changes. Like, for example, after he took over we didn't celebrate some Jewish holidays the way we had before. Until then, we had always had a big celebration in May on Israel's Independence Day. The teachers and the students would decorate the classrooms with balloons and blue-and-white Israeli flags. All eight classes would go out into the school yard and the principal, an Iraqi Jew, would give a long speech about the meaning of Independence Day. And then we'd sing these songs in Arabic, like this one—"It's the Independence Day of my country / The bird who sings, sings gladly today / Happiness reigns all over / From the valley to the plain." You see, I still remember it. Looking back now, I don't feel we should have been told to sing these things, I'm glad the Arab principal changed it. Today's kids

don't do this anymore, no more decorating the classroom, no more singing songs. They hang an Israeli flag from the school, and that's all. But
in my time we were ignorant. The teachers told us to decorate and we
decorated, they told us to sing and we sang.

If you look back on it now, knowing what we know now, you can
see that there were lots of things we didn't learn. You asked me if we
learned in school about the war in 1948. No, we didn't, not that I remember. Not in history class, and not in any other class. What I remember is that we learned about some of the older history here. Napoleon,
Herod, the Romans. And we learned about Hitler and someone else,
Musso-somebody. But, about the 1948 war here, how the Arabs and Jews
fought, and why there was a war at all—I tell you, I can't remember
learning about it at all. Did you learn in your time, Rafiqa? No, you see.
It's not something they taught. Now, yes, it's changed. Today's children
learn about these things. Today, almost every teacher in the school in
Abu Ghosh is an Arab. But in my time we didn't talk about these subjects, about the wars between Arabs and Jews—not in school.

2

Of course, just living in Abu Ghosh, all of us knew *something* about the
war in 1948. To this day, I can't say I know a lot, but I know about what
happened here, some of it, even though I was born after the war. All of
us here had family over on the other side, in Jordan. I can remember
when I was about ten years old, we went to Beit Safafa hoping to see
our relatives who were in Jordan.* I went with kids my age and some
aunts. Not with my parents, they didn't go that time. There were a lot
of people there shouting across the fences, trying to talk to their relatives.

---

* After the 1948 war the border between Jordan and Israel ran through the
village of Beit Safafa, in south Jerusalem; one part of the village was in Israel and
the other in Jordan, with fences separating the two parts. On holidays, Arabs from
Abu Ghosh and elsewhere in Israel would come to Beit Safafa with the hope of
seeing and shouting greetings to family on the Jordanian side.

Suddenly, my aunt Jalila said, "There's Leila—over there!" I had never met my aunt Leila, I only knew my mother named me after her sister. She yelled over to me, "Whose daughter are you?" I answered, "Amina's daughter—I'm Leila!" My aunt Leila began crying and crying, and I swear, I began crying too. Then Labiba—she's a cousin of my mother's—fainted. She had come with us hoping to see her brother who was a policeman on the Jordanian side. There were rumors in the village that he was dead, but she didn't believe the rumors. She came to look for him. She wanted to cross over to the other side and find him. The Israelis didn't let her, she got all upset, and she fainted. Finally, they sent someone to try to find him, and you know, he *was* alive! Labiba's brother came to the Jordanian side of the fence and the Israelis let her cross over to meet him. I can still see that scene before my eyes. We stood there watching the two of them embrace, all of us weeping. I tell you, I'll never forget that.

Naturally, we heard lots of stories about those over in Jordan. Nobody sat down and explained it all to us—how the war in 1948 started and why—but we learned things here and there. Jalila, my mother's sister, and now my mother-in-law, talked a lot about the war. She likes to talk and she had many stories. She was married to the *mukhtar,* Hammad R. You know that, right? She was over in Jordan for about five years and then she and the *mukhtar* managed to get back with their children. Walid was born here just before they left. He was six years old when his father died, but he still remembers him. And Jalila, she's always talking about the old days. Just yesterday, she was over here helping me make *maqluba,* and she was talking about the *mukhtar.*

I swear, my mother-in-law has had a hard life. Oh yes, she sure has. She was married to a man before the *mukhtar,* her cousin. He was no good, he was always looking for other women, so her father took her back home. But then fate brought her to the *mukhtar.* The *mukhtar's* wife died and he was left a widower with two children. He came immediately and asked for Jalila. He was fifty years old and she was eighteen. She told her parents, "I want someone to look after me now. No more young men, only an older man." So she married the *mukhtar* and she became a rich woman. She was no longer poor like my parents, no. She was busy all the time with the *mukhtar's* guests, but she had servants to help her. They had a fine house and lots of land. Five hundred dunams. Then the war came in 1948, and they lost everything. When they were over in Jordan, people robbed everything in their house. Furniture, rugs, silver, everything. You see this copper fruit dish here? Simple but fine, no? It's one of the few things they found in their house when they came back. All the rest was gone. The land, too. The Israelis took over everything except for a few dunams in the village. The *mukhtar* had to go to work as a laborer. That finished him. "God take me to you, I don't want to live anymore"—that's what Hammad R. prayed. Walid was in school that day when it happened. They came and told him, "Your father just died, he got hit by lightning." God had answered Hammad R.'s prayers. Poor Jalila and the children, though. There were six children and Jalila had to raise them without a husband. Somehow she managed it. Her sons are all fine men, important men in the village now. They are still seen as the sons of the *mukhtar,* the best *mukhtar* the village ever had. Before 1948, and after—Walid's father is known as the best.

⌣

What I know about the 1948 war, I learned from the stories of others. To this day, I still hear things I never knew. My mother has probably told you things that I, myself, don't know. I think we were very lucky that we survived, don't you? I can't imagine what our lives would have been like if my parents had left the village in 1948 along with my grandparents, and we had grown up in Jordan. Praise God, they stayed! Those who left had a hard time of it. When they came over here to visit after the 1967 war, we found that out. They hadn't done so well in Jordan, not at all.

I remember all that very well. You see, the 1967 war happened when I was already pretty old, I think I was about fifteen. Yes, right, it was when I was in eighth grade. I remember it, sure. My father had a radio and he was listening all the time. So we knew a war was coming, a big war. We were living in our new house, the one my mother is in today. It's a solidly built house. My father wanted to fortify it by putting sandbags around the windows and doors. He had us help him. He wanted the house to be well protected in case bombs were dropped. Some of the smaller children were put down in the storeroom to sleep. I can remember we were just finishing with the sandbags around the windows when a woman neighbor began shouting, "War! War! Head for the monastery!" Many people began running to the monastery, that's where they hid in the 1948 war and were saved. My parents didn't go this time. They thought our house was safe enough. Anyway, it didn't matter. All of Abu Ghosh was a safe place to be in that war. Nothing happened here. There were a few shots fired nearby on the first day, and a few times when we looked outside we could see planes overhead chasing each other. But that was it. They call it the Six-Day War, right? It was over in six days.

For us, the Israeli Arabs, it was a shock. We were listening to the radio broadcasts from Jordan and Egypt, and we were sure the Arab armies were going to win. That's what *they* said. They kept announcing Arab victories, one after the other. Lies, just lies, it turned out. It was disappointing, sure it was. I'm not going to lie to you and say we were hoping for Israel to win. Of course, we wanted the Arabs to win. Nasser was a hero in the village then. Everyone loved him, old and young. When Nasser and the Arab armies lost it made us all angry. We didn't believe it would happen. And in six days—who would have believed it?

Anyway, that was the 1967 war. Started and finished in one week. The only good thing that came out of it—at least, we felt it was a good thing in the beginning—was that suddenly we could again see all our family, all the people from Abu Ghosh who had left in 1948. My grandmother, my father's and mother's sisters, our cousins. Half of Abu Ghosh was over in Jordan, and suddenly they all came back to the village. They couldn't come to live, except for a few of them like my grandmother. The Israelis didn't let them stay. But they were allowed to come for long visits, for weeks or months.

Well, at first, we enjoyed this. My parents especially enjoyed it. Me, I found it strange. To be honest, almost all these relatives who had been living over in Jordan seemed different from us. I can't really explain it. They seemed like strangers in everything, how they talked and what they said. I had expected I was going to feel close to them, we were always hearing about them. But, they seemed like complete strangers to me. And they had this way about them that made you feel—I know my mother felt this—they expected things out of us. You know, one of them would say, "We don't have this kind of cleanser, or this soap over there." And another would say, "That orange juice concentrate, where do you get that?" Hinting, you see. And we were expected to go out and buy these things for them. We did, sure. We bought lots of presents, but they were always asking for more. I tell you, I didn't like it. I wasn't used to people talking in this way. And these were my relatives! They didn't give me the feeling I wanted to know them more. I guess they had a hard life over in Jordan, maybe they envied us. I just know that when these visits ended, we were all relieved. We'd had enough for the time being.

⁂

For me, when the 1967 war was over and all the visits stopped, I was looking to do something. But what could I do? I didn't want to get married, I was too young for that—only sixteen. What I really wanted was to continue in school. Well, a lucky thing happened. Just then, here in the village they opened up this one-year trade school for girls exactly my age. They gave courses in Hebrew, Arabic, math, and they also taught you how to sew. I was eager to go. I went to my parents and told them, but they refused. "Leila has gone to school long enough," my father said. I didn't know what to do, and then I figured I'd go to

Margalit. She was a nurse in the health clinic in the village, a Jewish woman who spoke Arabic. Everyone in the village respected her, my mother too. I went to Margalit, and I could see she was on my side. The next thing I knew, she had gone to my father and he agreed.

Your sister went with me that same year. I used to rely on her to help me with the math homework. She was smarter than me in that. Oh, that was a good year! I really enjoyed it. After that, I wanted to go on to high school too, but my parents were against my going to East Jerusalem. *Khalas,* that was it. There was nothing I could do about it.

Actually, what happened is that during that year in the trade school, when I was sixteen and a half, Walid came to request me. In a way I was surprised, and in a way not. Walid is my cousin, so I had seen him over the years. No, we never sat and talked, of course not. He's five years older than me, that's a lot of years when you're young. But we would visit his house, and they'd visit us. And sometimes we'd all go on outings, like picking olives together. Walid and I never said more than "hello" to each other. Still, there was something I could feel. This one time when we went olive picking—I was already fifteen or sixteen—I could sense he had his eye on me. Even from a distance I could feel it. I didn't say anything and neither did he. Then, one day, his sister came to visit me. She told me, "Leila, my brother wants to marry you. We all love you in our family. We hope you'll accept." I said to her, "Why has Walid chosen me? Why not my older sister Rana?" She answered, "No, Walid wants you. He loves *you.*" I wasn't against the idea, it was just that Rana and Zahira weren't married yet, and they were older than me. I didn't want to cause problems. And, naturally, it did cause problems. My mother was against my going first, she opposed the idea. If she had her way, she would have stopped it. Walid didn't give up though, and in the end that's how it worked out. My father and mother agreed. Nobody came and asked me what *I* wanted, but I wasn't against it. So it was agreed I'd marry Walid.

He and his family came over one day and made a formal request. It had already been agreed, but the custom was to make a formal request. Walid came with a *maska*,* this bracelet to put on my wrist. I knew it was going to happen, yet when they got to our house I suddenly ran into the other room. The whole thing embarrassed me. I didn't know what to do with myself. Then my uncle Khalil came and took me by the arm and led me back to the salon. I was brought to sit next to Walid, a formal request was made, and he put the *maska* on my wrist. I was sixteen and a half years old, too young to get married according to the law. You had to be seventeen. When we had the ceremony to sign the *kitab* a few weeks later, the *sheikh* told us he personally was going to hold onto the marriage contract until I was legal age. He didn't want to run into any problems. That's what he did, and then when I was seventeen we had our wedding party.

I had several months between the *kitab* and the wedding to get myself ready. I went to Tel Aviv and got everything there. Things were cheaper in the West Bank, but you got much better quality in Tel Aviv. In my time, the custom was that the bride wore seven dresses of different colors—white, black, red, pink, green, blue, and yellow. And there were matching shoes for the black, red and white dresses. These days the custom is different, right? The bride only wears one dress, a white one. Maybe it's more elegant this new way. I know the way I did it was fine with me. Today, they also don't ride a horse in the *zaffa* anymore. That's really a shame. That was a good custom. Although, the truth is, I didn't get to ride the horse. Oh, how I regret that! To sit up there looking at all the people, it's a special thing for a bride. I wanted to do it, but my father was a religious man, very modest in his ways. I didn't dare ask him to let me do it, and my parents didn't suggest it either. To this day,

---

* A *maska* [literally, something with which to catch] is given and received as an informal agreement that the two parties are planning to write the *kitab*. Like an engagement ring, its social purpose is to show others that the girl is already "caught."

it's the one thing I regret about my wedding. Everything else was fine, perfect.

After the party at my parents' house, a party for the women, I was brought over by the men in Walid's family to his house. That's where they had the men's party. Today, they no longer do it this way, no separate parties. They have one party for everyone. But back then, it was separate. Anyway, the party at Walid's house was enormous. Almost the whole village came because it was right before the elections in the village, and so all the men wanted to make an appearance. Walid and his brothers are important in the village, they were back then too. So, it was a big party. You know, music and dancing—the men doing the *debka*. I was there with some of the women in my family, we sat separately. Well, it went on and on—all afternoon. I could see that Walid was really enjoying it. I enjoyed it too, watching from the side. Really, I did. The only thing I was sorry about was the horse. I had wanted to ride over to Walid's house on the horse, sitting up there looking out at the people in my white dress. But except for that, everything was the way I wanted. Really, it was a fine wedding.

❧

After the wedding we went to live in my mother-in-law's house. No, there weren't honeymoons in those days. Not like today. Look, my daughter Lilian went to Greece with her husband. But that's a new custom. Honeymoons are for today's couples, we didn't have them. You had a few days of privacy at your mother-in-law's house and that was it.

For me, moving in with my mother-in-law was not what I expected. I knew her, sure, she's my aunt. Still, a mother-in-law is a mother-in-law even if she's your aunt. That's what I found out. My aunt, she's a different type than my mother, as different as the earth and the sky. She's more outgoing, she likes to go here and there. After her husband died she started smoking. How many women in Abu Ghosh do *that*? And when we were kids, she used to listen to these romantic dramas on the radio.

My mother would tell her it was an *eib,* that she was going to influence us to listen too—and, of course, we did listen in secret. Oh yes, Jalila was a different type, more open you could say. But, you see, once I moved into her house with Walid, I saw another side of her. My aunt started to take over, she became like a boss. I hadn't expected it. Everything Walid and I did, she had to be in on it. Where we were going, why we were going there, and when we were coming back—she had something to say about it. And money! Walid wasn't making much money in those days, so she was always critical about what we did with our money. She wanted to be the boss of the house, simple as that. I was really offended at first, but I didn't fight back. I decided the best thing was to leave it to Walid. Let him work it out with her, I figured. Yet in the beginning it was hard for me. I swear, with Lilian and the rest of my children, I wouldn't do that. I'm keeping out of things, not like my mother-in-law did.

Walid and I had been married about six months when I got pregnant. I was eighteen when I had Lilian, she's my first. How did I feel about having a girl first? Look, anyone who tells you it makes no difference is not telling the truth. A woman always wants her first to be a boy, even the second. A woman is given more credit if she has sons, that's the way it is in Arab society. Now that Lilian has grown up, I'm glad I had a girl. Daughters stay close to you, sons go off. But you're influenced by those around you. So, naturally, when Lilian was born I was disappointed. I had wanted a boy.

We called her Lilian instead of some Arab name because of Walid's brother, Qasem. Around the time that Lilian was born, Qasem had to break off his relationship with a girl named Lilian. He loved this girl very much, but she was Jewish. Actually, her father was Arab and her mother was Jewish. My mother-in-law opposed this relationship, and when Qasem said he was going to marry the girl, she became enraged. There was a big struggle, and in the end my mother-in-law got her way. Qasem was broken-hearted. So Walid wanted to ease his brother's heart, to do something that would at least keep the name in the family. That's what we did. We called our first Lilian, even though it's not an Arab name. We did it for Qasem.

After Lilian was born, I got pregnant right away. And again it was a girl. This poor child died, though. She got some kind of fever in her brain, and she died when she was one month old. That was her fate, what could we do? Immediately after that I again got pregnant, and this time it was a son—Samir. He's our oldest son, I'm Umm Samir. I'm the one who chose the name. I chose almost all the names after our first. I'd hear a name I liked on one of the television dramas, and I'd pick that. Walid didn't mind, not at all. He's easy about these things. So I picked the names for our sons. That's what I brought after the second girl, just sons. Six sons altogether. I had them all one right after the other, all of them in the hospital. Usually, Hadassah Hospital in Jerusalem. It's a fine place, a very good hospital. By the time I was about thirty years old, I had brought them all. Lilian is our only daughter, and now that she's married there's only boys here. Six boys, Walid, and me.

I brought the first five children when we were living at my mother-in-law's house. The last two I brought when we moved here, where we're living today. My mother-in-law *was* a big help to me with the children, I'll say that. I didn't know much about caring for babies. She told me what to do and I did it. With the first four, we massaged them with olive oil and wrapped them from top to bottom with a cloth. It's the traditional way. I wasn't so sure about this wrapping business, but my mother-in-law talked me into it. She said it was good for their bones and skin. I went along with it. With the last three I didn't do it, even though she was telling me I should. I did it my own way. Diapers alone, that's all. We didn't have Pampers, the diapers you throw away, like the Jews use. We couldn't afford them. So it was a lot of work. I was busy every minute in those years. It wasn't easy, not at all.

But, praise God, they all turned out well, at least so far. They're all good children, every one of them. These days Walid's been doing very well in his construction business, so we're adding onto the house. We've been here twelve years or so, and it's really a bit small for us. Now, each

of the boys will have his own room. It's better that way, right? It's different than when I was growing up, that's for sure.

Really, they're good boys, they deserve the best. They're not spoiled.
Even though they're boys, they sometimes help me out in the house. If
a guest comes, like when you're here, one of them will sometimes bring
the coffee. They're alright in this way. The only thing I wish is that one
or two of them, or all of them, would go off to college. Walid and I
encourage them to do it, but so far nobody has gone. With Lilian too,
we wanted her to go to college. But she couldn't get high enough grades
on her matriculation exam—she couldn't pass the English part—so she
didn't go to college. She wound up working in the clothing factory in
Jerusalem, where Qasem is a supervisor. Some of my younger sisters
worked there too. Lilian hated it, and I don't blame her. A year or so
later she got married, and now she's got two children of her own. She
married her cousin, Hamzi.

⌇

Cousin marriage—what do I think of it? Look, if you ask me, I'll tell
you the truth. It's not a good thing. I mean, my mother did it, I did it,
and so did Lilian, but it's best not to marry a cousin. Usually, I mean.
That's what the doctors say, and they're right. If you marry someone in
your family it can cause problems with the children's health, or their
personalities, or how clever they are. It's better not to marry so close,
even though until recently that's the way it was done. Parents married
their children to first cousins. These days, things are changing. In my
view, it's best to marry someone from outside the clan, even outside the
village. Walid says he doesn't care if it's outside the clan, but it should be
someone from the village. That way, you know better who the person
is. But look, these days the parents don't control it so much. Children
are much freer to choose who they want. Even girls are freer. If a girl
doesn't agree to the groom, she tells her parents "No," and that's it.
Lilian refused the first one who came, and if she hadn't wanted the

second—even though he's my brother's son—she would have refused too. A girl is much freer now, it's better that way.

And these days, the children know much more. They're not ignorant about life like I was when I got married. They learn in school. Today, they teach them about pregnancy and things like that. All my sons know about this. And Lilian knew too, before she got married. No, I didn't talk to her, I didn't tell her anything. She learned in school. And she learned at the clothing factory where she went to work. The women there were always gossiping, so she heard about sex and all that from them. I never discussed it with her, but I could tell before she got married that she knew about these things. I'm close to her—I was before she got married and I still am—so I could tell she wasn't ignorant. Not like I was. It's a different generation now, they're much more aware.

Lilian, she even teaches *me* things. She knows things I don't know. She supports me. Look, she's my only daughter, there's things she understands because she's a woman. Like recently, she was the one who supported me with something, with this problem. I'll tell you what it was. It happened a few months ago. You see, I got pregnant again. For a while I'd been taking pills to avoid getting pregnant, and then the doctor said I should take a break for a few months. I took a break, and I wound up getting pregnant again. It made me very upset. I don't want another. It's not a good thing to bring children after the age of forty. What, I'm going to go with my daughter and her friends to the baby clinic? No, no, not for me. I told my daughter and some of my sisters about it, and my mother found out too. Everyone knew, including my sons. They all told me to go on with it. "Yes, yes, bring another child," my sons said. My sisters said the same, and my mother told me, "Leila, it's *haram* to get rid of it. It's against our religion." The only one who supported me was Lilian. She told me I should go see her doctor, check it out on that ultra-machine, the one that looks like a television. Her doctor said maybe I'm not really pregnant, at my age it might be a "false pregnancy." I don't know about these things, but I knew I was pregnant. I could tell. "So, if you're pregnant, you can abort it at the hospital,"

Lilian said. "You've had enough children. Do what *you* want!" She was the one who sympathized the most with me.

I decided not to go for the abortion, but to do other things instead. I began to work extra hard around the house. I ran up and down the stairs, and I was jumping, jumping, jumping all the time. I also pressed my stomach hard with my hands. Walid knew what I was doing, but all he said to me is, "Leila, you're going to hurt yourself." Well, what happened is that the baby fell out. I miscarried. I wrapped it in a cloth and buried it in our yard, under a tree. Then, I went to the hospital and got cleaned up. And that was it. Nobody says anything about it now. Not my children, not Walid. My mother thinks I miscarried because I was upset about things, that's the way she sees it. Alright, I was upset. True. But now it's over and *khalas,* no more. I'm going to a doctor and get a contraceptive that I can use, one that will work. I don't want any more accidents like this one. No, no. No more pregnancies for me!

⤳

Don't misunderstand me, I like small children. I just don't want more of my own. But taking care of other people's children, doing it as a job—*that's* fine with me. I like it. You know that's what I do, right? I've been doing it for five or six years. The children I take care of now are all from Abu Ghosh. Three of them are my brother Khalil's children. Their mother is sick, she can't be with them now. Frankly, I don't like this arrangement, it was sort of pushed on me. I wish she could take care of them herself. But what can I do? The thing I like, really, is taking care of children *not* in the family, children of mothers who work and need a child caretaker during the day. This is the work I like to do. And it pays well too!

The way I started doing this was a little unusual. I started working with Jewish children. It is unusual, right? I tell you, I wasn't looking to do this work, it happened by accident. What happened is that Walid was involved in some project over in the Jewish settlement, Nataf. Walid gets along real well with everyone, Jews or Arabs, it doesn't matter. Anyway, this family he was doing some building for, the woman—her name is Haya—came to Walid and said, "We have no child caretakers in the settlement that I like. You don't happen to know a good one in Abu Ghosh, do you?" Walid said he would check into it and let her know.

So that evening he comes home and tells me. Actually, he told our neighbor who was sitting with me then. She immediately said she was interested. After she left I got mad at Walid. "Why not ask me?" I said. You see, the idea really struck me as something I wanted to do. All my children were in school by then and I had the time for it. I really wanted to do it. Walid said that since he was a building contractor there, he was embarrassed to suggest me. But I didn't let him get away with that. I pressed him, and finally he agreed. And that's how it started. Haya began bringing her daughter, Miriam, to me.

Haya is an unusual person, one of the Peace Now people, I think. She teaches at Hebrew University, and she used to bring Miriam to me three times a week. I took care of her for about a year. Oh, what a beautiful girl Miriam was! Like the moon. She was about a year and a half old then. I used to wash her, feed her, and take good care of her. I'd feed her our food, Arab food, and she'd eat everything. I'd put her in a little pool we have for children, she loved that. And my children would sometimes play with her too. We spoke Arabic to her. Haya wanted that, she wanted her daughter to learn Arabic. And she did. Haya and I became friendly too. She'd sometimes sit here and talk and eat with us, and sometimes I'd do her hair with henna for her. I really liked her.

During that year Haya began to tell her friends in Nataf about me. She made a real advertising campaign for me. The next thing I knew, others were coming. One, two . . . it got to where I had seven or eight kids from Nataf. They were all good kids, truly they were. There's been so many by now, I forget some of their names. Some would come only for a few hours a week, some came every day. I charged by the hour, four shekels an hour—or by the month, 550 shekels a month. It was good money, sure it was. Walid didn't mind that at all! Although, he's never asked me for an agora. "It's yours, do what you want with it," he tells me. He's very good about it. He even likes having the kids around, that's the way he is.

The one time he got angry, though, was when I made a bad mistake. It was the kind of thing that happens now and then, but I guess because it was with a kid from Nataf it bothered him more. It bothered me, too. What it was is that one of the kids, Smadar, got burned in the face. I was baking something in the oven, and Smadar came running over to me just as I opened it. She caught the oven door in her face, and she got a huge burn mark. I felt horrible. I went running with Smadar to the clinic here, but they were shut because of a strike. I took her to the office of a private doctor, but he wasn't there. I felt shaken up. Walid came in just then and started yelling at me, "Why don't you pay more attention? Why did you let this happen?" When the mother called and told me to send her daughter home that day with a neighbor from Nataf, I said to her, "I'm coming that way, I'll bring her myself." I wanted to talk to her in person. I went with my oldest son, and while we were driving there I had the thought, "They'll say I did it on purpose because the girl's Jewish and I'm Arab." But when we got there, the mother was not like that at all. She was very understanding. She could see the burn wasn't so serious and she said, "Relax, these things happen. It's happened to me too." She was very kind about it, but I felt awful.

These days I'm not working with any kids from Nataf. I think they now have some child caretakers there to bring their children to. I'm still in touch with some of the mothers and their children. Once in a while they drop by and say hello. Haya came here a few months ago with Miriam, I hadn't seen her in years. "This is Leila, she's the one who raised you," Haya told her. Miriam was a little shy with me at first, but she warmed up after a while. It was good to see her again. She's still a beautiful child, still like the moon.

I no longer have Jewish kids here who I take care of. Only Arab children from the village. That's too bad, really. I'd like to work with Jewish and Arab children together. That would be good. Maybe it'll happen. Like I said, I still have a good relationship with some people in Nataf. Though, you know, a while back one of my sons said something that shocked me. Maybe he was upset about something that day, I don't know. He said, "Those kids you've taken care of—the Jewish boys—one day they're going to be soldiers." I answered, "Yes, so?" I wasn't sure what he was getting at. And he went on, "Someday you're going to pass a checkpoint and one of them is going to stop you and say, 'Give me your identity card!'" I told him, "Listen, by the time they grow up, we're going to have peace here. And besides, they'd recognize me. Nothing like that will happen." That's what I told him, but I admit that when I thought about it more, it upset me. I mean, if such a thing ever was to happen it would hurt me, of course it would. I'm not saying that thinking about this has changed my mind about taking care of Jewish children. I loved those kids, and some of their parents were wonderful. I can't change the politics here, can I? Yet, sometimes you realize that it's all pretty awful, an awful situation to raise children in—ours and theirs.

◢

For me, politics isn't something I think about very much. Even though it's something that affects us all, I'm not very interested in it. I vote, yes. I supported Meretz* in the last election. Walid and I both did. They're the best, I think. They're the ones who are helping to bring the Arabs and Jews together, and the ones who are helping bring about peace. I supported them. So far, I think they're doing a good job.

It looks to me like there's going to be peace. If there is, it'll be good for the Arabs here in Israel. We Israeli Arabs used to get along much better with the Jews before 1967. Since then—and especially since the

---

* In the 1992 elections to the 120-member Knesset, Meretz won 12 seats (one of which an Arab occupies). It is the major coalition partner with the Labor party and, unlike the Labor party, supports the creation of a Palestinian state in Gaza and the West Bank.

Intifada—things have gotten bad between us and the Jews. We used to have relations with them, we'd visit each other on holidays. Now, hardly at all. We used to go wherever we wanted, with nobody stopping us for our identity cards. Now, they stop us. They're suspicious of us. This is no good. No good for us or them.

I'm not saying I'm against the Intifada. It *did* bring some results. Now, it begins to look like there's going to be a settlement. They've already given back Gaza and Jericho, and soon they'll give back more. At least, that's what they say. Look, I'm not a politician. I don't know exactly how the land here should be divided. But it has to be divided fairly. The Jews say it all belongs to them and their grandfathers. The Arabs say it's all theirs, it belonged to their grandfathers. So we have to make a division, a compromise. Let there be a Palestinian state on the West Bank and in Gaza, and a Jewish state here. That's fair, no? We in Abu Ghosh will stay here in the Jewish state. What, we're going to move over there? No, this is our village, our home. Our lives are good here, we'll all stay.

But let's finish this thing. Let's make a *sulha* and stop all the killing. A mother is a mother whether she's Jewish or Palestinian, all mothers hurt the same. So, *khalas,* let's make peace. That's what I want. And the way it looks now, it's going to happen. God willing, it will. That's what I think.

Umm Khaled

While most of the population of Abu Ghosh fled the village in 1948 to become refugees in Jordan, Umm Khaled and her family wound up where they had been before—in their four-room house in the center of the village, next to the monastery. All the other Arab villages lying within the Jerusalem corridor had been destroyed: Abu Ghosh was now surrounded by Jewish settlements. Umm Khaled and her husband went on raising their family within the cocoon of their village, adjusting, as best they could, to their new and uncertain status as Arabs in the state of Israel.

In this section Umm Khaled takes up her account of life in Abu Ghosh—from the period just after the 1948 war until the present. During this time her family increased from six to fifteen children (her oldest son died); almost all of them married and are now raising their own children in Abu Ghosh. With a clear eye she regards her family and reflects on some of the struggles, political and otherwise, they have endured over the last forty-five years.

❧

W hen the war ended in 1948 we were back in our house and my husband was still working in the monastery's fields. Because my husband had this job, we didn't lack for food. Cabbages, cauliflower, lettuce, plums, apricots, grapes—we had it all. Others in the village looked at us with an envious eye. Some of them had little to eat, and they had to go looking for work with the Jews. This was a hard time, believe me.

For us the hard part was not that we were hungry. We had enough to eat. But we were suffering from the loss of our families, our relatives. Most had fled and weren't able to sneak back, this way or that. We felt like part of our body had been taken away from us. Now and then, someone would work out their papers and get back. Like my two sisters and their families. My parents, though, didn't come back until just before the 1967 war. And my mother-in-law didn't get back here until after that war. By then so much time had passed, so many things had happened—but look, we had to go on without them. That was our fate, what else could we do?

Me, I kept bringing children. That was my fate, I kept getting a stomach. Twenty-one stomachs I had. I brought Muhsen, my sixth, during the 1948 war, and after that I brought the rest. My mother-in-law was no longer around to help me with the little ones. My two oldest daughters, Khawla and Zahira, helped me until they got married. And after that the younger girls helped out. That's the way I managed it. But I swear, it was easier raising children when I did than it is today. Sure, I had no washing machine with all the buttons, I had to wash clothes by hand in a bucket. No fancy stove either, for years I cooked over a fire. Still, I say it was easier then. Children didn't wear you out like they do today. When I cooked a meal the children ate—no complaints. Today, a mother cooks a meal and the children say, "No, I want a pizza. No, I want a hot dog." We didn't have any meat back then, we were poorer, much poorer, but we felt better. And if you ask me, the children grew up better. They weren't so hard to raise like today's children.

After I brought my tenth child—I don't know if you've heard this—I got some kind of paper that you hang on the wall from the Israeli government. The head of the government, Ben-Gurion, sent me this paper congratulating me for having ten children. Umm Issa and I were the only ones to get it in Abu Ghosh. And there was a check too, for 100 pounds, which was good money in those days. No, I never hung the paper on the wall. It's still in the closet. But the 100 pounds was good to have, really a fine surprise.

I'll tell you the truth, though. To have so many children, ten or more, is too much. It's hard on the woman. After she's had four, it starts to weaken her. Look at me today, I'm too weak sometimes to even get up and fix myself something to eat. I tell you, too many children is not good for the woman. Abu Khaled, blessed be his memory, wanted a big family. He was the only son, he wanted more and more children. So we kept having more. Some women told me that as long as I was breast-feeding I wouldn't get pregnant. I used to breastfeed for a long time, day and night. Maybe a year for the girls, and two years for the boys. I got pregnant anyway, so I don't believe that breastfeeding stops you from getting pregnant. For me it didn't work that way. I kept getting one stomach after another.

I brought most of the children at home, not in the hospital. After Khawla, my first, I brought them here in the village. There was a mid-wife here, a woman who didn't have any children of her own. She wasn't trained, but she knew her work. She did it because she was generous and she wanted to help out in this way. I never had to pay her for it. Later, after Leila—no, after Maysa—I started going to the hospital. This was about in 1960, and it was easier to get to the hospital quickly. So the last five or six I brought in the hospital in Jerusalem, one hospital or another.

I never lost one at birth, I was lucky in that. One of my daughters, Maysa—the first Maysa—died a few months after I brought her. We gave her name to the one who came after her. I wanted to keep the name even though we lost the baby. My husband went along with it. Usually, he and I decided together on the name, sometimes it was his idea and sometimes it was mine. Most of the time we named the children after someone in his family—his father or mother—or someone in my family. Khaled, our oldest son, is named after his father. My poor son, God bless his memory, died when he was eighteen years old. He had a bad heart, some kind of infection in the pipes of his heart. We took him to a German woman doctor in a Jewish settlement near here, and she gave us medicine. But we couldn't save him. He left us. My husband decided to call our son who was born after Khaled died by the same name. This time he didn't consult with me. He went and gave the officials the name Khaled. I was very upset by this. I couldn't call my new son by Khaled's name. It saddened me too much. I called him Khalil instead, and that's how we call him in the family, though in his identity card he's called Khaled, the way Abu Khaled registered him.

Besides Khaled and Maysa—the first Maysa—I lost four others before they were born. I miscarried four times, all girls I was told. Do I remember? Oh yes, each one. They all went between the third and fifth month. Always there was something that happened just before I miscarried. One time was when I went to bake *imtabbaq* [a type of blintze]. I walked to the oven with the dough on my head like a *fellaha*. I wasn't used to it and it tired me out and my back gave way. I began bleeding and that was it, I miscarried. Another time, I miscarried shortly after my mother had this accident. We were in the yard, I was doing the wash and suddenly I saw her fall and crack her head on the ground. Seeing her lie there in all this blood shocked me, and soon after that I miscarried. A third time, it was right after my father died. I had stopped eating for a couple of days, and I took two aspirin, and with all the hunger and sadness, I miscarried. The fourth miscarriage came after my daughter Khawla got engaged. I didn't agree to this groom. My husband didn't consult with me, he left me on the side. The rage I felt caused me to miscarry, I'm sure of it.

So that was it, four miscarriages. Together with Khaled and Maysa, I lost six. Fifteen are left, praise God. They're all grown up now and they have their own children. I don't really know how many grandchildren I have, maybe one hundred or so. And maybe thirty great-great-grandchildren. Fate has been kind to our family. Abu Khaled was one son—and now look! God be praised.

ط

Sometime after I had brought Leila, and after her, Hasan, my husband
got arrested. This was about 1955. The thing he got arrested for was
not something he did, but they took him anyway. What happened was
this. Somebody placed a bomb just outside a Jewish school not far from
here. The ones who did it must have been people from the village who
were collaborating with the Jewish police. They wanted to have a reason
to get rid of some of the important men in the village. My husband
wasn't a political man, but he came from an important clan and he had
a fine reputation. So, what happened was that as soon as the bomb ex-
ploded, police came rushing to the village. They surrounded our house,
broke in, and started looking here and there for evidence. They took
little things and made big accusations out of them. But what could they
prove? My husband was a religious man, he prayed and fasted. There is
no way in the world he would have done a thing like that. Well, there
was a trial for my husband and three others who were important political men in the village. No real proof was brought against them, so they
didn't keep them in jail. Instead, they banned them from the village for
six months.* All were sent out of the area to live in other Arab villages,
each one to a different village. My husband was sent north to Baqa al-
Gharbiya.

He was there only four months, not six. But for me, it was like four
years. Right after it happened I went to the wife of the president of Israel
to request that she do something. Khawla's husband advised me to do
this. He went to a lawyer, and the lawyer wrote up a letter that I brought
along with me. I also brought all my children. The president's wife didn't
speak any Arabic, so I couldn't talk to her. I gave her the letter. She said
she couldn't get my husband back, but she said something about trying

* Banishment—temporary or permanent—was a punishment meted out to
Arabs who committed political offenses, or were otherwise politically problematic
for the Israeli government.

to help us with money. That wasn't what I really wanted, and anyway, she didn't help us that way either. I heard that she did send some kind of inspector to the village to find out about us. He went to the grocery store to see if we were in debt. Only two days before I had paid our bill, so they told the inspector, "The family of Abu Khaled owes us nothing." I never got one agora from the president's wife. Nothing.

I did get to see my husband when he was in Baqa al-Gharbiya. I went twice. You had to get special permission from the police to go there. Back then, Arabs were not able to travel around Israel whenever they wanted. To go out of your area you had to have a permit.* I went both times with one of the men in the family and stayed a few days. My husband was managing fine there. The people in the village realized he wasn't guilty at all and that he was a good, religious man. Every day he was invited to someone else's house as a guest. He was living in a room of the house of a widow who had a son. This poor woman had just lost her daughter. The girl was killed in an accident right before she was supposed to be married. Having my husband there to look after helped her take her mind off things. She cooked for him, washed his clothes, fetched water so he could bathe and wash for prayers. She was good to him. My husband could have just sat around doing nothing—I think that's what the others did who were expelled—but he chose to work. He fixed an olive press they had in the village, and he ran it for them. He was good at those things. They stuffed money in his pockets for this work. He didn't want to take it, but they stuffed it in anyway. They really liked him. Later, a few months after my husband returned to Abu Ghosh, we went back to Baqa al-Gharbiya to express our gratitude to all the people. Especially to the poor woman who lost her daughter and

---

* After the 1948 war until 1966, all the major areas of Arab population were placed under the authority of the Israeli military government; travel between various districts in Israel required special permits. This regulation was strenuously applied against the Arab population in the first years after the war.

took such good care of my husband. Poor thing. She was still in a bad way. She had no husband. My heart went out to her.

❧

My husband returned to his work at the monastery, and things went on just like before. We continued to manage. Working in the monastery's fields gave us enough to eat, but still we had to have cash money for other things—clothes, shoes, medicine, lots of things. *Zalmati** wasn't getting paid enough for all of this. So my sons also had to go to work. Abu Khaled pulled Issa out of school after sixth grade to work in a cement factory, and Ibrahim and Hasan, too, left after eighth grade to work. That's how we were able to afford things. My youngest son, Khalil, could have gone to school, but *he* didn't want to. A teacher hit him in first grade, and he never went back. I tried to convince him to return, but he always refused. He works now as a waiter.

My older daughters never went out to work, they stayed at home helping me until they got married. They went to school a few years, third grade or sixth grade. Only my younger daughters went until high school, and then a few of them—Majda, Nadia, Butheina—went to work in a clothing factory in Jerusalem. We didn't need their money then, so they kept it for themselves to buy clothes or whatever. That was fine with me. Did I want them to go to college? No, I didn't. High school was good enough. I didn't want them leaving the village to study. Going to work at the clothing factory was alright, one of my sister Jalila's sons is a boss there. But if they went to the university, maybe they could get in trouble, maybe rumors would be spread about them. You know how it is. A girl raises her arm to scratch herself, and someone who sees her thinks she's waving to the man across the street. I didn't want this to happen to my daughters. So I say, better to get married after high school. I know you

---

* *Zalmati* [my fellow] is an affectionate expression by which Umm Khaled occasionally refers to her husband.

probably don't agree with me, you're college-educated yourself, and I know and respect your family. Yet we had ten daughters, and I say, better for them that they got married without going to college. If a woman has a good husband and she brings a few children, boys and girls, that's the best thing for her. She doesn't need to go to college for this, right?

The problem is, you don't always find a good husband. It depends on what your fate is. People think they can arrange it to go the way they want, but everyone has her own fate. God alone decides, not us. We try to choose good husbands for our daughters, but it's God who decides how it's going to be. In our family, some of my daughters had a good fate, and some not. Most did alright, but I'll admit it, some of my daughters didn't do so well with their husbands.

Majda, she's the one who really had a bad fate. And that happened even though we married her to someone we knew, a cousin. This cousin turned out to be a drinker and someone who roams around at night. Majda is always alone with her children. She looks terrible, she's so thin she looks like she's at death's edge. Her husband wastes their money. I had given her two gold bracelets as a wedding present, special bracelets that my father once gave me. Well, Majda never wore them. I wondered why, and then my husband and I figured it out. Her husband must have taken them and sold them. I tell you, I'd prefer it if she never got married at all rather than wind up with one like him.

With Leila, she married a cousin too, and she's had a good fate. I admit that I was against this marriage. Not because of Walid, her husband. But I didn't want Leila getting married right *then*. Her two older sisters, Zahira and Rana, hadn't married yet. That's not the way to do things. The older ones should go first. Others were pushing for this marriage. Walid was very insistent, and he got my mother to do his bidding for him. Even my sister Jalila wasn't for it. But my mother took over, and that was it. The decision was taken out of our hands. They signed the *kitab* before Leila was of legal age. It wasn't the right thing to do, but they did it anyway. Now, if you ask me, I have to admit that it worked out fine. Leila has had a good fate. Walid has been an excellent husband

and their children are all good. No problems. Leila knows how to raise children, she's very warm with them. She's even taken to raising other people's children, she's made a job out of it. I told her not to do it. Better to give her time to Walid and her own children. Yet she's done it her own way. From what I can see, she's doing fine. She and Walid are a good couple. I wish all my daughters had a good marriage like hers.

With my sons, I didn't get into it much. Abu Khaled took care of things. Mostly my sons have done alright, praise God. The one time I got into it was the time with Issa. He was the first of my sons to get married. This was shortly after the war in 1967. Issa told us that he wanted to marry outside the village. He told me to find him someone from East Jerusalem. The reason he wanted this was because he was *ikhweh fi al-ridaah* with too many girls in the village. You know what that is, don't you? You see when Issa was a baby, I wasn't able to breast-feed him. I was too upset at the time. One of my brothers, Marwan, had just drowned. I was so upset, no milk was coming out. So I had some other women in the village breastfeed him for a while. My husband was enraged at me afterwards because if you suck at the breast of someone who isn't your mother, then—this is according to our religion—that mother's children become *ikhweh fi al-ridaah*. They're like your own brothers and sisters, you can't marry together.* So, you see, Issa had too many "sisters" in the village, and for that reason he wanted me to find someone outside. I tried to help him. I went back to East Jerusalem and looked up families I had known when I was a girl. They sent me to houses where there were candidates, and I'd go there and drink coffee and talk with the girl and look her over. With the ones I liked, the parents refused for one reason or another. One family told me frankly, "We won't let our daughters marry anyone in Israel." This was only a little after the Six-Day War, you could understand it. In the end, I wasn't

---

* According to the Koran (Sura 4:22), children who have suckled from the same breast are forbidden to marry.

able to arrange anything for Issa. He had to marry a girl from here in the village, someone from our clan who was a few years younger than him and with whom he wasn't *ikhweh fi al-ridaah*. It worked out fine, they have nine children. That was his fate, you see. Even though I tried to work out something else, it didn't happen. Issa's fate was to marry in the village, and that's what happened.

⁂

The war in 1967—you want to know about that? Alright, I'll tell you. You probably don't remember. You were too young when it happened, right? Besides, nothing much happened here in the village. It wasn't like what happened over in Jerusalem or in the West Bank. *There* is where the war was. The people over there were the ones who suffered.

My mother, praise God, was no longer over there when the war started. We had brought her and my father back to Abu Ghosh in 1965. My father died after that, about a year later. It had taken us until 1965 to finally work out their papers, and then we brought them back through the Red Cross. No, it wasn't possible to visit with them between 1948 and 1965. They were over in the West Bank—you couldn't get there and they couldn't come her. My father was living off the pension he got from the English, and also there was some money coming from the English because my brothers had died when they were with the police. That was all they had, my father didn't work. They told us about this when they returned. While they were over there we didn't know about them. We did manage to see them once—from the distance, in Beit Safafa. This was in 1963 or 1964, during the Big Feast. Do you know how Beit Safafa was then? It was divided in two, one side in Jordan and one side in Israel, and with a fence on each side and a barrier in the middle. We heard that some Abu Ghosh people were coming to the Jordanian side of Beit Safafa on that holiday, and my husband and I went there hoping to see some of our relatives. His mother didn't come, but my parents were there with one of my sisters. My other sister had married, she didn't come. We shouted back and forth for about a half-hour. You could hardly hear each other. The place was full of people shouting, and police were all around. I felt terrible not being able to get closer. What could you do? I took off two gold bracelets I was wearing, they were thick and braided and worth a lot. I wrapped them in a scarf and heaved them. I shouted, "One is for you, mother, and one is for my mother-in-law." Praise God, they cleared both fences and landed at her feet. She took them, and that was it. The next time we saw them was when they returned to Abu Ghosh to live. I'm glad my father got to come back to Abu Ghosh before he died. He's buried here in the old cemetery. If they hadn't made it back then, my father, blessed be his memory, would never have seen the village again. After the Six-Day War would have been too late for him.

Anyway, you want to know how the Six-Day War was in Abu Ghosh, right? Well, it turned out to be nothing, but before it started we were all very scared. We remembered the 1948 war, and this had us worried. This time we knew what was happening. Everyone had a radio and some of us had televisions. We listened to all the talk, and we knew a big war was coming. We took all our money and bought supplies—flour, rice, sugar, fruit juices to drink, and chocolates and candies for the children if they started crying. We loaded up. We protected ourselves by covering the windows with sacks of flour and placing sacks of cement in front of the doors. And we even took two or three of our youngest children and put them in the storage room downstairs, where they slept on mattresses. We said to ourselves, "If the rest of us are killed by bombs, maybe these small ones will stay alive down there." I'm telling you, we were scared. We buried ourselves alive in our houses, waiting and waiting for the war to come. Then one morning it came. People outside began shouting, "War, war, war—it's coming now!" But, as soon as it came, it was over. What was it—five days, right? There was no shooting, no bombing, nothing here. In five days the Jews had beaten all the Arab countries, and that was it. Later, we found out how bad the war had been on the other side. Here in Abu Ghosh it was quiet, quiet. Nobody suffered a scratch in the village.

As soon as the war ended, *fathat al-dunya* [the world opened]. All of a sudden, we were able to go over to the Arab side, and our relatives were able to come here. We were living in our new house then, this one we're sitting in today. It's bigger than the old one we had in the center of the village. We had finished building it a few months before the war started. There's an upstairs and downstairs, more than four bedrooms. It's a good thing we had all this space, too. All our relatives from over there came, all the ones living on the West Bank. Those in Jordan couldn't come. We went ourselves to Nablus to get my mother-in-law who was ill. We brought her back here to live with us. Our other relatives came for visits—my husband's sisters, our aunts and uncles, our cousins. They came for weeks, months. I swear, after the 1967 War our house was filled with guests all the time. No matter how much food we cooked, it went immediately. Potful after potful of soup, rice. Half a sheep one day, a box of fish another day. It kept going on and on like that. They were our guests and we treated them right. But to tell you the truth, there was something about it that I didn't like. We began to get the feeling that our guests, our relatives, wanted to squeeze out of us what they could. We felt they were looking at us not in the right way, that they were thinking what belonged to us was partly *theirs*. They had left in 1948 and lost everything. Where they went, they didn't do so well. Not as well as we did. We still had our houses, our property and our land—*some* of our land. They envied us. No matter how much we fed them or bought them presents, it never seemed to satisfy them. Really, that's the truth.

When the visits stopped, finally, it didn't leave us with the feeling of wanting to go visit them immediately. Eventually we went, but not as much as you might think. More often, we'd go over to the West Bank by ourselves, to do things over there by ourselves. *Fathat al-dunya,* we wanted to see what was over there. Me, I went shopping over there. Cheap! I tell you, the prices were nothing compared to what we were paying here. It's the same today. Everything on the West Bank costs much less. I went over there right after the war and bought huge quantities. Sacks of meat, rolls of cloth, and boxes full of shoes for all the children. I continued going, at least once a month. For Butheina's wedding, I bought all the clothing, and even the white bridal dress over there. It was only 500 shekels, in Tel Aviv it would have been maybe 4,000. The quality was a little better in Tel Aviv, but that's some difference in price, isn't it? I swear, for us it was a good thing, it helped us out a lot being able to buy over there.

Oh yes, there were other reasons it was good for us that we could go to the West Bank and to East Jerusalem. You know, two of my daughters married men from over there, Nadia and Muna. Nadia lives over in the Old City, not far from where I grew up. She did very well, her husband is a fine man. But Muna's marriage isn't so good. They live with her mother-in-law and her husband's brother's family over in Al-Ram, just outside Jerusalem. They all live in the same house. Her mother-in-law controls all of them, and Muna's life is hard. What can you do? That was her fate. I tell her for the sake of the children she should stay strong, she shouldn't leave. Where's she going to go, back here? No, she has to stay. Maybe things will get better.

Maysa, she also married someone from over there, but he came to live in Abu Ghosh. His family is from here originally, but he grew up over in the West Bank. He's a good one, I don't know how he puts up with the situation—you know, Maysa is not well. I don't want to go into all of it, but after she brought her children she had some problems. Her thinking wasn't right, she wasn't able to manage at home. We went to some doctors here, but when that didn't work we decided to get some help for her over there. What kind of help? Well, we took her to a *sheikha* over in Artas, near Bethlehem. There're a lot of these healers over in the West Bank, and some are very good. I don't know if you believe in these things, but I do. I've seen things, oh yes, I have. I believe these healers can help. Especially sometimes when the doctors can't do anything. Like with Maysa, and like with my granddaughter Nabila. We took her too when we went. Nabila had this shaking in her arm and shoulder, she got it after a dog barked at her. She'd shake and shake, she couldn't stop sometimes. So we took both of them, Maysa and Nabila.

When we got to the *sheikha* she was busy, but she agreed to work with us. She was a young *sheikha,* only fifteen years old maybe. She was plump and white with a pretty face. I asked her, "Where did you learn what you do?" She answered, "I don't know how to read or write, but *they* do the writing for me." I asked her, "Who's *they?*" She said, "I have some helpers, some men, who speak to me in my head and give me instructions." The *sheikha's* mother-in-law was in the room with her, and she said, "Really, we didn't want her to do this, but she's got a gift for it." The mother-in-law—we heard this later—was a greedy one, she liked all the gifts and money the *sheikha* received. Anyway, the *sheikha* said to us, "Someone has performed some black magic on your daughter, they've put a curse on an apple tree. That's why she's been sick. She needs to come here four times." After that, she turned to my granddaughter and took care of her. She gave her mother a piece of paper with some writing on it and told her to dissolve it in water and then wash Nabila's arm with the water. If there was any leftover water, she said, that had to be spilled out in a clean place like in the garden, not down the drain. She also gave her mother a second bottle of water for the girl to drink. Well, they did all this, and you know, my granddaughter got better. Nabila doesn't shake anymore. The *sheikha* really helped her. It's amazing, isn't it? But, what happened with Maysa is that when we went back the second time to see the *sheikha,* she wasn't there. She was dead. They had killed her. Because of all the money her mother-in-law was taking in, people got envious. Some people from the village, or who knows where, killed this poor girl *sheikha.*

After that, we took Maysa to another *sheikha* in Nablus. She, too, said that a curse had been put on Maysa. "Who's the one who wanted to marry your daughter before her present husband?" When she asked this I had to stop and think. Then I remembered and told her, "Her cousin wanted to marry her but it wasn't fated to be." The *sheikha* said to us,

"Some woman has put a curse on your daughter." The *sheikha* gave us a *hejab** for Maysa and told us to come back once again. But when we got home, Maysa threw away the *hejab,* she refused to wear it. And to this day she's still suffering. We don't take her back to the *sheikha*s any more, even though there are some good ones over there. *Khalas.* Only God knows what my poor daughter's fate is going to be now.

2

These days we don't go over to the West Bank very much anymore. I still do a little shopping in Ramallah once in a while, but that's it. We don't go around visiting, or anything else. Not since the Intifada. At the beginning of the Intifada we got attacked once. In Nablus. We were on our way to buy *kenafeh* [a sweet cheese pastry] in Nablus, it's very good there. I was with my daughter Zahira and my son Ibrahim and his wife. Because we were driving an Israeli car, a car with yellow license plates, we got stoned. It scared us. We turned around quickly and came right back to Abu Ghosh. Since then, we go over to the West Bank much less. Who wants to get stoned, right?

If you ask me, I'll tell you frankly—I'm against this Intifada. We've had none of this stone throwing or Intifada here in Abu Ghosh, I'm glad for that. *Haram!* I don't agree with killing people, not these and not those. When I see on television or hear on the radio that someone got killed, it bothers me. It doesn't matter to me who it is, I'm against it. It's not God's way for innocent people to be killed. *Haram,* I swear. What we need here is peace, not killing. Right now, they are trying to make a *sulha,* Israel and the Arabs. That's good. Anyone who's against that is wrong. On television I see some people who are against peace, Jews and

---

* A *hejab* [literally, a veil or protective covering] consists of a piece of paper with Koranic phrases or symbolic markings. Typically, a traditional healer will give an *hejab* to a client with instructions to wear or carry it in an amulet, or to immerse it in drinking or bathing water, or to burn it and smear the blessed ashes on the skin.

Arabs. They're wrong. The Muslims who are against it, the Hamas people, they're wrong. To make a *sulha* is good. Why shouldn't we?

How long this is going to take, I don't know. Who knows? Only God. Maybe one year, maybe five, maybe fifteen. In the future there'll be peace. It can't keep going on like this, I don't think so. God willing, it will change. In our family, everyone is hoping for peace. We believe in making a *sulha*. Abu Khaled, he thought the same. He was a man of religion, against war. He had no involvement in politics. That wasn't his way, it isn't mine.

⌇

Abu Khaled left us six years ago. It doesn't seem that long, but it is. The days go by fast. Yes, that's his picture up on the wall. It was taken after we went on the *hajj*. That's him, that's how he looked—always with his white cap on. I swear, he was a good man, a special man. He loved his children and was never bored by them. He was someone with patience. He had worked with the monks, he was calm like them. Sometimes I'd ask my daughters and their children to go home already, or I'd discourage them from visiting. *Zalmati,* he was the opposite. He always wanted them to come, and when they were here he wanted them to stay longer. What a good man he was! God bless his memory.

He left us suddenly. He wasn't in the hospital or sick for a long while. He just went. He had strong stomach pains and he was urinating blood. This had happened before when he was tired or angry. I gave him some tea with *miramiya* [wild sage] to drink, and we thought it would pass by. When it didn't, we called the ambulance. On the way to the hospital he threw up, his tongue came out of his mouth, and he went.

We came back home. We washed him here. A man came and read the Koran. He was buried in the new graveyard up on the hill. My parents and brothers are in the old graveyard in the center of the village. I swear, I've never been to my husband's grave. Not my parents' either. It's permissible to go, but I've just never gone. Do I still keep things of his? A few things, very few. I gave away his clothes to the poor, and my children took his Korans—he had a few of them—and his prayer beads. I just have his picture that's up there on the wall, and also some old papers and a diary he kept when he was younger. I can't read these things. But I know that some of these papers—they're half-eaten by mice now—say that the ninety dunams down by Emwas belongs to him. And the diary, I really don't know what's in it. A little while back I asked my youngest son, Khalil, to read some of it to me. What was written there was something about this cow we used to have—when she got pregnant, when she brought a calf, what she ate, things like that. There was also something there from when he was twenty-one or twenty-two years old, but Khalil didn't read it to me. But look, who needs to read these things to remember him? I don't. He was a special man, I remember him every day. We were together more than fifty years, we had a good life together, and we had a good family. Fate was kind to me. God bless his memory.

Since he went, I've stayed here in the house with our youngest daughter, Suhad. Suhad's not married yet, and she probably won't get married either. She's twenty-seven now, I think it's too late. What do you think, Rafiqa? You're educated, maybe you'll meet someone educated who's older. Suhad, she only finished high school. She has this store on the first floor of the house, you know. She sells these household things that she brings from Tel Aviv. It's a way of making some money, she doesn't have to ask her brothers for anything. Besides working in the store, Suhad helps me in the house. Really, I couldn't manage without her. When my throat hurts, she makes me a drink of milk, egg, and honey. If I have some problem at night, she's got a telephone right in her room. She watches over me. Without her, I might have been dead already. Suhad's the one who is keeping me alive. I swear, God gave her to me as a present in order to help me now. That's what I think. And you know, it was Abu Khaled who insisted I have still another. What was I when Suhad was born—forty-five years old? I got a stomach and I had another child, even though I didn't want another.

It's *haram* to get rid of a baby once you have a stomach. What Leila wanted to do, it's forbidden. She got a stomach, and she started talking about how she didn't want it, and maybe she was going to do something to get rid of it. I told her, "Leila, it's forbidden, you must go on with it." Walid told her the same. Then, what happened is that she had a miscarriage. I don't know exactly how it happened, but it must have been because she was upset. She's busy taking care of Khalil's children these days. Khalil's wife is sick, so the three girls are staying with Leila. Leila doesn't really want that, and then she got a stomach too. It was too much for her. She miscarried. Yet, at least, she didn't go have something done. *Haram,* I tell you. Who knows who the baby would be? Maybe the baby would have been a present to Leila in her old age, like Suhad is for me. God alone knows. God alone decides.

For me, I'm glad I have Suhad. She will care for me until the end. I've also got two of my grandchildren who are coming to live here. They're going to live on the floor downstairs, next to Suhad's store, as soon as they're married. Jamal is Issa's son, and Amal is Rana's daughter. They're cousins. They'll be a good couple, I'm sure. I arranged this marriage. Jamal was always very close to me and Abu Khaled. He used to help us out a lot as a boy, and my husband put money away for him in the bank. I suggested to Jamal that he marry Amal, and he went along with it. They're getting married in September, and then they'll move in.

So, there's going to be a few more people around. That's good. I don't know how many more years I have left, but it will be good to have my grandchildren here, along with Suhad. I want to stay here in this house until the end of my time, in Abu Khaled's house. I feel good here. It's nice up here on the top of Abu Ghosh, isn't it, Rafiqa? You've been here all your life, right? It's a good place to live, good air. And you can see the whole village from up here. Abu Ghosh is a place blessed by God, don't you think?

EPILOGUE

To begin these closing remarks and introduce myself to the reader, I would like to describe an event that happened when I was two years old. I do not remember this event, but over the years my grandmother and parents retold it enough times that it became well established—branded, you could say—in my brain.

What happened was this. I was hospitalized in Jerusalem with a high fever, and I stayed there for several weeks. My parents were unable to visit every day since my father was busy as a construction worker, and my mother was also busy at home with my two brothers and two sisters. One day the mailman arrived with a letter written in Hebrew. The mailman could not read Hebrew much more than my parents, and so he read, "Your daughter has died, please come and get the corpse." My parents fell into shock and grief, and my father's mother went to calm them by saying, "Praise God that He chose to take a daughter, and not one of the sons!" My parents came to fetch my body. I greeted them with the joy of a two-year old who was not aware of her supposed fate. We returned to Abu Ghosh with me dressed in a new red dress and red shoes that my parents bought me along the way. And my grandmother, who had been preparing things at home for my burial, was amazed to see her granddaughter reborn.

Over the years I heard this story many times, and it came to have a special meaning for me. As regards my grandmother, I was often unkind to her. For years every request she made of me—for example, to bring her a glass of water—I'd remind her, "And who would be doing this for you now, if I, *the girl,* had died?" This was unfair. After all, my poor grandmother was not entirely to blame for her attitudes. The society she lived in led her to believe that girls are not as valuable as boys. It was Arab society, my society, that made my grandmother think it better that one like her should die rather than one of the other, fairer, sex. My poor grandmother went to her grave believing this, and while I have not ac-knowledged her in the book's dedication, I am sure today that she is as responsible for my wanting to do this book as anyone else I knew.

◢

Most women born in our society have similar stories, or ones much worse. The six women in this book all had to deal with the problem of being regarded as inferior because they are women. As their stories make clear, each responds to this problem in her own way, each with her own mixture of acceptance and rebellion. As we compare the stories of the mothers and daughters, the point that stands out for me is the huge, almost revolutionary, change that has taken place in our society since the time of my grandmother and, alongside it, just how far we have to go until inequality between the sexes disappears in all its forms.

In the introduction we outlined some of the main shifts that have occurred for women in the areas of education, work, and personal free-dom. What I would like to add here are some personal thoughts on these matters. Let me start with the area of education. It *is* true that today's women are far more educated than their mothers, and there can be no doubt that this development has caused, and will continue to cause, much stress in our society. Someone not born and raised in Arab society may find it hard to understand how deep the belief was—and in many places, still is—that men are the ones who know, and women are the ones who are ignorant. It is painful to see in our small sample how pervasive this thought is among the mothers (though Umm Abdullah, the youngest of the mothers, has started to fight against it). And it is encouraging to see that within the two college-educated women (Marianne and Samira) a new awareness has taken place. These women assume that they know about the world, about life, as much as men know—in some instances, even more.

It was a rewarding experience for me to feel how grateful the older women in this book seemed to be that somebody saw fit to ask about their lives. *They* knew that they had led interesting lives, but the idea that their stories might be worthy of putting in a book was not something they could imagine. I feel honored to have the possibility of bearing these stories, and I only wish that in translation we could catch the full richness of their colloquial storytelling styles. As for the daughters— particularly Marianne and Samira—they were not surprised that someone would want to put their ideas in a book. Both have a familiarity with books, and furthermore each felt she had something worth saying to a larger, anonymous, audience.

Education, and especially college education, has given Palestinian women a greater sense of authority, no doubt about it. The experience of leaving the family and going to college is one that opens women's eyes. Each girl who leaves her home to go to college offers a model for others who follow. In my village I was one of the first to go, and now most of my nieces are either going to college or thinking of going. The gap between us and those who do not go to college—for example, Leila—is profound. But I have seen that the increase in self-confidence in those of us who have gone to college has also benefited our sisters who have stayed at home. In a general way, they have benefited from our increased status. Leila is a person with strong opinions, and—to her mother's discomfort—she does not hold back from stating them to her husband. In the era of the mothers, such expressions were considered an *eib*. In this respect, we *have* come a long way.

The problem I see now is that women's growing educational status has not yet brought about sufficient gains in their status within the family. In short, women are still expected to be housewives and mothers in all the traditional ways, even if they are working full-time jobs outside the house. I know that in the West women struggle with this problem too, but they have already won battles that we have yet to fight. In Palestinian society, men rarely share with their wives in taking care of small children and in housework—as Samira and her husband do. Leila is far more typical of village women, and Marianne (a city woman who is not yet married) still takes it for granted that she will be the "homemaker." I think we are a generation or two away from real change in this area, though it does seem to me that we are moving slowly in the right direction.

Another area in which progress has been slow is that of courting and marriage. True, there have been some gains. The three mothers (and Leila) all had husbands chosen for them, while Samira and Marianne assume the right to choose their own partner—with their parents' approval. The main problem now, as I see it, is that our society does not accept the possibility of men and women meeting publicly, dating each other in an open way and getting to know about each other before marriage. For women who live in the cities, or for Christian Arab women (whose families traditionally are more Western-oriented), there is somewhat more freedom. Yet for village women the restrictions are great, and women who break them are risking a great deal, sometimes even their lives. Even for college-educated women, like Samira and Marianne, one can see how repressive the family and society are when it comes to dating and courting. Each has felt it necessary to be highly secretive, and one can see how humiliating this is. The usual result of all this repression is that Palestinian men and women wind up marrying someone they hardly know. And, of course, this often leads to marital unhappiness. Speaking personally, as an unmarried woman, I can only say that sometimes I despair about the possibility of women in our society ever attaining the level of personal freedom in this area that seems to me a basic right and necessity.

⭒

This brings me to another point I want to discuss: the decision to participate in a book with my friend and colleague, Mike Gorkin. Mike talks about it in the preface, and we mention it in some of the chapter notes: for me to go about openly with him and interview Palestinian women was to expose myself—*and* my family—to social disapproval. Obviously, I knew this when I started. The kind of comments that Umm Mahmud made to me (see the dialogue) were predictable; she was even more tactful than others. I am grateful to my parents: they were willing to expose *themselves* to potential criticism of this type and, even more, did not put upon me the burden of doing this project in secret.

Now that we have done the book together, I sense that criticism may be coming my way from another source. Some of my Palestinian women friends may blame me for doing this project with a male outsider, and one who had (as he admits in the preface) some underlying difficulties in working with me as a Palestinian woman. Why did I not choose to do this book with a Palestinian woman? For me, the answer is simple. The idea for the book came from Mike. When he turned to me, acknowledging his need for a female insider to work with—someone to help with the interviews, and also to give another perspective on the material—I had no hesitation. I had always wanted to speak out about the situation of women in our society and to recount the kinds of stories that I have heard all my life—stories that convey the vitality and richness, often unrecognized, of *all* generations of Palestinian women. A book on mothers and daughters seemed like an excellent place to do so. And I had no hesitation about working specifically with Mike. We had already worked together on an article about traditional healers in Palestinian society, and I admired his book, *Days of Honey, Days of Onion: The Story of a Palestinian Family in Israel.* I trusted that whatever difficulties we ran into—and there were some, as he stated in the preface—Mike would deal with them frankly and fairly. I feel my trust was well placed. Mike's "blemishes" (and mine too, of course) are more clear now, but my friendship with him remains. If I have offended anyone by my "collaboration" with Mike, I can only say that I, at least, feel no regrets.

❧

In working on this book, I faced specific difficulties with each of the pairs, and other general difficulties that are part of doing fieldwork in Arab society. Let me start with the last point. As an Arab doing fieldwork in Arab society, I had to deal with the fact that in our culture it is extremely difficult to maintain a line between one's role as an interviewer and one's personal relationship to the interviewee (some of the essays in *Arab Women in the Field: Studying Your Own Society,* edited by Soriya Atorki and Camillia Solh [Syracuse: University of Syracuse Press, 1988], discuss the problem). Once I began to ask personal and intimate questions—and receive answers to them—I found myself put into the role of friend. Rather than "friendly interviewer," I was becoming "a friend who was interviewing." Mike and I discussed this problem, and I understand that for Westerners this difficulty also exists, yet not to the same degree, I think. For instance, with Marianne I found myself immediately in the role of friend. She was going through a difficult period in her life, and she chose to confide in me. I could not say no and I did not want to do so. And I believe that if I had refused the demands of friendship, Marianne would have been offended and less willing to participate in the study. Mike and I decided on a working rule that helped me draw a line between interviewer and friend: that is, to use only what was said on tape. Yet trying to remain an interviewer and also a friend often made me feel torn between the work and the friendship. I do not think there is a clear solution to this conflict, and it is all the more difficult if you happen to be an Arab doing fieldwork in Arab society.

With Leila and her mother, the problem was even more complicated because we are from the same village. Their willingness to participate in the study was already a signal that they considered me "a friend," even though I had never before visited either of them. The advantage of my immediate acceptance was obvious. Leila and Umm Khaled talked about intimate matters more quickly than the other pairs. Also, because I am from their village, I had heard stories about members of their family and I was able to ask about some of these events. For example, I knew about Abu Khaled's arrest and "banishment" in the 1950s, and was able to ask about it and receive Umm Khaled's interesting recollections. However, the restrictions placed on me as a "daughter of the village" also meant that there were a number of topics that I had to avoid. I could not ask about sexual matters, for instance. It was difficult enough to ask women not from my village; with Umm Khaled and Leila it was absolutely unacceptable for me to do this. Even inquiring about Abu Khaled's death was on the edge of what I felt I could ask, because "a friend" does not ask things that make another uncomfortable. As a person who has lived all my life in Abu Ghosh, and who expects to be there after the book is published, I could not do anything that would make these people too uncomfortable. Maybe Mike and I made an error in choosing to work with a couple from my village, but I hope the interesting material that came out of my interviews with them makes up for the restrictions I felt obliged to follow as a native daughter.

With Umm Abdullah and Samira I came up against another problem—one I did not have with the other pairs. It is the complex problem of being a Palestinian who lives in Israel. In brief, we who live within Israel and our fellow Palestinians in the Occupied Territories share our culture, but our political fate has been different. We are a discriminated minority within Israel, and that fact makes us feel our Palestinian identity more. Yet we are not under occupation, and as citizens of a materially developed society we enjoy some of its benefits. And above all, we have the benefit of not having lost our villages and homes. Visiting Samira and Umm Abdullah was, therefore, difficult for me. They personally made me feel comfortable and welcomed. But driving through their refugee camp with my yellow Israeli license plates—not blue plates, showing residence in the territories—I sensed the suspicious eyes of those around us. And yes, I worried for the safety of my Jewish colleague. The time I spent visiting with Umm Abdullah and Samira was the most extended and intensive contact I ever had with those living in refugee camps. I found myself wondering at times what my life would have been like if my parents, who fled in 1948, had not been able to return to Abu Ghosh. Listening to Umm Abdullah's and Samira's stories filled me with admiration for their personal courage and strength. But mixed in was a certain sadness, both because they *are* like me and also because they *are not.*

In the most basic way, though, Umm Abdullah and Samira—and Umm Khaled and Leila, and Umm Mahmud and Marianne—are unquestionably like me. We are all women. Despite my particular differences with each of them, I felt throughout the adventure of coming to know them that our existence as women held us together. This, after all, is a book of women's stories—Palestinian life as viewed through the eyes of women. It is being published in English, and I am glad that English-speaking people, women especially, will be reading these stories. I want others to know about us. But I also hope that someday these stories will be available in Arabic. I want my mother and sisters and friends to read these "lives." My father and brothers, too. And of course, if she were still alive I would want someone to read these stories to my grandmother, who was illiterate. I am sure she would enjoy hearing them. Indeed, it would give me great pleasure to read them to her myself. And if she asked, I would bring her a glass of water—this time without saying a word.

—*Rafiqa Othman*
October 1995

CHRONOLOGY

SIGNIFICANT EVENTS IN THE RECENT HISTORY OF ISRAEL / PALESTINE

1517–1917	Rule of the Ottoman Empire over Palestine.
1917–18	British capture of Palestine from the Turks during World War I. (In 1922, the League of Nations gave the British a mandate to rule Palestine, which they exercised until their exodus in 1918.)
1917	Publication of the Balfour Declaration (November), a letter from the British foreign secretary to Lord Rothschild, lay head of London's Jewish community, stating that the British government "viewed with favor the establishment in Palestine of a national home for the Jewish people," adding that it should be "clearly understood that nothing shall be done which may prejudice the civil and religious rights of existing non-Jewish communities in Palestine."
1936–39	Widespread rebellion by the Arabs in Palestine against British policies, and especially British concurrence in the establishment of a Jewish homeland. During the revolt, Arabs fought against the British and the Jews.
1947	Announcement of the Partition Agreement (November) whereby the United Nations decided to divide Palestine into two states, one

Jewish and the other Arab. The Jews accepted the agreement, the Arabs opposed it.

1947–49   Civil war between Palestinian Arabs and Jews from the time of the Partition Agreement until the exodus of the British and declaration of the Jewish state on May 14/15, 1948. Thereafter, until armistice agreements were signed in 1949, the war was also between Israel and five Arab states—Syria, Lebanon, Iraq, Transjordan, and Egypt. During this period approximately 370 Palestinian villages and towns were destroyed and some 600,000 to 760,000 Palestinians became refugees, mostly in the Gaza Strip (captured by Egypt during the war) or in the eastern sector of Palestine (captured by Transjordan, which in 1948 became Jordan). Only 160,000 Palestinian Arabs remained within the expanded borders of the new Jewish state.

1964   Formation of the Palestine Liberation Organization (PLO). Yasser Arafat's Fatah faction, one of several constituent groups of the PLO, has been the main faction since the late 1960s.

1967   The June 1967 War or Six-Day War. During the war, Israel captured the Gaza Strip and Sinai Peninsula from Egypt, the Golan Heights from Syria, and the eastern sector of Palestine from Jordan.

1973   The October War or Yom Kippur War. During the war, Egypt and Syria attacked Jewish positions in Sinai and the Golan Heights. As part of subsequent disengagement agreements, some border changes were made in both areas.

1979   Signing of the Egyptian-Israeli Peace Treaty (March) by Anwar Sadat, president of Egypt, and Menahem Begin, prime minister of Israel. As part of the treaty, Israel agreed to return all of the Sinai to Egypt.

1982   The Lebanon War (June–September). Israel invaded Lebanon, primarily in an effort to expel the PLO from its bases on Lebanese soil and to help create a Lebanese government more favorable to Israel.

1987   Eruption of the Intifada (December) in Gaza and the West Bank. The uprising is considered to have ended with the signing of the Declaration of Principles for Self-rule in the Territories (September 1993).

1991   The Gulf War (January–February). During the war, the United
            States and its allies defeated Iraq and thereby removed Iraqi forces
            from Kuwait.

1993   Signing of the PLO-Israel Declaration of Principles for Self-rule
            in the Territories (September), by Abu Mazen, a senior PLO
            official, and Shimon Peres, foreign minister of Israel, in Washing-
            ton, D.C., at a White House ceremony.

1994   Agreement on the first stage of self-rule for Palestinians (May). It
            established autonomy for Palestinians living in the Gaza Strip and
            the West Bank town of Jericho (and is sometimes referred to as
            "Gaza and Jericho First").

1995   Agreement on the second stage of self-rule (September). This
            agreement calls for extending autonomy to West Bank areas where
            the majority of the Palestinian population live.

GLOSSARY

As many readers may be aware, the Arabic language contains several sounds that are not found in English. We base our transliterations of Arabic on the scheme recommended by the *International Journal of Middle East Studies* but omit all accents or diacritics. Our hope is that these transliterations will allow readers familiar with the original to identify Arabic terms but will not slow down readers who know no Arabic.

abu	father (of)
agora	Israeli currency (plural, agorot); there are 100 agorot in a shekel
baruda	a type of rifle
dinar	Jordanian currency (as of this writing, a dinar equals approximately $1.45)
dunam	about one-fourth of an acre
eib	shame
Fatah	the faction of the Palestine Liberation Organization (PLO) headed by Yasser Arafat; Fatah is an acronym for Palestine National Liberation Movement
fedai	guerrilla fighter (feminine, *fedaiya;* plural, *fedaiyin*)
fellah	peasant (feminine, *fellaha;* plural, *fellahin*)
hajj	pilgrimage to Mecca; a man who has made the pilgrimage is respectfully referred to as Hajj, and a woman as Hajja

Hamas	the leading Muslim fundamentalist organization in the Occupied Territories
haram	forbidden
intifada	literally, shaking off; colloquially, uprising; specifically, the term is used in reference to the Palestinian uprising that began in December 1987 in the Occupied Territories of the West Bank and the Gaza Strip
kitab	marriage contract
khalas	finished, done with
kuhl	ash and other ingredients used as a salve for eyes
mahr	dowry, bride price
maqluba	a chicken, rice, and eggplant dish
mukhtar	village headman
pound	Palestinian currency (until 1948); also, Israeli currency (1948–80)
shabab	fellows, guys
Shabak	a Hebrew term, now well known by the Palestinians, it is an acronym for Sherut Bitahon Klali, the Israeli internal security services
sheikh	a Muslim religious official or teacher. Colloquially, the term is also applied to traditional healers (feminine, *sheikha;* instead of plural *shiukh/sheikhat,* we use an English plural in -s)
shekel	Israeli currency since 1980 (as of this writing, 3 shekels are the equivalent of $1.00)
sulha	peace agreement; a *sulha* may be between individuals or families or countries, and is typically arranged by a mediator
suq	market
sura	chapter; specifically, a chapter from the Koran
tabun	outdoor oven made of mud, clay or stone
tawjihi	high school matriculation examination in the West Bank and Gaza
thawb	long-sleeved long dress (instead of plural *athwab,* we use an English plural in -s)
umm	mother
zatar	wild thyme
zaffa	wedding procession